PRAISE FOR EDUCATION NATION

"I strongly believe that education is the single most important job of the human race. I'm very excited that *Education Nation* is adding to the tools we are giving educators and many others to make change in their own communities."

> —*George Lucas*, *founder and chairman, The George Lucas Educational Foundation (from the Foreword)*

"This book provides an outstanding overview of where we stand in the history of learning technologies, what current initiatives are most promising, and what challenges and opportunities we face in the near future."

> —*Christopher Dede*, *Timothy E. Wirth Professor in Learning Technologies, Harvard Graduate School of Education*

"How fortunate we are that Milton Chen has decided to share the lessons he has learned along the way on his incredible learning journey. As we just begin to unlock the methods of teaching our kids in a 21st Century context, this book should be embraced by every caring educator and parent who wants to do right by our kids."

> —*Gary E. Knell*, *president and CEO, Sesame Workshop*

"Milton Chen is a visionary and global leader in education. Emphasizing creativity, technology-enabled learning, project-based intellectual adventures and social/emotional intelligences, *Education Nation* encompasses the well-being of the whole child and the major shift to student-centered learning. Chen is a masterful storyteller and collaborator. His ideals continue to inspire and push our own boundaries to do what is right to help kids—and to never give up."

—*Susan Patrick, president and CEO, International Association for K–12 Online Learning (iNACOL)*

"Milton Chen has had an extraordinary perch for learning how media and technology can spark innovation and redefine teaching and learning. *Education Nation* provides a new vision of what is now possible, with vivid examples from real schools."

—*Linda Darling-Hammond, Charles E. Ducommun Professor, Stanford University and codirector of the School Redesign Network*

"This is a great book, Milton Chen is truly a gifted writer who has a unique ability to illustrate in words what the rest of us can only imagine. I found myself "seeing" in my mind what was written on the page. His writing is inspirational and leads us to see that there is no better time than now for creating a New Day for Learning."

—*Dr. An-Me Chung, program officer, C. S. Mott Foundation*

EDUCATION NATION

PUBLISHED WITH SUPPORT FROM

THE GEORGE LUCAS EDUCATIONAL FOUNDATION

The George Lucas Educational Foundation, founded in 1991, is a non-profit operating foundation committed to providing tools, resources, and inspiration about what works in public education. Through *Edutopia*, its mission is to empower and support education reform by shining a spotlight on innovative and successful learning environments. *Edutopia* embraces six core concepts of project-based learning, comprehensive assessment, integrated studies, social and emotional learning, teacher development, and technology integration. To find and share solutions, visit Edutopia.org.

EDUCATION NATION

Six Leading Edges of

Innovation in our Schools

MILTON CHEN

Foreword by George Lucas

JOSSEY-BASS
A Wiley Imprint
www.josseybass.com

Published by Jossey-Bass
A Wiley Imprint
989 Market Street, San Francisco, CA 94103-1741—www.josseybass.com

Readers should be aware that Internet Web sites offered as citations and/or sources for further information may have changed or disappeared between the time this was written and when it is read.

Limit of Liability/Disclaimer of Warranty: While the publisher and author have used their best efforts in preparing this book, they make no representations or warranties with respect to the accuracy or completeness of the contents of this book and specifically disclaim any implied warranties of merchantability or fitness for a particular purpose. No warranty may be created or extended by sales representatives or written sales materials. The advice and strategies contained herein may not be suitable for your situation. You should consult with a professional where appropriate. Neither the publisher nor author shall be liable for any loss of profit or any other commercial damages, including but not limited to special, incidental, consequential, or other damages.

Jossey-Bass books and products are available through most bookstores. To contact Jossey-Bass directly call our Customer Care Department within the U.S. at 800-956-7739, outside the U.S. at 317-572-3986, or fax 317-572-4002.

Jossey-Bass also publishes its books in a variety of electronic formats. Some content that appears in print may not be available in electronic books.

Library of Congress Cataloging-in-Publication Data

Chen, Milton.
  Education nation: six leading edges of innovation in our schools/Milton Chen; foreword by George Lucas.
    p. cm.–(Jossey-Bass teacher)
  Includes bibliographical references and index.
  ISBN 978-0-470-61506-5 (hardback)
  1.   School improvement programs–United States. 2.   Educational innovations–United States. 3.   Educational technology–United States. I.   Title.
  LB2822.82.C434 2010
  371.2'090973–dc22

                                                                2010011067

Printed in the United States of America

FIRST EDITION

HB Printing 10 9 8 7 6 5 4 3 2

CONTENTS

ACKNOWLEDGMENTS

MUCH OF THIS BOOK is my effort to "curate" my favorite stories in recent years from the Edutopia.org Web site, my "best of" collection from Edutopia's amazing wealth of resources documenting innovation in schools. My first debt of appreciation goes to the many talented colleagues at The George Lucas Educational Foundation (GLEF) who produced the inspiring content on Edutopia.org and in our *Edutopia* magazine. The editorial and Web production work has been led by David Markus and Jim Daly as editorial directors; Ken Ellis, executive producer for documentaries; Cal Joy, director of Web development; and Cindy Johanson, our new executive director. As a foundation founded by a filmmaker, GLEF's distinctive work is in making documentary films to capture what innovation looks like in the classroom. The films are supported with explanatory articles, interviews, and resources. Many of the examples I describe in this book are linked to those films and are best understood by seeing the teachers and students in action.

I also express my gratitude to the board of directors at The George Lucas Educational Foundation—George Lucas, Steve Arnold, Micheline Chau, Kim Meredith, Kate Nyegaard, and Marshall Turner—who provided a unique organization and resources for us to do this creative work. I thank them for providing me with the time to reflect on our body of work and to write this book.

I also thank Amy Borovoy, Laurie Chu, and Sharon Murotsune from the Edutopia staff for their help in assembling the images published here. For more than three years, Sharon served as my executive assistant, coordinating the communications and travel that enabled me to visit a number of the schools and projects profiled and talk to their pioneering educators. A talented artist at LucasArts, Greg Knight, did the illustrations for the Visions 2020 piece (pages 167 and 168 in the photo insert). I also thank my colleagues from the Fulbright New Century Scholars program, who broadened my horizons to understand that the issues of improving schools in the United States are shared globally.

A number of valued colleagues read portions of the manuscript and provided many insightful comments to improve it: Christopher Dede of Harvard Graduate School of Education, Ted Hasselbring of Vanderbilt University, and Şusan Patrick of iNACOL, all members of GLEF's National Advisory Council; Steve Arnold of the GLEF board; John Bransford and Susan Mosborg of the University of Washington; Pedro Hernández-Ramos of Santa Clara University; Kevin Kelly of San Francisco State University; Chris Livaccari of the Asia Society; Joe Morelock of Oregon's Canby School District; and Kathy Shirley of the Escondido School District in California. Any errors of fact are solely my own.

This is the third book I've worked on with the publishing team at Jossey-Bass, who again demonstrated their expertise and professionalism. Kate Gagnon, associate editor; Justin Frahm, production editor; Dimi Berkner, marketing director; and Lesley Iura, publisher, have all been a pleasure to work with. From the design of the book to its organization and selection of images, we started out with good ideas and our collaboration made them better, practicing a twenty-first-century skill we want students to develop.

My wife, Ruth Cox, has always been my first and most honest reader. Working in the academic technology group at San Francisco State University, she's an expert on technology use in higher education. This year, we celebrate our silver anniversary together. Through these twenty-five years, she has been an actress, lecturer in psychology, and mother to our daughter, Maggie, who is now embarking on her own career. We also share the same birthday, a statistical miracle signifying that it was all meant to be. As a teacher, parent, and partner, she knows how to put "the edge" into education and life. I lovingly dedicate this book to her.

FOREWORD

I DIDN'T ENJOY school very much. Occasionally, I had a teacher who would inspire me. But as an adult, as I began working with computer technology to tell stories through film, I began to wonder, "Why couldn't we use these new technologies to help improve the educational process?"

Twenty years ago, when we started our foundation, we could see that digital technology was going to completely revolutionize the educational system, whether it liked it or not. Technology is a virus that is changing education, just as it has changed nearly every industry, including my own in filmmaking and entertainment. Twenty years from now, when every student has his or her own computer, educational systems will be using technology in much more powerful and pervasive ways. When knowledge is changing so rapidly, it doesn't make sense to spend $150 on textbooks that students only use for fifteen weeks. From the beginning, we wanted our foundation to show how to best use these new technologies.

THE GOAL OF EDUCATION: USING INFORMATION WELL

When we first started out, we asked, "What are the most important things students should learn?" Our answer focuses on three uses of information: we want students to know how to *find* information, how to *assess* the quality of information, and how to *creatively and effectively use* information to accomplish a goal. When I was a student, information was contained in the encyclopedia, a reputable source. But fifty years later, when information is on someone's Web site, it's not clear whether it's reputable or true. So, from among many sources, students need to assess for themselves which information is most factual and useful.

Then, students need to take that information, digest it, and do something creative with it, whether it's designing a multimedia presentation or a rocket to the moon. Instead of just asking students to spit information back, schools should be asking them, "What can you create with the information you've found?"

Social-emotional learning also becomes very important. In today's world, it is not enough to know how to use information well. Students also have to learn how to cooperate, to lead, and to work well with different types of people. These skills are keys to being successful in a career and to having a civilized society. Students need to learn how to become wise human beings, emotionally and intellectually.

TEACHERS AS COACHES AND WISE ELDERS

Teachers play critical roles in connecting the social-emotional and intellectual realms. They become students' guides, coaches, and "wise elders." When technology is employed, teachers are freed from standing in front of the class and presenting information. We've got Google for that. Now, they can spend more time developing deeper personal relationships with students. They can pat students on the back, call them by name, and encourage them to work harder. Like Plato or Aristotle, they can inquire, "Why do you think that's true?" These are things no computer will ever do well. In my experience, there's nothing more potent in education than a teacher who truly cares about you.

THE YOUTH ARE BUILDING THE PATH

Changing education is a long-term challenge and takes generations. The next generation of youth is going to accept this change completely. They have taken over technology and run with it while schools are trying to catch up. On Facebook, students are talking to Russian and Chinese kids, comparing notes, and collaborating on projects. They know there's a real world out there that adults know little about. They are realizing, "My little cocoon isn't my little cocoon anymore."

Today's youth are building a pathway to change education. I see the difference in my own daughters, who are thirty and twenty-one. They speak different languages and think differently from each other. My younger daughter's generation lives in the Internet world and is tied into a different reality than my older daughter and me. We still like to look up the movie schedules in the paper!

THE FUTURE OF TECHNOLOGY

The potential of digital technology is vast. We have barely tapped into it. Eventually, there will be a new delivery system for instructional materials, with all the relevant and best-quality textbooks, curricula, documentaries, and faculty presentations. It will be broken down into specific categories so students and teachers can search topics very quickly. It will include the vast repositories of places like the Library of Congress, the Louvre, and our best universities. And it will be safe for students, teachers, and parents.

Schools will benefit from advances in simulation technology, making it more affordable. In universities, medical students use digital cadavers to simulate the human body. Eventually, high school students will have a simpler version to learn human anatomy and physiology. School versions of high-end computer-aided design programs will enable students to build a house on a Florida beach and see if it could withstand a Category 5 hurricane. After studying the geology, engineering, and science, there's nothing better than being able to push the button and see what happens. Nothing would get students' attention more than that!

EDUTOPIA'S ROLE

At Edutopia, our job is to produce and disseminate information about the most innovative learning environments, addressing core concepts of project-based learning, cooperative learning, technology integration, comprehensive assessment, and teacher development for implementing these practices. When we first started, we quickly learned about fantastic schools, teachers, and situations where student learning is off the charts. But they're not well known and therefore not replicated.

Today, there's a growing consensus that technology and new practices can help students learn faster and enjoy learning. We want Edutopia.org to be the place where educators can find out about these practices and put them to work. Our "Schools That Work" online features provide detailed information to help the broad audience needed to change schools, from state capitols and universities to schools and Main Street, where parents urgently want a better future for their children.

In the past few years, Edutopia has seen rapid growth in the numbers of exemplary schools and creative learning settings. Dr. Milton Chen, who led our foundation for twelve years as executive director and continues as senior fellow, has had a unique vantage point for following these trends in innovation. In *Education Nation*, he has done a fantastic job acting as Edutopia's curator, assembling this exhibition from the large collection of stories from our Web site and other sources. His unique and personal perspective, dating back to his years at Sesame Workshop, provides the narrative weaving these stories together, with Web links to resources and films showing engaged students and effective teachers in action. As one educator said about Edutopia, this book can be a valuable "idea factory" for creating twenty-first-century schools.

I strongly believe that education is the single most important job of the human race. I'm very excited that *Education Nation* is adding to the tools we are giving educators and many others to make change in their own communities.

GEORGE LUCAS
Founder and Chairman,
The George Lucas Educational Foundation

PREFACE
MY LEARNING JOURNEY
FROM THE LONGEST STREET
IN THE WORLD
TO A GALAXY
LONG AGO AND FAR, FAR AWAY

I'VE ALWAYS BEEN FASCINATED by the ability of children to learn in creative, powerful, accelerated, and joyful ways. This fascination started for me as a teenager and has carried me over a thirty-five-year career devoted to designing, researching, and advocating for educational media and technology. Like the MIT Media Lab's Seymour Papert, I've always believed that these tools, especially in the guiding hands of teachers and parents, could serve as "wheels for the mind."

My own personal odyssey has led me from working at Sesame Workshop in New York City to KQED, the PBS station in San Francisco, and the past twelve years as executive director of The George Lucas Educational Foundation in the San Francisco Bay Area. Looking back, I appreciate that it's been a unique journey and a fortunate one. Thanks to the numerous versions of *Sesame Street* now shown in the Middle East, Africa, Europe, Latin America, and Asia, I sometimes say my career has taken me from the longest street in the world to a galaxy long ago and far, far away. I begin by sharing my "learning journey," since it frames and colors my views of where education is and where it needs to be as we end the first decade of the twenty-first century.

My journey began on the south side of Chicago, where I spent my childhood. To this day, living in San Francisco, many people are surprised to hear that's where I grew up, since, in fact, there were not many Asian families in the Midwest. Just after World War II, in 1945, my father, Wen-Lan, came with a group of mining engineers to study coal mines in West Virginia and Pennsylvania. He stayed on for graduate school at Penn State and was joined by my mother, Shu-Min, a music student, in 1949. Although they had married in 1945, they were separated for the first four years of their marriage.

When I became interested in the history of Chinese in the United States, I was surprised to learn that the five-year span in which my parents immigrated was the *only* five years, post–World War II, when Chinese could come to the United States. In 1945, China was an ally against the Japanese; in 1949, the Communists won the civil war and China became the enemy. Born in 1953, I was indeed a son of global events and a historical U.S.-China relationship that opened the door for my parents to come here and quickly shut it, forcing my parents to sever ties to their families and make a life in the Midwest.

Decades later, my mother told me that my maternal grandfather, whom I never met, had been, in the Chinese phrase, a "social educator" who had studied sociology and created a community learning center in their small farming village in the 1930s, first providing books to teach literacy and later bringing in a new technology called radio as an electronic source of awareness of a wider world. I like to think we share a common gene for educational innovation and using new methods to bring learning to a broader group of learners.

I have always seen education through the lens of social justice, which I trace back to early experiences attending a racially integrated school, Frank Bennett Elementary School, on the far south side of Chicago. (Though I never thought about it as a boy, I've learned Mr. Bennett was a lawyer and member of the Chicago City Council and Board of Education in the early 1900s, with the new school dedicated in his name, two years after his passing, in 1927.) In a class photo from 1961 (see page 153), half of the children are white, half of them are black, and there's me and Janis Miyamoto. My class was a dramatic shift from Bennett's history as an all-white school.

But although our school was integrated, every day when the school bell rang and we walked back to our neighborhoods, I, along with the white children, walked a few blocks to our homes, while the black children had to walk further, over the Dan Ryan Expressway, to their neighborhood. Integrated school, segregated community. When I was eleven and our family decided to move to the suburbs for better schools, a neighbor came and asked my father whether we were, in fact, selling our home to a black family. We helped to integrate that Roseland neighborhood in the 1960s, the same neighborhood where a community organizer named Barack Obama worked during the 1980s.

I got bitten by this bug of innovative learning early on. It might have happened during my high school years, during those hot and muggy August days in the forest preserves near Chicago, where my first job was working as a YMCA day camp counselor. On those field trips, where we hiked, made campfires, roasted hot dogs, and fished in the ponds, I saw my group of 12 eight-year-old boys come alive, their boundless energy fueling endless curiosity about the trees, fish, and insects. We chose to call our group "The Dirty Dozen," and they lived up to their name.

In the fall of 1970, I went to the right college for the wrong reason. I went to Harvard with a vague idea of becoming a public interest lawyer, perhaps working on educational issues such as desegregation and student tracking. During my sophomore year, I started working as a research assistant at the Center for Law and Education on campus, then headed by a young civil rights lawyer named Marian Wright Edelman, now known as the distinguished and courageous founder of the Children's Defense Fund.

That year, I saw a small note in a Chinese American newsletter, saying that the Children's Television Workshop was looking to diversify its group of advisors. *Sesame Street* had launched in 1968, to tremendous national publicity; its founder, Joan Cooney, and its tallest character, Big Bird, appeared on the cover of *Time* magazine. Like millions of children and parents, I was taken with the creativity of the program, its blending of Muppets, a multiracial cast, music, animation, and films to deliver a core curriculum to preschool children. I had read that *Time* article in high school and even fashioned a speech for a contest on the new role of the "mass media" in education. I could think of nothing more exciting than getting involved with this national phenomenon.

As a college sophomore, I hardly qualified as an advisor, but I wrote to Joan Cooney anyway. To my surprise, she wrote back and told me I was in luck. (To this day, I try to write back to every student who writes me.) Their major curriculum advisor was Dr. Gerald Lesser, a Harvard professor of education and psychology, just across campus, and I should go talk to him. At the time, Gerry Lesser was a rare academic interested in harnessing television to teach. From our first meeting, I was disarmed by this casual and welcoming Harvard professor in his trademark tennis shoes, corduroy slacks, and appealing knack for describing early childhood development in plain English. This unique skill stood him in good stead in persuading TV writers and performers to understand the show from the child's point of view.

Sam Gibbon, one of three producers for the series, recalled the early curriculum seminars:

> Gerry would come into these meetings of gray beards from all over the country, [academics] who were accustomed to defending their turf.... He'd take off his coat, loosen his tie, and roll his sleeves up. He would introduce everybody and say something about their work. There would be sixty people in the room and he would introduce every single one of them, calling them by their first name. It was an amazing feat of memory. [Professional] titles were out the window, and he'd say, "Any good idea is as good as any other good idea, and it doesn't matter where it comes from."[1]

At the tender age of nineteen, working with Gerry, Dr. Courtney Cazden, a reading expert, and a small group of graduate students, I started watching kids watch *Sesame Street* and *The Electric Company* reading series, studying how they absorbed lessons from a medium thought to have no redeeming educational value. From *Sesame Street*, they learned concepts of letters, numbers, shapes, and sorting quickly and enthusiastically, debunking the conventional wisdom of those days. Some "experts" skeptically asked how a TV-delivered curriculum could teach counting from 1 to 10 to preschoolers, when kindergarten teachers were having difficulty teaching numbers in person? Today, the *Sesame Street* curriculum teaches preschoolers to count from 1 to 40.

Sesame Street has been the first and biggest game changer in the past forty years of educational innovation. In a few short years, it went from a twinkle in Joan Cooney's eye to daily broadcasts on PBS, reaching millions of preschoolers, at a "cost-effectiveness" of only a few cents per child per program, achieving the kind of scale and impact that educational policymakers in the multichannel age of the Internet still wish for.

In 1974, I wrote my senior honors thesis for my major in social studies on the economic, regulatory, and cultural factors affecting the quality of children's television, with Sam Gibbon, by then a lecturer at Harvard, as a thesis advisor. Even back then, I was interested in the future path of media for education, during the "Golden Age of the Commercial TV Networks." I wrote, "Of future interest is the burgeoning development and use of a number of technological innovations ... cable television, open access channels, video capabilities and videocassettes for individual homes, portable video cameras for use in homes and schools, three-dimensional or holographic television. ... [Television] will be a two-way communications system of over one hundred channels, used by different groups—including children—who produce their own programs and communicate with each other."

Okay, so I was off by a few hundred channels and we're still waiting for holographic television, but at least I foresaw the future of children having technology in their own hands and using it to tell their own stories. After graduating from Harvard, thanks to a traveling fellowship, I set off on my first trip abroad, with a project to study children's TV at the BBC and other public broadcasters in Europe.

I joined Sesame Workshop in 1976, working in the public affairs department, writing press releases, editorial backgrounders, and occasionally answering viewer mail. One of the more colorful letters we received was from a man excoriating *Sesame Street* for exposing tender preschool minds to the idea that two men could share the same bedroom, albeit in separate beds. We wanted to write a short, terse reply: "Dear Sir: Bert and Ernie are not humans. They're puppets." That fall, I went to work in the research department and helped to develop pre-science segments for *Sesame Street* and a new science series that became known as *3–2–1 Contact*.

The further stops along my journey took me to a graduate program in communications research at Stanford and a brief teaching stint at the Harvard Graduate School of Education. For my doctoral dissertation, I studied differences between Bay Area high school girls and boys in their use of computers. Back in the early 1980s, computers were mainly large desktop machines or terminals attached to mainframes. A few "microcomputers" were making their way into the classrooms for use as word processors or playing games. My survey found there were no differences in the grades that males and females achieved in courses using computers, from science to computer programming, but girls selected those courses less often. It was an early lesson in differences in early exposure, adult mentoring, and the social environment that affects girls' and boys' uses of computers.

With a decade as education director at KQED-San Francisco and twelve years as executive director at The George Lucas Educational Foundation (GLEF), I've worked for more than three decades in educational media and technology, broadening opportunities and environments for child-centered learning and engagement. Along the way, I've had the amazing opportunity to learn from and work with an amazing range of creative educators and media professionals, some well known, such as Joan Ganz Cooney, Fred Rogers, and George Lucas, and many more working in schools, universities, afterschool programs, foundations, and nonprofits.

And now we've arrived at a multichannel, Web world with the world's knowledge available at our fingertips, whenever learners are ready, any time, anywhere. This new world of learning will only get deeper, richer, and easier to access, with new forms and environments. Think back on just the past three years of the Web and the rise of video-sharing via YouTube, social networking with Facebook, and Twitter communities, and just imagine what the next decade will bring. While school boards struggle with policies to allow or block these new media from their schools, educators and students are moving at Internet speed. They are adapting Ning to create online communities to share best teaching practices and wikispaces to enlarge the physical classroom into virtual space, allowing classroom discussions to continue online during evenings and weekends. And students are instant messaging, Facebooking, and tweeting to help each other with the homework due tomorrow.

With all of the tools the Internet has brought to our fingertips, it's a great time to be a student! And an exciting moment in history to be a teacher. But for many more students and teachers to capitalize on these opportunities, many individuals and groups across the nation must band together and advocate for a very different kind of school, dramatically different from the schools we all attended and from the schools envisioned in most "school reform." We need a movement.

When George Lucas is asked, "Who's the audience for Edutopia?," he always responds, "Everyone with an interest in improving education." Every educator—teacher, principal, or school board member—parent, and student can become part of the movement by making learning a more engaging and enjoyable experience each day. And every education advocate in a business, community organization, college, university, or foundation can "think bigger" about what is now possible and share that vision in their organizations. And all these groups of stakeholders need to connect their efforts with each other.

I hope this book can be one of many handbooks for this movement. Our work over the past decade at Edutopia has shone the spotlight on an amazing army of change agents working hard, often alone or in small groups, to revolutionize how students learn in their communities. I see them at every education conference and, especially, at conferences focusing on technology. These change agents come from strikingly different backgrounds, from all states, from first-year teachers in their twenties to senior citizens who refuse to retire, from musicians to scientists, kindergarten teachers to college professors, and students themselves. Yet they share the same passion for creating the new world of learning made possible through new collaborations and redefining when, where, and how learning happens.

You may feel you are already part of this movement. If you don't, I invite you to sign up. One simple way is to join one of many online communities devoted to reinventing schools, such as ours at Edutopia, Classroom 2.0, Scholastic's TeacherShare, or many others. Others are creating their own using the platforms of Facebook or Ning. You'll quickly learn the first and most reassuring lesson in joining a movement: you are not alone.

EDUCATION NATION

INTRODUCTION
THE VISION OF AN EDUCATION NATION

*We must regrind our lenses to monitor the periphery, the edges
of our business. At these edges lie our richest opportunities for
value creation. If we adjust our lenses accordingly, then we will
begin to see something remarkable: The edges will reshape and
eventually transform the core.*

JOHN HAGEL III AND JOHN SEELY BROWN

IMAGINE AN "EDUCATION Nation," a learning society where the education of children and adults is the highest national priority, on par with a strong economy, high employment, and national security. Where resources from public and private sources fund a "ladder of learning" for learners of all ages, from pre-K through "gray." Where learners take courses through the formal institutions of high-quality schools and universities and take advantage of informal experiences offered through museums, libraries, churches, youth groups, and parks as well as via the media.

Where our national and state leaders, not just in education, but in business, sports, and entertainment, use their bully pulpits to extol the value of learning for individuals of all ages. And where the citizens take full advantage of the opportunities to embrace lifelong learning. This society would begin to educate and support mothers and fathers with parent education classes during the prenatal period, as provided by Geoffrey Canada's Harlem Children's Zone. Leaders would emphasize the importance of a healthy body for a productive mind, as First Lady Michelle Obama has done with her Let's Move! campaign against childhood obesity. Policymakers would confront criticism from the press and the public, as some governors and superintendents have, to

1

ensure that every student has access to the digital tools required for learning in this decade.

The United States is not yet this nation, although many leaders, organizations, and commissions have articulated many aspects of this vision. And many millions of Americans manage to achieve it for themselves and their families. But many more millions do not. The past two decades of failing to modernize our schools, increase high school graduation rates, and achieve college success for a much higher percentage of students are threatening the future of the nation. The drumbeat of statistics about our outmoded educational system reverberates through every education conference. Among those depressing facts and figures, I find the clearest indictment of our failure to improve schools in these three:

1. Of 50 students behind in reading in first grade, 44 will still be behind in fourth grade.

2. An American student drops out of high school every 26 seconds, a total of 6,000 each day.

3. Thirty years ago, the United States ranked 1st in the quality of its high school graduates. Today, it is 18th among twenty-three industrialized nations.[1]

From national defense to environmental defense, from national security to economic security, every major issue of our day depends on our capacity to educate our citizenry to a much higher level than generations past. Every nation is only as good as its educational system. In the midst of a continuing economic recession, the United States is slowly awakening to this hard fact.

Other nations are making more progress toward this ideal. Finland, Singapore, and South Korea have highly selective recruitment methods for new teachers. In South Korea, primary teachers must score in the top 5 percent on their college entrance exams. In Singapore, only 20 percent of those who apply to become teachers are selected and paid a salary during at least part of their training.[2] Australia's national and state leadership has moved aggressively to create a national broadband network and provide each student with a laptop computer. England and Canada have developed systems of performance-based assessments that go far beyond what multiple-choice tests can measure.

What would it take to create an Education Nation? It would take greater political will than we have mustered to confront the barriers to modernize our schools. It would take a shift in the cultural values of families and communities. And it would mean bringing to scale the pockets of educational innovation that exist in many schools and other learning environments around the country. For the past several decades, this innovation has been occurring at the edges of our school system and is growing. When these multiple edges converge and move to occupy the center, an Education Nation will be born.

PUTTING THE "EDGE" INTO EDUCATION

For a while, I've been saying that we need to "put the edge into education" and create a sense that teaching and learning are exciting, contemporary, and cool. As its most important enterprise, education should be "on the cutting edge" of society, technology, and culture, rather than trailing other sectors. *Sesame Street* and *The Electric Company* made learning hip. President Barack Obama has called for this same cultural shift, proclaiming that we want students to believe that "it's cool to be smart."

However, schools function as a large, bureaucratic system, based on politics, preservation of the status quo, and daily routines. The school year is one nine-month-long ritual, punctuated by semesters, holiday and spring breaks, and the long summer vacation. With the high stakes we have placed on end-of-year tests, much of the spring semester is consumed by test preparation. While technology has accelerated change around the globe during the past decade, and other nations are instituting major changes in their schools, our American school system still seems to lumber along, blissfully ignorant of its anachronistic ways.

Nothing seismic ever seems to happen to our schools (and I don't mean wishing for another earthquake here in San Francisco). If you listed adjectives to describe American schools, *edgy* wouldn't be one of them.

One rare example of a sudden jolt to the system was NetDay, held on March 9, 1996, when business, parent, and community groups self-organized to wire schools to the Internet. John Gage, then chief science officer at Sun Microsystems, now at the investment firm of Kleiner Perkins Caufield & Byers, was one of the founders. He told me a story of the Los Angeles Unified School District, the nation's largest, hearing of this effort and wanting to schedule some meetings. Gage told them NetDay had one rule: "No meetings." Everything a community group needed to wire a school was on its Web site at netday96.com. Volunteers would show up at schools on that Saturday, as President Bill Clinton and Vice President Al Gore did in the Bay Area. In just one day, 20,000 volunteers helped wire 20 percent of California's schools, with 2,500 wiring kits donated by phone companies. Gage has proposed an exciting new project, to send similar groups into schools to audit how the buildings use water and energy, a "green school audit" to engage students in learning about energy conservation in the very buildings where they spend their days.

But generally, it's been extraordinarily difficult to put the "edge"—indeed many edges—into the American school system. In the Olympics of school systems, we are world champions of educational inertia. Partly due to our system's decentralization, its fifty states and more than 14,000 school districts have proven remarkably resistant to large-scale change. Beyond ironic, the United States, the world leader in innovation and technology, is endangering its own future by ignoring what it knows about education. Through international comparisons, such as the PISA (Program for International Student Assessment) exam in which nations such as Singapore, Finland, and Korea excel, the United States can now trudge up the medal stand to claim the dubious honor of propping up a second-rate school system that is immune to the very innovations it has invented.

There is no sadder testament to this fact than the schools in the San Francisco Bay Area, the home of Silicon Valley. Most operate as if they had been locked in a time capsule from thirty years ago, with the same courses, schedules, and classrooms where teachers stand in front of their students and deliver what they know. In fact, given California's long decline in state educational funding, its schools during the 1970s were comparatively better than today's, as documented by journalist John Merrow in his aptly titled documentary, *First to Worst*.[3]

Within an hour's drive of the campuses of Google, Apple, Intel, Cisco, and many other companies that brought us the world of digital information we now inhabit, you would be hard-pressed to find a single school in which every student and teacher has 24/7 access to the tools those companies have created. Google has created a free, ultra-high-bandwidth network in its headquarters community of Mountain View, California, but students within its schools don't have the simplest devices to access the network.

The Silicon Valley culture of technology-based creative design, engineering, marketing, and collaboration is also missing in its surrounding schools. The children who are fortunate to have parents who work in those companies may use those tools at home, but not in their schools. And considering that California now educates 12 percent of our nation's children, this disconnect between American ingenuity and educational immunity is unraveling our nation's future. The United States has a long way to go to becoming an Education Nation.

INNOVATION ON THE EDGES OF THE SCHOOL SYSTEM

But the game is not over yet. There is still hope that America can bring its spirit of innovation to its schools and become the Education Nation of its aspirations, where No Child is Left Behind and all children have a chance to complete high school and go on to college. In fact, in the recent past, American schools have had a history of innovation happening at the edges of its system. Founded in 1991, The George Lucas Educational Foundation (GLEF), also located in the San Francisco Bay Area, has been examining these edges, researching and documenting the work of pioneering schools and school leaders. It is not coincidental that founder and chairman, George Lucas, also founded Lucasfilm, a company synonymous with technological innovation in filmmaking and entertainment. As George says in his Foreword to this book and in an introductory film to GLEF's work, in the course of creating digital tools for visual effects, sound design, and video games in the 1980s, "I began to wonder, "Why couldn't we use these new technologies to help improve the educational process?"

Since 1997, our foundation, through its Edutopia media, has been documenting the "edges of educational change," showing how leading-edge schools, first small but now growing in number, have changed their curriculum from textbook-based to project-based learning, enabling students to investigate important problems and projects relevant to their own lives and communities, sending them into inner cities, historic sites, farms, lakes, and streams. Many community experts and partners, including businesses, universities, government agencies, and nonprofits, are helping these schools to explode learning beyond the four walls of the classroom.

These schools are equipping students and teachers with modern digital tools for thinking, communicating, and collaborating, benefiting from the exponentially increasing power of technology and rapidly declining costs. They are increasing "learning time" through better use of hours during the school day and extending into afternoons, evenings, weekends, and summers. After-school programs are continuing learning beyond the last bell, providing creative experiences missing from the school day and giving more help to students who need it. Districts are elevating the profession of teaching, paying teachers more, and demanding better results. The edges of innovation are growing and moving from individual pioneering teachers to entire schools and districts, thanks to a growing cadre of principal and superintendent leaders. Eventually, these edges will envelop the center. These edges are what this book is about.

In their perceptive book, *The Only Sustainable Edge,* John Hagel III, a business strategist, and John Seely Brown, former director of the renowned Xerox Palo Alto Research Center (PARC) and an advisor to

GLEF in its early years, have described the importance of businesses paying attention to innovation at "the edges" in several senses:

> In particular, we must regrind our lenses to monitor the periphery, that is, the edges, of our business. At these edges lie our richest opportunities for value creation.... So what do we mean by the edge? First, we mean the edge of the enterprise, where one company interfaces or interacts with another economic entity.... Second, the edge refers to the boundaries of mature markets ... where they may overlap, collide, or converge. Third, we touch on geographic edges, especially those of such emerging economies as China and India....
>
> Finally we refer to the edges between generations, where younger consumers and employees, shaped by pervasive information technology, are learning, consuming, and collaborating with each other.... These edges will become the primary source of business innovation and therefore fertile ground for value creation.... If we adjust our lenses accordingly, then we will begin to see something remarkable: The edges will reshape and eventually transform the core.[4]

GLEF'S EDUTOPIA: TELLING STORIES FROM THE EDGES OF SCHOOL INNOVATION

Edutopia's unique role in the redesign of American education has been to utilize media—especially documentary film, supported by articles, resources such as lesson plans, and interviews with school leaders—to showcase these edges of innovation. Many of the places I describe in this book were first chronicled in a film or article on Edutopia.org. Our stories have invited an audience of mostly American, but increasingly international, educators, policymakers, and parents to pay attention to these interesting places "on the edges" of their school systems.

Frequently, I have had the experience of showing educators exemplary programs in or near their own districts they were unaware of, such as showing a film to San Francisco educators about Build SF, an unusual half-day program in which high school students work with architects to learn about design and building. One of the hallmarks of traditional systems is they don't do a very good job about communicating what's new and "edgy." While these programs may have been geographically right under the audience's noses, they were mentally far away.

There are four special strategies we employ at Edutopia in our mission to document and disseminate these stories. The first is that we stay positive. We acknowledge the many inherent problems in our schools, and education journalism chronicles them in great detail. But GLEF believes that, for schools to improve, we learn more from understanding success than focusing on failure. And there are many interesting lessons to be learned from what didn't work on the road to success.

The second is using documentary film as our own "leading edge," to show visually what cannot be communicated in words. The look on the third grader's face when she sees a butterfly emerge from its chrysalis. How students genuinely enjoy working and collaborating with each other. When I speak to groups, I always show our documentaries and, invariably, that's what the audiences remember.

Third, we focus first on what these innovations look like in the classroom, in what teachers and students *do*. So much of educational reform discussion is conducted at a general level, on the matters of national, district, and state policy. So, while we might all agree that teachers should be paid more or receive more professional development, Edutopia aims to answer the question: What should teachers be paid more to do? How should they act and teach in the classroom?

And fourth, we strive to present all of our material in clear language, free of jargon, comprehensible to a parent as well as a professor. The education profession conducts its affairs in an esoteric language, sometimes called "educationese," an unwieldy combination of fancy words and awkward acronyms that parents, journalists, and school board members often have difficulty penetrating. To qualify as a speaker of Education as a Second Language (the other ESL), you would need to define how differentiated instruction could benefit ELL and FRL students, especially if they have an IEP. And how professional learning communities can scaffold their achievement using Bloom's Taxonomy. (For those new to Education as a Second Language, the abbreviations stand for English language learner, free or reduced lunch, and individualized education program.)

This language barrier prevents a larger community of consensus on where our schools should be heading. If parents, in particular, understood and demanded more innovative schools, school board members who count on their votes would listen more attentively.

We once published an article in which a professor wrote that teachers needed to possess "pedagogical content knowledge." Kate Nyegaard, one of our board members, noticed this and said, "What does that mean? I'm a school board member responsible for funds for professional development and could allocate funds for it." I said, "I think that means teachers need to know their subjects and how to teach them." Nyegaard said, "Well, why didn't you say that? That I understand!"

ABOUT THIS BOOK

This book is my effort to summarize what our foundation has learned from our search for those pockets of innovation on the edges. I describe in these pages six "edges" that developed slowly during the 1990s but are now accelerating in their growth. Edge 1 sets the foundation for the others: the edge of our educational thinking. The other five build on the first and how we think about who, when, how, where, and why we educate. They represent the edges of curriculum, technology, time/place, and teaching. The last may be the most influential: the youth edge of today's digital learners.

These edges of education parallel the edges of business described by Hagel and Brown, such as schools creating partnerships with universities, museums, and others to add value to the learning process; districts and states recognizing the limitations and obsolescence of the traditional education market and harnessing new opportunities through, for instance, online learning; the influence of geography, in adapting educational models from Europe and Asia and globalizing the American curriculum; and the biggest edge of all: the current generation of digital learners bringing new habits of learning and communicating as they progress through their schools. With the growing power and popularity of handheld mobile devices, these young learners are carrying this change in their pockets.

Like a museum curator assembling an exhibit from a large collection of artifacts, I've had to be selective in my examples. They are located in a diverse range of cities, suburbs, and rural areas across the United States, revealing that the edges are not limited by geography. But these are not the only ones. Our Edutopia.org Web site is a deep archive of films and stories from hundreds of schools around the nation, and many from abroad. Our documentary films have profiled more than 150 schools and programs. I hope you'll take the time to look at the links I've listed in this book, which link to other related stories on the Edutopia site and others. The innovations I describe are best understood by watching the films of these classroom in action. All of the links can be found in the Selected Web Sites at the end of this book and also online here: www.Edutopia.org/educationnation.

I also hope you'll engage in the conversation in the Edutopia online community, bringing in your own perspective, examples, and resources. This book is the executive summary for the deeper story of innovation at Edutopia.org and other places on the Web. Most of all, I hope this book can help you start, or continue, important conversations and actions on how all of us can create an Education Nation.

1

THE THINKING EDGE
GETTING SMARTER ABOUT LEARNING

From the standpoint of the child, the great waste in the school comes from his inability to utilize the experiences he gets outside the school in any complete and free way within the school itself; while, on the other hand, he is unable to apply in daily life what he is learning at school.

JOHN DEWEY, "WASTE IN EDUCATION,"
The School and Society, 1899

THE FIRST EDGE, the Thinking Edge, is the most fundamental: modernizing our *thinking* about education. The most basic prerequisite to creating an Education Nation is changing our thinking about the enterprise itself—the learning process, the role of students, teachers, and parents, and what is possible today given the opportunities afforded by technology. As we know from efforts to change politics, religion, and even our personal relationships, changing our thinking can be the most difficult thing we human beings can do, especially when our opinions are firmly rooted in personal experience. As my colleague, Dr. Allen Glenn, professor and dean emeritus of education at the University of Washington, puts it, "The biggest obstacle to school change is our memories." We all think we know what a school is and how a classroom is organized, since we spent eighteen years in them during our formative years. It's hard to imagine anything else.

Unfortunately, we're not very smart about learning. For a field devoted to improving the teaching and learning of children, we grownups aren't getting smarter fast enough about how to do this.

In this chapter, I discuss how updating our thinking can build on some well-known and articulated philosophies about how children learn best, such as the child-centered approach of John Dewey. While his beliefs are popular with progressive educators, they are still not widely shared, especially among policymakers who don't have much time or appetite for readings from the history of education. Dewey's views stand in marked contrast to a top-down system of education, in which policymakers prescribe what, when, and how information is to be transmitted to young minds. If futurist and computer scientist Alan Kay is right, that "point of view is worth 80 IQ points" is true, we need to "regrind our lenses" to adopt some new points of view to boost our educational IQ. We need to know where to look.

I also discuss moving beyond ten simplistic "either/or" ways of thinking toward "both-and" syntheses and recent research by Carol Dweck at Stanford on imbuing children with mental models of their own learning: "mindsets," as described in Dweck's book *Mindset: The New Psychology of Success*. Maybe it shouldn't be so hard. We instinctively use the correct mindset when we think about sports and the arts. We just need to apply those views to education.

 From Dewey to Duncan

Chicago, Illinois

John Dewey is often referred to as the father of the progressive education movement for his advocacy of child-centered teaching and connecting "school life" to real life. John Mergendoller of the Buck Institute for Education calls him "St. John." I like to connect Dewey to the history of his time and his arrival in the 1890s as a young professor of philosophy and psychology from New York at a newly created University of Chicago. The university had been founded by John D. Rockefeller, whose oil fortune had grown rapidly, as a Baptist institution of higher learning for that burgeoning city on what was then the "western" edge of the American frontier. Dewey started an elementary school called the University Elementary School, which he later renamed the Laboratory School, known for many decades for its quality education for children of university faculty and other residents of the Hyde Park neighborhood. Dewey intentionally used the word *laboratory* for his school, intending it to resemble other university labs where the most promising theoretical ideas could be developed into classroom practices.

In 1899, John Dewey articulated his ideas on schooling in a series of three lectures called "The School and Society" to parents of the Lab School.[1] Since he was speaking to parents rather than to a more academic audience, his points are especially clear and concise. In my own talks, I recommend these speeches, republished in 1990 by the University of Chicago Press, to parents and education students. The modernity of Dewey's writings is striking, expressing the sentiments of many education leaders, especially teachers, today. Dewey spoke to two key themes that resonate powerfully with the role of school in this twenty-first century.

The first is the critical importance of schools to larger societal goals and especially the success of the American democracy. Only thirty years after the Civil War, Dewey described the importance of equal educational opportunity for all children and how the success of our still-fledgling democracy would hinge upon it: "What the best and wisest parent wants for his own child, that must the community want for all of its children. Any other ideal for our schools is narrow and unlovely; acted upon, it destroys our democracy. All that society has accomplished for itself is put, through the agency of the school, at the disposal of its future members."[2]

He connected individual growth to societal growth: "Here individualism and socialism are at one. Only by being true to the full growth of all the individuals who make it up, can society by any chance be true to itself. . . . Nothing counts as much as the school, for, as Horace Mann said, 'Where anything is growing, one former is worth a thousand re-formers.'"[3]

Secretary of Education Arne Duncan has a little-known personal connection to John Dewey. His mother ran an after-school tutoring program in a church, serving African American families. In an article in *Parade* magazine, Secretary Duncan described his own family's preparation for that day: "No day of the year held more anticipation for my sister, brother, and me than the first day of school—and our mom and dad made sure we never took it for granted. Every year, we had to neatly lay out our new pencils and notebooks the day before school. On my first day of kindergarten, my dad strapped me into a child seat on the back of his bicycle and pedaled to the schoolhouse door to guide my first step into the brave new world of teachers, principals, and classmates."[4]

That schoolhouse was, in fact, John Dewey's Lab School at the University of Chicago, where Duncan's father was a professor of psychology. As a boy, Arne Duncan literally walked in Dewey's footsteps. More than a century after Dewey's lectures to parents, as secretary of education, Duncan went on to closely echo Dewey's words: "While much has changed since then, the singular impact of education has not. Education still holds the unique power to open doors in American society—and parents today, as in earlier generations, have the ability to help make those dreams of opportunity a reality. Education remains 'the great equalizer' in America. No matter what your zip code, race, or national origin, every child is entitled to a quality education."[5]

A second major theme urged by Dewey was to connect school learning to children's lives, a theme that underlies each of the six edges of this book. As early as the 1890s, the institution of school was already isolating the classroom from the rest of society and undermining the natural curiosity of children, leading to a long century of censoring student interest that continues today. In a section called "Waste in Education," Dewey wrote:

While I was visiting in the city of Moline a few years ago, the superintendent told me that they found many children every year who were surprised to learn that the Mississippi River in the textbook had anything to do with the stream of water flowing past their homes. . . . It is more or less an awakening to many children to find that the whole thing is nothing but a more formal and definite statement of the facts which they see, feel, and touch every day. When we think that we all live on the earth, that we live in an atmosphere, that our lives are touched at every point by the influences of the soil, flora, and fauna, by considerations of light and heat, and then think of what the school study of geography has been, we have a typical idea of the gap existing between the everyday experiences of the child and the isolated material supplied in such large measure in the school.[6]

Dewey knew what so many educators know today: if we just allowed children to ask and seek answers to questions they naturally ask, they would lead their own learning into many domains. Back in 1977, I was research director for a major new project that would become the PBS children's science series, *3–2–1 Contact*. In the early stages, we thought of it as "the curiosity show" and sought to build the series around children's questions. We went out to local schools in New York City and gathered questions from eight- to twelve-year-olds. Here is a sampling of them:

Why do people get sick?

How does your body know when it's time to grow?

How do we talk?

How is a chimpanzee smarter than a porpoise?

How does a kangaroo jump?

Who is the tallest man or woman in the world?

How hot is a volcano?

How do you make: paper, chalk, glass, cartoon characters, telephones, buildings?

How does it work: calculator, camera, light bulb, magnet, clock, TV?

It is amazing how an obvious question children naturally ask can lead to many threads of investigation and increasingly sophisticated answers. One more question a child asked us, "What makes spring and summer?," was posed in a film to Harvard seniors, on the day of their commencement, phrased as, Why is it hotter in the summer and colder in the winter?

This innocent question, which we experience every year for as long as we've been on the planet, stumps many adults and even our supposedly best and brightest college graduates. In the film, *A Private Universe*, produced by the Harvard-Smithsonian Observatory, the Harvard seniors clearly had no idea, although some were quite glib in giving wrong answers. Having been in their position, wearing my graduation robe in Harvard Yard on a sunny June day in 1974, I guarantee I would have stumbled through an uncertain reply, as well.

I won't divulge the answer but encourage you to take this chance to investigate it. Before you race to Google it, see if this question doesn't take you back to a sense of being a human being living on this Earth and how far our educations have taken us from Dewey's admonition that children should investigate "the facts which they see, feel, and touch every day."

Try mulling it over with some friends. Comparing ideas with other people and seeing how they think energizes the learning process. Group work is an important feature of student-centered classrooms. Students benefit from hearing and reading how other learners are thinking. Unfortunately, most of us were schooled in classrooms where "No Talking" and "Do Your Own Work" were the dominant rules. Just as

Robert Putnam chronicled the decline of American community in his best-seller, *Bowling Alone*, our schools have mandated "learning alone."

When you've figured this one out, noting the importance of diagrams and visual models for understanding this phenomenon, pick a few of the other questions posed by the children we studied. Better yet, ask today's children for questions they're curious about or find your own "inner child" and come up with your own. Some of my favorites, which I'm still investigating, relate to items I carry around in my pocket and use every day. How does a cell phone work? A digital camera? An iPod? You can begin to appreciate how an entire curriculum could be built around a sequence of these investigations. Advocates of project-based learning call these "driving questions," questions that may seem simple in phrasing but lead to deep and complex investigations.

Kids ask obvious questions related to history and the humanities, too. As a boy driving about town with his parents in Modesto, California, George Lucas noticed many different types of churches. He asked his mother, "If there is only one God, why are there so many different religions?" This simple yet profound question could occupy weeks of investigation into history and comparative religion, whether the questioner is ten, twenty, or fifty years old. While the question was off limits in George's school in the 1950s and might be in most schools today, its relevance to the pressing issues of today's domestic and global conflicts could not be overstated.

Dewey's own question remains a driving question for creating an Education Nation: Could we design a school system in which every child could investigate the "facts which they see, feel, and touch every day"?

EDUCATION AND ECSTASY

George Leonard was a senior editor for *Look* magazine in the 1960s and reported on topics ranging from brain physiology to schools. A common thread was the untapped reserves of human potential. "In 1964," he wrote, "I spent six months interviewing leading psychologists and brain researchers on the subject of the human potential. They all agreed that most of the innate capability of most people is routinely squandered. It was clear that our mode of education itself was a major cause of this tragic waste."[7]

He cofounded Esalen, which continues today at Big Sur, California, as a community devoted to mindfulness. He served as an Army Air Corps pilot and was an aikido master. Leonard could have been the intellectual descendant of John Dewey three generations later. They shared the same DNA about learning. Leonard not only communicated that education should serve the natural curiosity of children, he also emphasized that learning is fundamentally a joyful activity, something that activates our higher impulses. As human beings, we are meant to love learning.

His 1956 account, "What Is a Teacher," based on weeks spent in Decatur, Illinois, with second-year teacher Carolyn Wilson and her students, accompanied by photographs by Charlotte Brooks, became a classic.

> A yellow haired boy flings up his hand. A tearful boy with a crew cut pulls away from Carolyn Wilson's embrace, resisting forgiveness. A doleful little girl nestles in the curve of Carolyn's body. And, on page after page, the teacher is there, struggling cheerfully against impossible odds, bolstered by unsubstantiated hope, saying "There is good in every child."[8]

This experience was one of many that led Leonard to call for a radical change in schooling. After writing trenchant pieces for *Look*, Leonard compiled his ideas in a 1968 book whose title married two words rarely spoken together, before or since: *Education and Ecstasy*. He wrote:

> The most common mode of instruction today, as in the Renaissance, has a teacher sitting or standing before a number of students in a single room, presenting them with facts and techniques of a verbal-rational nature. Our expectation of what the human animal can learn remains remarkably low

and timorous.... All that goes on in most schools and colleges today ... is only a thin slice of what education can become.

Leonard foresaw the dawn of a new age of learning, in which:

> Average students learn ... present day subject matter in a third or less of the present time, pleasurably rather than painfully.... Provide a new apprenticeship for living, appropriate to a technological age of constant change.... Many new types of learning having to do with crucial areas of human functioning that are now neglected ... can be made part of the educational enterprise. Much of what will be learned tomorrow does not today even have a commonly accepted name.... Almost every day will be a "teachable day," so that almost every educator can share with his students the inspired moments of learning now enjoyed by only the most rare and remarkable. Education in a new and greatly broadened sense can become a lifelong pursuit for everyone. To go on learning, to go sharing that learning with others.... Education, at best, is ecstatic.[9]

The book was serialized in three issues of *Look* and reached 34 million readers. Leonard received more than 5,000 letters from them, many wanting to start new kinds of schools. Nearly twenty years passed from the book's first publication to its second edition in 1987. Leonard wrote that he had resisted updating it, since the school system had proven remarkably resistant to change and so little change had come to pass. However, in the Foreword of the second edition, he wrote:

> In the late 70s, something quite unexpected happened. I began getting letters, phone calls, and visits from computer experts at universities, in Silicon Valley, at AT&T Information Systems. A new technology was coming online that

would make ... the visionary school ... possible, not in the
realm of science fiction, but in the near future.... I'm
also happy that some truly innovative computerized systems are presently coming on line. The Education Utility,
for example, is designed to beam an electronic information
system into schools, just as telephone service is wired into
our homes.... The Utility could provide individualized, self-
paced computer learning programs along with a classroom
management system and access to a wide variety of reference
materials.[10]

That Utility is now the Internet, providing students around the globe
with access—far beyond the early, text-based networked systems—to
the world's best sources of knowledge, including films, music, and
presentations by experts in many languages. Technology has surpassed
even Leonard's vision two decades later.

In a 1984 article in *Esquire*, entitled "The Great School Reform
Hoax," Leonard laid out an eleven-point agenda for schools that, a
quarter-century later, could easily be a manifesto for many groups
creating twenty-first-century schools. It included:

- Start individualizing education as soon as possible, in every respon-
  sible way possible.
- Initiate a large-scale curriculum development program.
- Pay teachers more and treat them as masters.
- Use computers to teach more than just how to use computers.
- Institute tough, consistent rules concerning dangerous or disrup-
  tive behavior.
- Get parents and the community involved in the schools.

But his eleventh point stands as the key to the previous ten:

Make school exciting, challenging, and vivid. This is the
most important point of all. The preschooler is a voracious

natural learner. Having just performed the most awesome learning feat known on this planet—the mastery of spoken language—the child goes off to school, only to get some stunning news: In this place, far too often, learning is dull! Here is the underlying truth that few expert observers are willing to confront: Most schools are dreary, boring places....

We must consider the possibility that students are justified in being bored, that we have been too cautious and unimaginative, that we have let our schools stagnate in the backwaters of our national life. Perhaps the moment has come to show our young people that school is where the action is, intellectually and physically, that the classroom as well as the playfield is a vivid place, a place of adventure and surprise, of manageable ordeals, of belly laughs–a place, in short, of learning.... Education is hard work, and that is true. But it is also great fun, an everlasting delight, and sometimes even ecstasy.[11]

I agree. In the halls of Congress, state capitols, district offices, and school hallways, the education conversation has been far too "cautious and unimaginative." About ten years ago, after I had joined the Lucas Foundation, I invited George Leonard, who lived not far from our campus in Marin County, to attend one of our foundation's events. He clearly saw the connection between his writings from the 1960s through the '80s with our work at Edutopia. Later, my wife and I had the chance to take a workshop led by him and his wife, Annie, at Esalen. In an aikido demonstration, he asked the young men in our class to form a line and charge at him. Even in his eighties, he deftly maneuvered around them and flipped them onto the mats.

George Leonard passed away in early 2010, as I was writing this book. We owe him a debt of gratitude. So, thank you, George Leonard, for proclaiming a Declaration of Independence from timid words and modest thinking about education, teachers, and students.

TEN EDUCATION WARS TO CEASE FIRE: FROM EITHER/OR TO BOTH-AND THINKING

Many worn-out ideas can be found in the turf battles, political disputes, and "education wars" that continue today. Albert Einstein is credited with this statement: "The definition of insanity is doing the same thing over and over again and expecting different results." The past few decades of roundabout school reform should be enough to drive most people who care about education insane.

While test results have made it abundantly clear for decades that the academic performance of American students has been declining, especially during secondary school, under No Child Left Behind, the United States stepped up its testing regime to report these sad results, over and over again. Or as Robin Williams puts it, "Redundant, redundant, redundant." School districts have responded to poor test results by subjecting students to more intensive drilling, tutoring, and staring at the same worksheets, textbooks, and whiteboards that didn't work in the first place. In many classrooms, trading chalk for dry-erase markers might be the biggest change one could point to. Even that shift might be hard won. Years ago, my colleague, John Richmond from the U.K.'s Channel 4, was visiting classrooms, checking on whether teachers were using their award-winning educational programs. One of them politely told him, "My dear Mr. Richmond, here in our school, we're still getting used to colored chalk."

In the education wars, such as the battle between emphasizing "basic skills" versus "higher-order thinking skills," experts dig in their heels, sharpen their opposing points of view, hone their debating skills, and publish their op-ed pieces. Instead of spinning our wheels in these timeworn debates, it's time to issue a cease-fire, step back, and think harder. In fact, as in most debates, both sides make good points. Practicing an important "twenty-first-century skill," we need a greater consensus that synthesizes these "either/or" debates into a more inclusive and bigger-picture "both-and" understanding.

The table below lists ten "either/or" debates and their opposing points of view that continue to generate more heat than light, resulting in a waste of precious time, resources, and policies, and, most of all, little impact on student learning. The right-hand column reconciles these extreme views into a smarter synthesis, acknowledging both sides and integrating them into a bigger picture of learning.

Turning Ten Either/Or Debates into Both-And Syntheses

EITHER	OR	BOTH-AND: THE SMARTER SYNTHESIS
Phonics skills	Whole language	Both are critical to reading. What kinds of rich linguistic environments support both?
Computational skills	Mathematical thinking	Both are critical in mathematics. What types of problems and experiences engage students to want to calculate and think mathematically?
Tests	Authentic assessment	Both are important in assessing and improving student learning. What kinds of tests are useful? And what larger assessment programs can improve learning?
Teacher-centered instruction	Student-centered learning	Teachers are vital in a student-centered classroom, but they play a different role when technology is the platform for content and collaboration.
Academic learning	Social-emotional learning	Students' heads are connected to their hearts. Both need to be engaged for productive student learning.

(*continued*)

Turning Ten Either/Or Debates into Both-And Syntheses (*continued*)

EITHER	OR	BOTH-AND: THE SMARTER SYNTHESIS
Learning in nature	Learning with technology	Understanding the natural world involves collecting and analyzing data. Handling data involves technology.
Reading	Media and technology	Media and technology can support reading, online and in print, in new ways, through enlivening text with images and music and aiding students in analyzing their own reading.
Face-to-face instruction	Online learning	The added value of face-to-face interactions becomes even more important in online learning. Face-to-face can happen online through videoconferencing and in person.
Twenty-first-century skills	Core curriculum	Exercise the "new skills" of creativity, collaboration, and global thinking within a redesigned core curriculum integrating the humanities and sciences.
Enjoyment in learning	Hard work of learning	If students have a choice and voice in what and how they learn, they'll work harder at it. Find what they enjoy doing, such as arts or sports, and connect learning to it.

HYBRID THINKING FOR EDUCATIONAL INNOVATION

Just as the hybrid gasoline-electric motor has brought innovation to automobiles, turning either/or into both-and thinking can create new approaches to fuel educational performance. There are many examples of break-the-mold hybrids in education; many of them relate to media and technology. *Sesame Street*, which celebrated its fortieth anniversary in 2009, is perhaps the best known, but it confronted many doubters during its early years who thought only in terms of what had been. "Television is the enemy of learning," they reasoned, setting up an extreme dichotomy. "It's full of violence and kids spend far too much time with it. It would be foolhardy to use TV to teach."

But *Sesame Street* presented an entirely new design for a children's TV show, one that was unimaginable based on the past. It brought together new talent, from Jim Henson's Muppets to TV writers, musicians, educators, and researchers who had never collaborated before. It combined humor, puppets, animation, songs, a diverse cast, and comprehensive preschool curriculum, focused on both cognitive and social skills. It used a TV format that relied on detailed "message design," high production values, and repetition—the TV commercial—and applied it to sell numbers, letters, and learning.

That's my definition of how innovation happens: take the best elements of what has been, integrate diverse sources of knowledge and talent, and create a breakthrough that hasn't been imagined before. In its creative assembly of these factors, *Sesame Street* is a quintessentially American production that has gone around the world and back. Now seen in various formats in more than 100 countries, from translations of the American series to coproductions with producers, animators, and puppeteers from countries such as South Africa and China, as well as a unique partnership between Israel and Palestine, *Sesame Street* is "the longest street in the world." Like a hybrid car, this TV vehicle may have outwardly looked like a TV show, but its inner workings fundamentally changed the future of media in education, returning enormous social benefit in the process. To paraphrase one of its most famous songs that teaches classification, "One of these shows is very much not like the others."

Today the world of online learning is hybridizing the value of face-to-face (FTF) instruction with the potential of multimedia teaching. It is combining the value of what teachers and learners can do together in real, synchronous time with the added value of what can be done individually and in groups offline and online, asynchronously. The research on online learning is finding that FTF sessions continue to be valuable. When teachers and learners have a chance to meet in person, the learning bonds between them are strengthened, improving their online exchanges, motivation, and trust. Now that learners can actually see and talk to each other online through videoconferencing, this new type of virtual meeting—FTF online—will improve the educational and cost-effectiveness of online learning.

There are many more either/ors in education. You can turn this "Table of Ten" into a game for your next faculty, school board, or professional development meeting. Add to the list and come up with some new educational hybrids of your own that build on the strengths of seemingly opposite points of view and compensate for their weaknesses. This activity exercises some twenty-first-century thinking muscles that students need as well: the ability to evaluate differing, sometimes conflicting, points of view and create a new, more contemporary and powerful perspective. Create some new HEVs, hybrid educational vehicles, that can take us further down the road to designing new schools and dramatically increase the mileage we've been getting out of our educational thinking.

FEED THE ELEPHANT, DON'T WEIGH THE ELEPHANT

I was at a meeting in New York when a colleague told a story of visiting India, where an educator there asked her, somewhat skeptically, "In America, you test your students a lot, don't you?" She replied that, indeed, the United States has a national policy that required testing of all students in certain grades. The Indian educator said, "Here, when we want the elephant to grow, we feed the elephant. We don't weigh the elephant."

Now, I've never been to India and I've never tried to weigh an elephant. But this strikes me as the most concise and sound educational policy advice I've heard: concentrate on what we should be intellectually (and physically) feeding our children and not just on measuring their mental weight. As our nation has found, burdened by the regulations of No Child Left Behind, it's incredibly hard to weigh an elephant accurately. The obsession with testing is slowing down an already lumbering educational system, at a time when we need to be speeding up. (I promise only one more elephant metaphor.)

If we were to emphasize feeding our students' brains, what would we feed them? Most answers would focus on content in the language arts, science, or math and how it should be taught. But what about telling students something about the very nature of learning, intelligence, and brain development itself? Why not teach students about how their own brains develop, that the brain is the most marvelous and complex human organ, and how learning is the nourishment their brains need to grow and develop?

A "GROWTH MODEL" OF INTELLIGENCE

Research has found that teaching children to appreciate their brains motivates them to learn and expend greater effort, with improvements in mathematics learning. These profound results came from studies by Stanford psychologist Carol Dweck and her colleagues, Lisa Blackwell at Columbia and Kali Trzesniewski at Stanford, published in *Child Development* and promoted in a story on National Public Radio.[12,13]

Dweck and her colleagues conducted two studies, the first showing relationships between students' theories of intelligence, their motivation to learn, and their academic achievement. In the first study, the sample included 373 junior high students in four successive groups from a New York City secondary school. The students were "moderately high achieving, with average 6th-grade math test scores at the 75th percentile nationally; 53% were eligible for free lunch." The sample was 55% African American, 27% South Asian, 15% Hispanic, and 3% East Asian or white.

Those students who held a "growth model" of intelligence agreed more often with statements such as "You can always greatly change how intelligent you are" and disagreed with statements such as "You have a certain amount of intelligence and you really can't do much to change it." They also valued learning more strongly (agreeing more often with statements such as "An important reason why I do my school work is because I like to learn new things") and believed more strongly that effort leads to positive outcomes ("The harder you work at something, the better you will be at it"). Faced with academic difficulties, such as not doing well on a test, they were more likely to redouble their efforts rather than blame their lack of intelligence or the fairness of the test.

This growth model of intelligence was related to higher mathematics achievement in the fall of seventh grade and in the spring of eighth grade. That junior high math grades could be affected by students' beliefs about themselves as learners should compel the attention of a nation anxious to improve mathematics achievement. The researchers related this potent relationship between students' beliefs and their academic performance to this critical period of adolescence. It's an important time to help teenagers develop a positive self-image about themselves as learners.

In a second study, the researchers studied whether this positive "growth model" of intelligence could be taught. In a different New York City junior high, with a similar racial mix but involving students with lower achieving and poorer backgrounds, ninety-one students were assigned to experimental and control groups. Both groups received instruction during eight 25-minute sessions on brain physiology and study skills. The experimental group, however, was "taught that intelligence is malleable" through, for instance, "vivid analogies [of] muscles becoming stronger." "The key message was that learning changes the brain by forming new [neurological] connections, and the students are in charge of the process."[14] All students had the same math teacher, who was unaware of which students were assigned to which group.

Math grades typically decline during the junior high years, but students who were taught to think that their brains and greater effort could increase intelligence reversed the expected decline, while students in the control group continued to decline. In the NPR interview, Dweck described how seriously students took this neurological learning: "When they studied, they thought about those neurons forming new connections. When they worked hard in school, they actually visualized how their brain was growing."[15]

Their math teacher gave these accounts of two students who had been taught the "growth model":

> L., who never puts in any extra effort and doesn't turn in homework on time, actually stayed up late working for hours to finish an assignment early so I could review it and give him a chance to revise it. He earned a B+ on the assignment (he had been getting Cs and lower).

> M. was [performing] far below grade level. During the past several weeks, she has voluntarily asked for extra help from me during her lunch period in order to improve her test-taking performance. Her grades drastically improved from failing to an 84 on her recent exam.[16]

Two sentences near the end of the *Child Development* article summarize its message to educators: "Children's beliefs become the mental 'baggage' that they bring to the achievement situation.... A focus on the potential of students to develop their intellectual capacity provides a host of motivational benefits."[17]

A note about elephants: one thing I do know is that their gestation period is about eighteen months. Let's spend the next year and a half giving birth to a new "national educational mindset," based on expanding students' minds and their own understanding about how to use them.

STUDENTS: FEED YOUR BRAINS AND WATCH THEM GROW

The research by Carol Dweck and her colleagues and its implications for education and parenting has been published as a book, *Mindset: The New Psychology of Success.*[18] It details how children can be taught to "feed their own brains" through understanding that their intelligence can be grown and how this mindset improves their academic performance. I asked Dweck about her recommendations of what teachers and parents can do. In an e-mail interview in February 2007, she recommended the following strategies:

- Teach students to think of their brain as a muscle that strengthens with use, and have them visualize the brain forming new connections every time they learn.

- When teaching study skills, convey to students that using these methods will help their brains learn better.

- Discourage use of labels (*smart*, *dumb*, and so on) that convey intelligence as a fixed entity.

- Praise students' effort, strategies, and progress, not their intelligence. Praising intelligence leads to students to fear challenges and makes them feel stupid and discouraged when they have difficulty.

- Give students challenging work. Teach them that challenging activities are fun and that mistakes help them learn.

I asked Dweck to comment on implications for educational policies that would support this kind of teaching.

> Teachers themselves should be seen as capable of growth and development, and policymakers should support teachers' efforts to grow. Teachers should also receive within-school mentoring in areas in which they are weak. The idea should be that all teachers have strengths and weaknesses, but that all can develop their skills in weaker areas. Teachers should also be rewarded for motivating love of learning and improvement in low-achievement students, not simply playing to children who are already high achievers.

Teachers whose students improved most in our workshops were those who devoted extra time to students who asked for help. Teachers need the time and leeway to devote this kind of attention to their students. Finally, this kind of teaching is about learning. American curricula often try to jam too many different topics into each year. For example, American high schools try to teach fifty to sixty science topics per year, as opposed to nine in Japanese schools. To show students how to learn and how to appreciate the growth in their understanding, we need more depth in what we teach them.

I asked her to comment on the role of technology in helping children express their intelligences.

Because our workshop was so successful, we obtained funding to develop a computer-based version called Brainology.[19] It consists of six modules teaching study skills and teaching about the brain. In the module on the brain, students visit a brain lab and do virtual experiments. For example, they could see how the brain formed new connections as it learned. They see online interviews with other students their age, keep an online journal, advise animated student characters how to study, and take mastery tests on the material at the end of each module.

We pilot tested this program in twenty New York City schools with considerable success. Virtually every student reported that they changed their mental model of learning and were doing new things to make their brains learn better, learn more, and make new connections.

Dweck's research mirrors Edutopia's core concepts such as project-based learning, teacher development, and technology integration. The teacher behaviors Dweck recommends are frequently seen and described in our articles and videos, depicting teachers setting high expectations for all students, with resulting strong achievement for students of all backgrounds. For example, in *Learning by Design,* our documentary on the Build SF Institute, teachers and architects are seen pushing San Francisco high school students to improve their building designs and devote greater effort and persistence.[20]

Edutopia's coverage of teacher development also emphasizes policies that provide more time for teacher collaboration and focus on student work, as well as more support for teacher mentoring. Edutopia's column, "Ask Ellen," written by Ellen Moir, executive director of the New Teacher Center in Santa Cruz, California, highlights these practices and policies.[21] Dweck's Brainology software illustrates a key benefit of technology in helping students visualize relationships and connect with other learners.

A NATIONAL CAMPAIGN TO TEACH BASKETBALL FROM TEXTBOOKS

If the United States has not yet earned the title of "Education Nation," it definitely qualifies as a sports-obsessed nation. The World Series, the Super Bowl, and the NBA finals all occupy a large portion of our nation's mindshare for months. Add in collegiate and high school sports, and you've got game, big time, on the brains of Americans. If we could get half as exercised about scholastics as sports, our schools would rapidly improve.

Until that happens, let's consider the lessons of sports for learning. While we may not be very smart about what real learning is, we're quite bright when it comes to sports.

Let's take the example of what we know about the teaching and learning of basketball and apply those lessons to schools. The shortcomings of what textbooks can teach and what "authentic learning" really is would quickly become apparent. I learned this analogy many years ago from an eminent science educator, Dr. Roger Nichols, who served as director of the Boston Museum of Science in the 1980s. Dr. Nichols felt so strongly about reaching children early with the excitement of science that he gave up his faculty position at Harvard Medical School to lead the Museum of Science during the last chapter of his career.

As a young assistant professor of education at Harvard, I took my graduate students to visit the Museum of Science and meet with Dr. Nichols. In discussing the need for hands-on science learning, Nichols asked us to imagine parents at the dinner table asking their young son or daughter that perennial question, "What did you learn in school today?" The child shrugs, as they often do, and says, "We learned to play basketball." The parents then ask, "How do you do that?" The child answers, "Well, we sat in the gym and the teacher passed out these books and we turned to chapter one, about passing the basketball. We learned there are three types of passes—the bounce pass, the chest pass, and the one-handed pass."

"Okay," parents would say, wanting to know more, "what happened next?" The child continues, "We read the next chapter about dribbling. And another chapter on shooting. We learned there's the set shot, the bank shot, and the jump shot." After a few minutes of this recitation, most parents, growing increasingly exasperated, would challenge: "But did the teacher ever give you a basketball and take you on the court to play?" "No," the child sighs. "We just read the book until the bell rang."

Nichols said that parents in America would never stand for this, for sports to be taught to their children solely through memorizing terms and reading about what athletes do. Sports require performance, watching others perform, and observing oneself performing. Sports coaches and athletes routinely make use of videotape analysis of games to improve performance. Yet millions of parents settle for science, mathematics, history, and other subjects taught through rote memorization of definitions from textbooks, while their children never get a chance to actively perform real science or history.

Powerful science and mathematics education moves students out of the classroom and into collecting data in fields and streams, at traffic intersections, and in their larger communities. Following the teachings of John Dewey, students could begin by seeking answers to the obvious questions they encounter every day in their own lives, such as, "Where does the water in your house come from? Where does it go to? And how can you measure its quality?" The learning of history should immerse students in original documents, photographs, and music, as the Library of Congress's American Memory collections do so well.[22]

So, I humbly propose a new national campaign to teach basketball with textbooks. If the ensuing parental marches on school board meetings, mass expressions of outrage, and enraged school board debates lead to energetic discussions about active hands-on, minds-on learning in academic subjects, this short-lived campaign will have been very worthwhile. It will have made us smarter about what authentic learning is all about and moved us closer to creating the kind of curriculum an Education Nation needs.

In the next chapter, I discuss how the smarter thinking and ideas from this chapter are being translated into better approaches to curriculum and assessment—the Curriculum Edge.

EDGE

2

THE CURRICULUM EDGE
REAL LEARNING
AND AUTHENTIC ASSESSMENT

What's your definition of a great school? Make it short and make it measurable. Here's mine: Do students run into the school in the morning at the same speed they run out in the afternoon?

FROM A CONVERSATION WITH PAUL HOUSTON, FORMER
EXECUTIVE DIRECTOR, AMERICAN ASSOCIATION
OF SCHOOL ADMINISTRATORS

THE CURRICULUM EDGE represents the growing trend of transforming and reorganizing the most fundamental educational activities: what students are taught and how their learning is assessed. This edge recognizes that today's curriculum has not kept up with the rapid pace of change in every discipline. The very definition of what a course is, how it is organized, and what it covers needs to be reconceived for advances in twenty-first-century knowledge. In particular, fields of knowledge have become more integrated rather than siloed; but many courses continue to teach mathematics separately from science, English distinct from history, and foreign languages apart from world culture. Universities, by reflecting research on the frontiers of knowledge, are integrating courses across the disciplines, and schools need to keep up with the times. These subject matter silos prevent students from seeing the relevance of courses and concepts, leading them to justifiably pose their most frequently asked question: "Why do I need to know this?"

Fortunately, the Curriculum Edge is driving a wedge into a growing number of schools, especially high schools, across the nation. Curricula that integrate across disciplines naturally occur in places where rigorous project-based learning (PBL) has been implemented. The Buck Institute for Education defines project-based learning: " . . . students go through an extended process of inquiry in response to a complex question, problem, or challenge. While allowing for some degree of student 'voice and choice,' rigorous projects are carefully planned, managed, and assessed to help students learn key academic content, practice 21st Century skills (such as collaboration, communication, and critical thinking), and create high-quality, authentic products and presentations."[1] Since students' exploration in the course of doing projects, such as the building of robots, doesn't stop at the borders between science, mathematics, and engineering, PBL is becoming increasingly recognized as a more effective course paradigm. Some excellent resources for understanding and designing project-based curricula and professional development include the Buck Institute for Education's PBL Handbook and PBL Starter Kit, as well as Suzie Boss and Jane Krauss's Reinventing Project-Based Learning.[2]

In this chapter, we look at places around the country that are redefining the curriculum to provide projects and experiences that are relevant to students' lives, their communities, and the larger world. More comprehensive approaches to curriculum also address its delivery through media beyond text, teaching students to communicate through images and sound. Curriculum issues also focus on students' hearts, as well as their minds, to connect their social, emotional, and academic development. And we raise our sights abroad, to nations such as Canada and Australia, for school systems that have implemented entirely new assessment systems to measure this deeper, authentic learning. Just as project-based learning takes students far beyond what they can learn while sitting at desks and filling out worksheets, like an underwater camera, these new performance-based assessments reveal a depth of student knowledge below the surface of simple test scores.

Research on the Benefits of Project-Based Learning

While project-based learning has been practiced for decades, it has gained new momentum with technology tools used for analyzing and presenting information and collaborating with others. To support the growing interest in PBL, in 2007, The George Lucas Educational Foundation commissioned a literature review of innovative classroom practices, such as PBL, cooperative learning, and teaching for deeper understanding in mathematics, science, and literacy. This review, led by Linda Darling-Hammond, includes chapters by Brigid Barron of Stanford, David Pearson and Alan Schoenfeld of Berkeley, and Elizabeth Stage of Berkeley's Lawrence Hall of Science and was published as *Powerful Learning: What We Know About Teaching for Understanding*.

In a summary published on the Edutopia Web site, Barron and Darling-Hammond reviewed numerous studies and found that

1. Students learn more deeply when they can apply classroom-gathered knowledge to real-world problems, and when they take part in projects that require sustained engagement and collaboration.
2. Active-learning practices have a more significant impact on student performance than any other variable, including student background and prior achievement.
3. Students are most successful when they are taught how to learn as well as what to learn.

They referred to studies such as the University of Wisconsin's School Restructuring Study, in which 2,128 students in twenty-three schools were taught using inquiry-based methods, resulting in significantly higher achievement.

In assessing several hundred studies of cooperative learning, Barron and Darling-Hammond documented the benefits of students working in pairs or in groups on collective tasks. They emphasized that effective implementation of project-based and cooperative learning, especially the need for teacher development, is critical. They noted that "teachers may think of project learning or problem-based teaching as unstructured and may fail to provide students with proper support and assessment as projects unfold." They cited the need for "developing group structures to help individuals learn together; creating tasks that support useful cooperative work, and introducing discussion strategies that support rich learning."[3]

Not Your Father's Biology Class

Naperville, Illinois

Today's biology course shouldn't be like your grandfather's, your father's, nor yours. Most of us took biology in our freshman year in high school; it was a survey course in which we memorized the classification of flora and fauna and the names of the parts of a cell. The most memorable events in my biology class, circa 1966, were looking at cells under a microscope, including pricking our fingers with a needle, looking at our own blood cells, and learning our blood types. Almost all students took freshman biology, but as science courses advanced through chemistry and physics, the numbers dropped.

The work of scientists in the newer fields of neuroscience and biotechnology, among others, have resulted in the ranking of biology as the most complex of the sciences. In the 1980s, Nobel Laureate in physics Leon Lederman, working at Fermilab near Chicago, saw that science education was not keeping pace with the science he wanted students to learn. He founded the Illinois Mathematics and Science Academy (IMSA), a selective high school for talented science students, grades 10 to 12, which received a 2009 Intel Schools of Distinction award. In a 2007 *Edutopia* magazine column, "Out with the Old, In with New Science," he explained his view:

A vast majority of public high schools are teaching science using a curriculum developed in the nineteenth century. This threadbare approach follows a sequence, designed by a national commission in about 1890, in which students study biology first, then chemistry, and then physics in eleventh or twelfth grade—if at all. More than a hundred years ago, this was a plausible sequence justified by the notion that the study of physics requires a higher level of mathematics than biology does. In 2006, however, this is an absurd line of reasoning. . . .

Today, we know that the disciplines follow a natural hierarchy. Think of it as a pyramid: The base is mathematics, which does not rest on or need any of the other disciplines. But physics, the next layer of the pyramid, relies heavily on the science of numbers—so much so that physicists have, in desperation, invented subbranches of mathematics.

Above physics sits chemistry, which requires physics for the explanation of all chemical processes. . . . Because everything is made of atoms, some sense of their structure and function should be part of early science learning. . . . When the molecules studied are sufficiently complex, we are verging into molecular biology.

Changing the sequence, however, is only the first step in creating a twenty-first-century curriculum. Ninth-grade physics must be taught without the usual emphasis on algebra. . . . Grasp of concepts is key, and the use of these concepts in chemistry and biology is promised. The broad application of such laws as those of motion and gravity is also a feature that is natural to physics and very difficult in ninth-grade biology.

The deep connections between disciplines imply a profound change in professional development as well. I suggest that an estimated 20 percent of teachers' time should be devoted to collegial interaction devoted to creating new learning strategies. Part of this discussion should focus on the need for storytelling . . . to explore science more fully: how it works, how it doesn't work, the nature of science, some of its history, and something about who does it and how it is done. This approach will reduce the content in each of the disciplines, but it is an essential trade-off.

The United States is unique among the world's nations in its absence of centralized educational management. We have 50 states, 16,000 school districts, and 25,000 public high schools. In the twenty-first century, there is a crucial need for coherence in a national education strategy.... A revolutionary update of our antiquated approach to teaching science is a great place to start.[4]

IMSA's curriculum reflects this up-ending of the biology, then chemistry, then physics "layer cake" of high school science. Its courses reflect modern knowledge and prize depth over breadth. Instead of year-long survey courses, IMSA has semester-long classes on topics that enable students to dive deeper into biochemistry, environmental chemistry, applied engineering, evolution, biodiversity, and ecology. This structure is reflected in the English curriculum as well, with focused semester courses such as "Portraits of Creativity," which examines the lives of creative people in the arts and sciences; "The Idea of the Individual," in which Dostoevsky's *Crime and Punishment* is compared to Shakespeare's *King Lear*; and "World Literature: Modern World Fiction," which draws upon readings from Chinua Achebe and Ryunosuke Akutagawa, the author of *Rashomon*, as well as Jorge Luis Borges and William Faulkner.

While we're revising STEM (science, technology, engineering, and math education) at the high school level, let's do the same thing from elementary school on. Dr. Seymour Papert of MIT's Media Lab fired the same salvo across the bow of all of K–12: "We teach numbers, then algebra, then calculus, then physics. Wrong! Start with engineering, and from that abstract out physics, and from that abstract out ideas of calculus, and eventually separate off pure mathematics. So much better to have the first-grade kid or kindergarten kid doing engineering and leave it to the older ones to do pure mathematics than to do it the other way around."[5] Start by having the youngest students use their hands to make things, such as Lego robots, buildings, and vehicles, learning to apply mathematics and science principles, rather than first serving them an austere diet of abstract rules of arithmetic.

FROM TEXTBOOK-BASED TO PROJECT-BASED LEARNING

Many educators around the nation and the world understand that project-based learning, as opposed to textbook-based learning, is the curricular structure to harness student engagement, lead students to learn in deeper and more meaningful ways, and allow students choice in what and how they study. When curriculum, instruction, and assessment shift out of the covers of the textbook and into the real-world context of projects, everything changes. Instead of superficially "covering the curriculum" as chapters in a textbook, students and teachers need to *uncover* the more complex issues revealed through the structured inquiry of projects. In investigating open-ended questions, students must decide for themselves which sources of information are most valuable. Making this shift calls for a revolution in every aspect of teaching and learning and is requiring decades to achieve.

For more than thirteen years, Edutopia has chronicled PBL and its benefits, dating back to an early "Edutopia classic," Jim Dieckmann's fourth- and fifth-grade classroom and an insect project at Clear View Charter School in Chula Vista, California, in San Diego County.[6] The project featured prominently in The George Lucas Educational Foundation's (GLEF) first documentary, a one-hour film titled *Learn & Live* hosted by Robin Williams.

Students collected insects in their backyards and schoolyards, researched them via the Internet, talked with expert scientists via videoconference, produced reports, and made presentations. One of the striking innovations was the ability of the San Diego State scientists to show the students' insects to them under a scanning electron microscope to analyze detailed anatomical structures of their jaws, wings, and legs.

Learn & Live was distributed on VHS cassette in 1997, a sign of how quickly times have changed. That film has been reformatted in five media over thirteen years: VHS cassette, PBS broadcast, CD-ROM, DVD, and now video over the Internet. Since then, while Internet and videoconferencing technologies have become much more powerful, cheaper, and pervasive, the insect project feels as groundbreaking today as it did back then. Just two years later, a National Science Foundation grant created Bugscope at the University of Illinois, making this project available to any school with an Internet connection. Students collect insect specimens, send them to the university, and control a $600,000 electron microscope to view their insects.[7]

The insect project took about six weeks. Most projects run between two and six weeks, and occasionally a teacher will string a few of them together. But the ultimate role of project-based learning is not to be implanted within a traditional curriculum, but to *supplant* the old curriculum with a new way of organizing entire courses.

This coursewide approach to PBL is still rare and has been frustrated by assessment systems based on memorization of information. Until assessment frameworks change, it will be a rare school board, superintendent, principal, or teacher who throws caution to the winds and experiments with entire PBL courses in the hope that students can also pass the tests.

Project-Based Learning in Advanced Placement Courses

Bellevue, Washington

In 2007, during the height of No Child Left Behind, The George Lucas Educational Foundation decided to invest in a project that would cut against the grain of current thinking. As chairman, George Lucas initiated this effort to develop a complete project-based course. He understood that, to gain credibility, such a course could not only assess student learning based upon the typical PBL measures of rubrics, reports, and presentations. To persuade policymakers and critics of project learning, student achievement needed to be measured against a standardized test. What better test than what many consider to be the gold standard of high school student achievement, the College Board's Advanced Placement

(AP) exam? Since other funders of educational research did not seem willing to support research and development on project-based learning, although GLEF is not a grant-making foundation, we saw the opportunity to get something started.

Led by Steve Arnold, GLEF cofounder and vice chair and former Lucasfilm games executive, we contacted a distinguished research group and experts in how people learn at the University of Washington, the Bellevue, Washington, school district, and then-superintendent Mike Riley. Riley was a far-sighted and progressive school leader, a "digital superintendent" who understood the power of technology in the hands of students and teachers. Riley himself used a laptop in our meetings to quickly call up data on student AP performance and course taking. Encouraged by the district and university researchers' enthusiasm, we agreed to fund the first year of the project.

During 2008–2009, the Knowledge in Action (KNAC) project was launched at three Bellevue high schools. Our goal was to deliver a complete, year-long AP U.S. Government and Politics course using project-based learning and to assess student outcomes on both the AP exam and measures of deeper learning. Drs. John Bransford and Susan Mosborg at the University of Washington LIFE (Learning in Informal and Formal Environments) Center signed on as the principal researchers for the study, working with Bellevue district curriculum staff, teachers, and other University of Washington faculty in the learning sciences, political science, and teacher education.[8]

‣ A Curriculum for AP U.S. Government and Politics

The AP U.S. Government and Politics course outlined by the College Board covers six major topics: constitutional underpinnings; political beliefs and behaviors; political parties, interest groups, and the media; institutions of national government (Congress, the presidency, federal government and courts); public policy; and civil rights and liberties. In the KNAC version, however, these topics were not simply taught in a linear order but were threaded together in a set of five "project cycles" spanning the year-long course. The projects were:

1. *A Government for Ixlandya.* Students become members of a UN Task Force advising a new fictional nation emerging from a dictatorship on the design of a constitutional democracy.

2. *Making a Difference.* Students interact with government and community leaders to propose public policies.

3. *111th Congress.* Students use an online simulation, LegSim, developed by University of Washington political science professor John Wilkerson, to act as new members of Congress, join committees, and propose legislation.

4. *Election 2008.* Students act as party strategists advising candidates in the November election.

5. *Supreme Court.* Students act as justices or attorneys arguing cases before the highest court.

Throughout the projects, students developed their expertise in simulations and tasks requiring teamwork. They used the Internet for research, visited with local officials, made presentations, received feedback from experts, and developed their responses to a course master question: What is the proper role of government in a democracy? Using formative assessment, teachers and students periodically reflected on and revised their work. Students also used Flipcams to document their course experience. At several points in the year, Edutopia's documentary crew collected classroom footage and interviews.

A "quasi-experimental" research design compared an AP course taught as a more conventional, textbook-based class with one organized around the projects. Two studies were conducted: Study 1 compared outcomes for students from two higher-achieving high schools. Study 2 compared students from a lower-performing high school with students from the higher-achieving, conventionally taught classes in Study 1.

Results from Year 1 were quite encouraging, despite a teachers' strike at the start of the school year, which limited class time. In Study 1, the PBL students from the high-achieving school performed significantly better on the AP American Government and Politics exam, scored from 1 (low) to 5 (high), with passing scores of 3, 4, and 5. It was notable that many more of the project-based learning students scored higher 4's and 5's than students in the conventional course.

All students were also given a "Complex Scenario Test" before and after the course. Each version of the test required students to frame and solve a simulated, real-world problem of participating in a democracy, such as giving policy advice to a member of Congress. In Study 1, the project-based learning students also performed significantly better on all four dimensions of this assessment. The PBL students rated their own engagement with the AP course higher on two of four dimensions of classroom community.

In Study 2, PBL students from the moderate achieving, less advantaged school performed as well on the AP test as students from the higher-achieving school who took the traditionally taught course. These PBL students also outperformed students in the traditional course on all four dimensions of the Complex Scenario Test.

These findings offer some initial, tentative support for the hypothesis that a rigorous project-based AP course might enable a broader range of high school students with more diverse backgrounds and learning styles to be successful at rigorous upper-level high school work. The KNAC team is making use of classroom videos to understand the activities and interactions to emphasize further.

In Year 2 of the study, during 2009–2010, with additional support from the Bill & Melinda Gates Foundation, the project-based AP U.S. Government course will again be offered and assessed against a matched sample of conventionally taught classes. A second AP course in science will be designed, with the intention of offering both AP courses in an urban district with higher proportions of students from low-income backgrounds.

Sadly, Mike Riley passed away suddenly during the first school year of the project. His enthusiasm and leadership in getting it off the ground was crucial. He had joined the College Board as a vice president and would have been a tremendous ally in infusing project-based learning into the next generation of Advanced Placement exams. He was a shining example of superintendents who are working tirelessly against bureaucracy and long odds to bring our American school system into the twenty-first century.

AUTO MOTIVES AND DRIVING INSPIRATIONS

One of my all-time favorite Edutopia stories was the July 2007 cover story of *Edutopia* magazine, showing young African American teens fist-bumping each other while standing next to a shiny, bright red sports car.[9] If you didn't know *Edutopia* was a magazine about educational innovation, you might have thought, "Well, that's nice. These boys are congratulating each other about buying a sports car." But as you learn from the article, "Auto Motive: Teens Build Award-Winning Electric Cars," these high school students designed and built that electric car, which they dubbed the "K-1 Attack." And they won the student division of the Tour de Sol, the nation's oldest and most prestigious competition to design alternative fuel vehicles, two years running.

Teens from the inner city of Philadelphia, or any urban center with high poverty, aren't supposed to be able to do this. Simon Hauger, formerly the group's academic teacher, cites a familiar, yet always shocking, statistic: "Half of these kids are dropping out of school and of the 50 percent who don't drop out, only 20 percent can pass the state test." While national commentary focuses on inner-city "dropout factories" and federal Race to the Top funds are requiring states to turn around these schools, how did these West Philly students defy those statistics and achieve far beyond what most imagine? What made the impossible possible?

The Automotive Academy

Philadelphia, Pennsylvania

This is the story of a special "school within a school," the West Philadelphia High School's Academy of Applied Automotive and Mechanical Science. Its secret lies in redesigning the high school curriculum to be relevant to sophisticated, real-world knowledge; conveying that curriculum in projects that students find compelling and inviting; recruiting a cadre of teachers with complementary, real-world expertise of their own; creating a team-based culture of students working alongside their faculty toward a common goal; and employing a new "learning day" including evenings, weekends, and summers.

Any one of these changes represents a major overhaul to the current system. The Automotive Academy fired on all of these pistons at once. This new type of high school experience brings many of the innovation edges of this book into sharp relief, symbolized by one very cool car. The fact that these students are learning design and engineering skills that might one day lead to a new American auto industry ought to attract the attention of policymakers and auto executives. It's encouraging that Ford Motor Company has come calling and invited the students to visit their labs.

The Academy's courses include a mix of the conventional mathematics, science, and shop classes, attended by 140 students. But the real action is in the turbo-charged electric-vehicle club, where fifteen students, known as the EVX team, design and build cars. Hauger, a mathematics and physics teacher and electrical engineer, started it as an after-school program in 1997, became an academic teacher, and has returned to directing the after-school program.

His efforts to move the program into the school day were frustrated by the difficulties of doing interdisciplinary project work within a constrained school schedule. Instead, the program morphed into other "learning time" outside the school day, including an intensive summer program, when students conduct research projects related to automotive design and engineering. Hauger says, "It's what we envision the school to be. Kids and teachers sit down together and ask, 'How can we do it in an interesting and innovative way to engage kids' passions and curiosity and address fundamental academic content?'"

Over an eight-week summer term, in which students were paid stipends, they researched the chemistry behind biodiesel fuels, learning that a by-product of making fuel from soybeans is soap. A partnership with Drexel University has been valuable, enlisting college students to teach computer-aided design for a three-wheel vehicle. Toastmasters International was brought in to tutor students on their presentation skills for final projects. Compared to his students, Hauger admits, "I still can't present that well. When you think about skills to be successful, that's definitely one of them."

A fan of the Big Picture project-based high schools, also profiled on Edutopia.org, Hauger credits his teaching team: "The reality is the small group of adults who are really good at this. The framework allows us to tap into students' creativity. This week in the shop, a student said, 'I don't know how to do this.' We say, 'Let me show you how I use the chop saw.' We never say, 'Since you don't know how to do that, let me find a student who does.' The project creates the need for students to learn all sorts of things, there's always problem-solving going on, great learning opportunities constantly come up. The first and most essential ingredient is the development of relationship with these kids."

Hauger also acknowledges the creativity of his students: "Add to that this mix of teenagers who think very creatively, who don't under-stand certain aspects of design and physics. They come up with some off-the-wall ideas. Most of them aren't realistic. They always see things in ways we don't and once in awhile, something great comes up," like the look-and-feel of the K-1 Attack. "Nobody had thought about making a bad-ass hybrid vehicle. As adults we thought about fuel economy. The kids understood the reality that in 2001 and 2002, the vehicles didn't have a wide appeal. One of them said, 'My grandmother might drive a Prius, but I wouldn't drive a Prius. Let's make an obnoxiously fast electric motor and use the diesel engine for fuel economy.'"

The West Philly EVX team was so successful in the student competitions, they decided to move up to the big leagues. In the fall of 2009, they entered the Progressive Insurance X Prize, a multistage competition with teams from Fortune 500 companies vying for $10 million in prize money to build a super fuel-efficient automobile with mass appeal that can get 100 miles to the gallon. The announcement of Michigan as the host state for the road performance events, to be held in 2010, included Lieutenant Governor John Cherry, Patrick Davis of the U.S. Department of Energy, and Peter Diamandis, chairman of the X Prize Foundation.

Hauger described the approach of his team: "We asked, 'What does a young urban city driver need?' Affordability and it has to look good. You're driving in the city under 50 miles per hour. We designed the Ford Focus as a plug-in-hybrid that can drive on electric power only. We started with an existing chassis to make sure it's affordable and meets safety standards. We wanted a small, lightweight, aerodynamic car and the Ford Focus fits those criteria." For assistance with the detailed business plan required, the team turned to a group of Drexel University MBA students for a plan to create manufacturing jobs in the city.

Surely, in this world-class competition, a group of high school students wouldn't make the first cut, but of 120 initial teams, 43 were selected for the road competition. There, among them, were the high school students from West Philly. They appeared in October 2009 on the *Today* show, in a segment reported by Jenna Bush Hager.[10] When she asks them about their neighborhood, one boy responds, "A lot of drugs and violence and a lot of bad situations, had I thought a little differently, would've turned out really, really bad. I'm talkin' jail time."

Making the group of forty-three is an amazing accomplishment, but don't bet against the EVX team just yet. Their business and technical/design plans were among the handful that did not require any modifications. To find out how the team ultimately did, check out the X Prize link.[11] The team also entered the alternative vehicle category and is designing a sports car to beat the land speed record of 132 miles per hour set by a Toyota Prius. They're betting theirs will do 160 mph and still get 100 mpg.

The *Edutopia* article also told one of the most inspiring stories I have ever read about a student achieving against very long odds. Terrie Gabe was part of the 2006 team that made modifications to the K-1's suspension and body and enabled the K-1 Attack to snare the championship for a second year in a row. As writer Ginny Phillips described it in the *Edutopia* article:

> Terrie Gabe . . . was 17 when she dropped out of 10th grade after her mother died. She went to work full-time to support herself and her younger brother, and enrolled him in the automotive academy. She'd been out of school for two years when he died. That's when Gabe decided she wanted to go back to high school, and asked to be admitted to the automotive academy—growing up around her uncles' auto shops, she loved cars. She couldn't afford to stop working, though, so she switched to the night shift, working from 11 p.m. until 5:45 a.m., then coming straight to school for her 7 a.m. class.
>
> During her first go-round in traditional high school, Gabe had skipped school frequently to go to work and had

earned C's and D's. But she graduated from the academy in 2006—having worked 40 to 45 hours a week between classes—at age 21 with straight A's and no absences.

In his wonderful book *The Element,* Sir Ken Robinson, a noted arts educator, used an unusual event in Death Valley to describe how education should be a matter of providing the right climate for students to thrive:

A few hundred miles away from my home in Los Angeles is Death Valley, one of the hottest, driest places on earth. Not much grows in Death Valley, hence the name. The reason is that it doesn't rain very much there—about two inches a year on average. However in the winter of 2004–5, something remarkable happened. More than seven inches of rain fell . . . something that had not happened for generations. Then in the spring of 2005, something even more remarkable happened. Spring flowers covered the entire floor of Death Valley. . . . Death Valley was alive with fresh, vibrant growth. . . .

What this proved, of course, was that Death Valley wasn't dead at all. It was asleep. It was simply waiting for the conditions of growth. . . . Human beings and human communities are the same.

A video of one of Robinson's talks, along with a transcript, is available on the Edutopia site.[12]

Like a dormant seedling in Robinson's story, Terrie Gabe was just waiting for the right conditions to flourish as a learner. She certainly had the persistence and drive, but she came close to succumbing to the harsh conditions of her life and first high school. All she needed to thrive was the lush rain of a new learning environment. And instructors who knew how to nurture her growth. As Simon Hauger points out, these new conditions align too rarely and might not last.

Terrie reflected on her achievements that year: "It was a tremendously fun year, hands-on, challenging. I was given the chance to do something I was interested in, working hands-on with cars and hands-on with teachers and other students. I've never had that experience as part of a team." Her statement summarizes the value of project-based learning and cooperative learning and how they lead to new types of student-teacher relationships. If we all agree that every high school senior should be able to express those same sentiments, we should put in place the experiences that will get them there. Terrie Gabe's resilience and success in the face of such personal tragedy should inspire the creation of many more of these schools.

LINKING HIGH SCHOOL, COLLEGE, AND CAREER

Philadelphia's Automotive and Technology Academy is one of 28 Philadelphia Academies operating in 16 high schools serving 4,500 students. The Academies began in 1969 as a response to the urban riots of the 1960s. Philadelphia business and community leaders came together to develop a new model to steer teenagers toward education and jobs rather than violence. The National Academy Foundation, based in New York City, coordinates a national network of more than 500 Academies in 41 states and the District of Columbia. They operate in 385 public high schools in 177 districts and include 253 Academies of Finance; 98 Academies of Hospitality and Tourism; 132 Academies of Information Technology; and 13 Academies of Engineering.[13]

These Academies are not a new form of the old vocational education, where high school students identified as not "college material" were trained for jobs in the construction, electrical, or mechanical trades. As the Automotive Academy indicates, their goal is not to train a student to fix a car, but to design the car. This Academy approach prepares students for postsecondary education, including community or technical college and four-year colleges and universities, boosting their longer-term career prospects, which improve dramatically with a college degree. The Academy approach is not necessarily focused on preparing students for work in the business sectors emphasized. The goal of the workplace internships involved is to give students experience in a professional environment, provide them with mentors, and help them relate their school learning to the real world.

While it is estimated there are more than 3,000 career academies operating around the country, they range in quality and rigor. The goal is to combine rigorous academic and technical curricula with workplace internships that work in tandem, integrating learning across the school and the workplace. This integration is not easy to achieve with traditional curricula and schedules, as Simon Hauger's experience reveals, and some workplaces are less prepared to involve high school students. A rigorous academy model requires close communication between high school faculty and employer mentors.

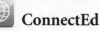 **ConnectEd**

California

One of the most ambitious efforts to continue the development of this model and bring it to scale is the work of ConnectEd: The California Center for College and Career, a nonprofit organization founded in 2006 with major support from the James Irvine Foundation.[14] In just four years, ConnectEd has become a leading organization in the state and the nation, lending coordination, leadership, and vision to bring the career academy concept into the twenty-first century. The organization identifies four core components for a program of "Linked Learning," formerly known as "Multiple Pathways":

1. A challenging academic component preparing students for college and other postsecondary programs, with four years of English, mathematics including algebra, geometry, and statistics, two years of science, three years of social studies, two years of foreign language, and one year of visual and performing arts

2. A demanding technical component of four or more technical courses

3. A work-based learning experience, including internships and virtual apprenticeships, and

4. Support services such as counseling and tutoring

I joined ConnectEd's board of directors in 2008, believing that this model offers the best hope for reinventing California's high schools in a state that educates 13 percent of the nation's students. ConnectEd is working with ten partner districts, including Long Beach, Pasadena, Sacramento, Los Angeles, San Diego, and Stockton, to implement high-quality Linked Learning academies in fields critical to California's economy: biomedicine and health sciences, finance, information technology, entertainment, hospitality and tourism, law and justice, and others. Linked Learning enables students to exercise choice among pathways that connect to their interests and to work alongside professionals in careers they might contemplate. The curriculum redesign of Linked Learning is informed by modern advances in these fields and includes an emphasis on project-based learning, cooperative learning, and the integration of technology. Dr. Gary Hoachlander, president of ConnectEd, says that "this work is about changing high school and ways of reengaging students to help them better understand why they need to master academics. It is powerful in helping students make meaning."

Coordination among the ten districts includes the development of an online platform, ConnectEd Studios, to enable students and teachers to access curriculum units and resources, plan projects, connect with industry professionals, and publish portfolios of work. This type of "educational Intranet" is valuable not only for students and faculty who use it, but for making the work visible to the larger group of stakeholders, including administrators, parents, school board members, and legislators. Technology can make innovation public, solving one puzzle of why many innovations go unnoticed.

As one example, the ConnectEd Web site includes a gallery of videos showcasing the experience of students. These student profiles personalize the rationale and the research behind Linked Learning. At the Space Technology and Robotics Academy (STaRS) in Lompoc, senior Trae Vernon plans to go on to college in civil engineering. STaRS students intern at nearby Vandenberg Air Force Base, whose rocket launches they grew up witnessing. Now, they are learning the skills to work there. As a basketball player, Trae is interested in translating what he's learned about design and engineering into becoming an architect for NBA arenas.

Ana Sical almost didn't make it to the Construction Tech Academy in San Diego for tenth grade. As she recounts her attitude at her first high school, "It was kind of just show up to school, I was always late, always absent. Then I came here, they almost didn't want to let me in. . . . Here I see there is a future for me, so I actually apply myself." In the video, she is shown using computer-aided design software to design buildings. Her principal describes how she has taken advantage of job shadows and internships. She graduated as a class valedictorian. The first in her family to attend college, Ana is at San Diego State University on full scholarship, where she is majoring in construction management. Once students get on the right path, it is amazing how rapidly they can progress.

In a third video, Obed Hurtado, a student at the Arthur Benjamin Health Professions High School in Sacramento, learns about the characteristics of light in physics class, principles that are reinforced when his class visits the Center for Biophotonics at the University of California, Davis. There, they learn about the user of lasers as surgical scalpels and examine how different colored lasers interact with tissue. Students and teachers wear scrubs to school, which Obed says gives him a feeling of "helping others and becoming a leader." He plans to work in radiology. His English teacher, Marsha Stanley, assigns the class to read *The Hot Zone*, the 1994 bestseller about the *Ebola* virus, and encourages Obed when he's struggling by telling him she wants him to be her doctor. The video gallery includes commentary by Jack O'Connell, state superintendent of public instruction, on the promise of Linked Learning and a segment about its approach to hands-on, integrated curriculum.

Evidence of Outcomes: Career Academies

More than 90 percent of National Academy Foundation (NAF) students graduate from high school—compared to 50 percent in the urban areas where most NAF Academies are located.

Four out of five NAF students go on to college or other postsecondary education.

Fifty-two percent of NAF graduates earn bachelor's degrees in four years—compared with 32 percent nationally.[15]

Of those who go on to postsecondary education, more than half are the first in their families to go to college.

Ninety percent of students report that the academies helped them to develop career plans.

Eighty-five percent of five- and ten-year alumni are working in a professional field.

Career academy graduates sustained $16,704 more in total earnings over the eight years following high school than non-academy group members who were also studied—11 percent more per year.[16]

Young men from career academies experienced increased earnings over eight years totaling $30,000—17 percent more per year than non-academy group members studied—thanks to a combination of increased wages, hours worked, and employment stability.

An increased percentage of career academy graduates live indepen-dently with children and a spouse or partner eight years following high school—young men, specifically, reported positive effects on marriage and parenting.

In a study by ConnectEd and the Career Academy Support Network of the University of California, Berkeley, 50 percent of students in California's partnership academies completed the courses required for University of California admission (known as the "a-g requirements") compared with 39 percent of graduates statewide. Academy students were also more likely to pass the California High School Exit Exam (CAHSEE) in 2005, including 71 percent of African American students compared with 55 percent African American students statewide. Graduation rates were also higher, 96 percent of Academy seniors compared with 87 percent statewide.[17]

GOING GLOBAL: LEARNING BECOMES INTERNET-IONAL

By now, the ability to think globally ranks high on everyone's list of critical twenty-first-century skills. In the Framework for 21st Century Learning, published by the Partnership for 21st Century Skills (P21), "global awareness" is described as one of five interdisciplinary themes, along with four other new "literacies"—financial and economic, civic, health, and environmental—that should be integrated across the traditional subject areas. The framework defines global liter-acy as "using 21st Century skills to understand and address global issues; learning from and working collaboratively with individuals representing diverse cultures, religions, and lifestyles in a spirit of mutual respect and open dialogue in personal, work, and community contexts; and understanding other nations and cultures, including use of non-English languages."[18]

The P21 site also lists the Web sites of leading organizations working on global learning, such as North Carolina in the World; Wisconsin's Strategies for Achieving Global Literacy; Primary Source, a Boston-based group; the Asia Society; the International Education and Resource Network (IEARN), one of the earliest advocates of global learning for all youth; Dickinson State University's Global Awareness Initiative from North Dakota; and Brown University's Institute for International Studies. More than twenty-five states have initiatives to advance global learning and are members of the States Network on International Education in the Schools working with the Asia Society and the Longview Foundation. An interactive map of these initiatives can be found on the Asia Society's education Web site.[19]

While educators and policymakers are responding to the "flat world" we live in, today's generation of students is also expressing widespread interest in learning about the rest of the globe. Thanks to the Internet, today's youth are easily connecting with peers in other countries and accessing different sources of international knowledge, from BBC World News and Al-Jazeera newscasts to chatting with Italian teenagers over Shared Talk or Skype to learn Italian, as one of our staffer's daughters does. Today's students are having international experiences at their fingertips, earlier in their childhoods. They will be our first truly global generation. For them, the Internet has made learning "Internet-ional."

Starting in 2004, Edutopia created a partnership with the Asia Society to document some of the best American schools leading the way to students' global futures. We produced documentary films, articles, video interviews with leaders in international educadtion, and two DVDs documenting schools and students,[20] including:

Walter Payton College Prep High School in Chicago, where students study one of five languages, including Chinese, for all four years. Their distance learning center enables live videoconferencing with students around the globe, from South Africa to China, and students participate in home-stay exchanges. The Chinese

Ministry of Education has funded Confucius Institutes at universities to support learning of Chinese language and culture. Payton has the only one located at an American high school.

San Antonio's International School of the Americas, whose curriculum includes visits to local museums, trips to Mexico, and competing in the Model United Nations. Our film showed how one enterprising teacher, confronted with the cost of buses for field trips, got her bus driver's license to enable her to use the city as her students' classroom.

John Stanford International School (JSIS) in Seattle, a K–5 elementary school where language immersion in Spanish and Japanese starts with the youngest students. For educators who believe that immersion programs give short shrift to other areas of the curriculum, JSIS demonstrates how learning a second language goes hand in hand with reading, math, and other subjects. Bilingualism travels in both directions: the school also offers a Bilingual Orientation Center to help immigrant children learn English.

Choctaw students in Mississippi who share stories with indigenous students in Thailand, through IEARN's First People's Project. Thanks to their teachers and tribal elders, students learn about their stories, histories, and sports and share their knowledge with the wider world. Upon learning of the needs of their Internet pen pals in Thailand, they organized a drive to donate blankets to them.

Portland, Oregon's K–12 Japanese immersion program (Japanese Magnet Program). Like JSIS, JMP is based on research that young children's brains are wired for language learning and that second language learning can encourage cognitive development. In the fifth grade, students learn to use Japanese word processing software to compose e-mail, host Japanese students, and visit them near Tokyo. Eighth-graders go to Japan for a two-week residency to complete an interdisciplinary project.

High Tech High in San Diego, where students learn DNA testing procedures on meat samples to investigate poached meat in African markets. They and their teacher traveled to Tanzania to hold a workshop for local game officials on the identification of bushmeat. Team teaching between humanities and science teachers is common, such as the Waterways to Peace project, where connecting African politics to water scarcity led to creating a model plant for water purification.

Dylan, a thirteen-year-old from New Hampshire who participated in ThinkQuest, the Oracle Education Foundation's international competition for youth-produced Web sites. One of Edutopia's 10 Digital Generation profiles, Dylan worked with teens in Argentina, Japan, and India who never met but produced an award-winning Web site, Sentenced for Life, on animal cruelty.

One of the benefits of connecting American students to their peers in other countries is that they quickly come to understand their lives in one of the world's most affluent nations. When they learn that much of the world lives on $3 a day or less, they gain a new appreciation of their place in the world. In 2003, we published one of our earliest global stories of Parkland High School students in Winston-Salem, North Carolina, connecting online with students in Moldova. (*Mea culpa*: I had to look it up on a map; it's one of the former Soviet Socialist Republics.) The Moldova schools had electricity for only a few hours every day when they could use the Internet. As student Sarah Gathings said, "I'm poor but I'm rich compared to them. When my mom gives me $5, I think, 'This ain't enough.' But if they had it, they'd be grateful for it. I'm not grateful for everything I have and I should be."

This growth in global learning in American schools is one of the most exciting parts of the Curriculum Edge, and it is made possible by the Technology Edge. Many school districts are incorporating global content across multiple subject areas, from the obvious courses in the humanities, history, social studies, foreign language, literature, music, and world culture classes to the less obvious STEM fields, which have also gone global in study of environmental issues and the history of math and science. (For instance, the Maya were the leading astronomers and mathematicians of their day.) This Curriculum Edge involves creating new courses to teach lesser-known but critical languages for the future, such as Chinese and Arabic.

Among the many organizations providing curriculum, professional development, and other resources for global learning, I discuss two that have national and global scope and whose Web sites provide a wealth of online content and assistance to educators: the Asia Society in New York City and the National Geographic Society in Washington, D.C.[21]

The Asia Society's education site contains a wealth of information on these schools and others, as well as their national initiatives, which include the Partnership for Global Learning, model schools, the role of afterschool programs, curriculum units and lesson plans, and the Chinese Language Initiative. The site includes a nice interactive map showing policy initiatives in close to two dozen states, including California, Wyoming, Nebraska, Georgia, Connecticut, and Vermont. It gives resources and advice for teachers who want to fund trips to take their students abroad, a key step on the road to global understanding.

The National Geographic Society's reputation for excellence in teaching about global issues and high-quality materials and professional development are well known. Its Education Network provides educator subscriptions to *National Geographic* magazine and access to an online community. Its Education Foundation focuses on partnerships with schools and universities and has led a move to "rebrand" geography education under the banner of "geoliteracy," defining it as "the ability to reason about the world to make personal, professional, and civic decisions. It is essential for life in today's complex and inter-connected society."

The foundation supports the Geographic Alliance Network of state educators, both K–12 and higher education, and has led the My Wonderful World campaign, organized through a coalition of nonprofits and businesses to support work in schools and universities. National Geographic Xpeditions is a great source of lesson plans, activities, and maps, part of the Thinkfinity searchable database of standards-based lessons from eleven leading national organizations, such as the Kennedy Center for the Performing Arts and the Smithsonian National Museum of American History.

Both the Asia Society and the National Geographic Education Foundation have regular e-newsletters to keep readers current with the latest developments.

In 2003, Edutopia profiled teacher Eva LaMar's teaching of what she also called "geoliteracy," where third-graders at Tolenas Elementary School in the Bay Area studied the ecology of the local marsh and visited Rush Ranch to learn about the history of their town, including a working blacksmith shop. Their studies integrated history, science, and art as they were mentored by high school students to create videos and Web sites of their work. LaMar later moved to Oregon, where she codirects the Geo-Literacy Project.[22]

CHINESE IS THE NEW FRENCH

I've watched, with interest and some bemusement, the growth of interest in the teaching of Asian languages and culture in American schools. I myself have struggled to learn Mandarin, taking three years in college and graduate school and occasional trips to Taiwan and China that have refreshed my speaking, but not my reading or writing. I started studying the language in the 1970s, anticipating a day when I might travel to China and be able to speak to my aunts, uncles, and cousins, whom I didn't meet until I was twenty-seven. It has been very gratifying to be able to converse with them and with Chinese educators there.

It has also been revealing to talk to American educators who resist implementing Asian language courses out of a belief that Chinese is too difficult for students to learn (as if high school courses in Spanish or French are sufficient to master those languages). With the rise of China as an international power, I believe the U.S.-China relationship is now most important bilateral relationship Americans have and that the teaching of Chinese language, culture, and history to Westerners is vital to global peace and security.

Across the country and the world, Chinese language learning is exploding. What had been a mysterious and arcane language studied only by Asian specialists is now the subject of fast-growing course enrollments in schools and universities. A *New York Times* article on January 21, 2010, reported that a study by the Center for Applied Linguistics estimated that about 1,600 American public and private schools are teaching Chinese, compared with about 300 ten years earlier.[23] However, that study noted a troubling decline in the teaching of other foreign languages, such as Russian, Japanese, and especially German and French, in secondary schools. The article reported that Trevor Packer, vice president at the College Board, believed that, in just three years, its AP exam in Mandarin, first administered in 2007, may surpass AP German as the third most popular AP foreign language, behind Spanish and French.

With trained Chinese language teachers in short supply, the Chinese government is providing teachers to American schools. The Freeman Foundation has funded six universities to develop teacher training programs for Chinese. From first-graders in immersion programs to MBAs seeking high-paying postings in Shanghai, learning Chinese has become trendy. These new courses are taking advantage of online courses and modules, such as those offered by Active Chinese and Go Chinese.

Through its Chinese Language Initiatives, the Asia Society in New York tracks the growth of Chinese language teaching, offering advice for starting programs in local schools, aid for teachers seeking certification, and a national conference. The society is creating a program of Confucius Classrooms, a network of 100 exemplary Chinese language programs in American schools utilizing an online community, professional development, and partner schools in China. These schools will, in turn, act as resources for other schools in their regions. Vivien Stewart, formerly vice president and now senior advisor for education at the Asia Society, believes that "there will be great opportunities for online and blended courses in language teaching. State virtual high schools are seeing demand for languages. In an online Mandarin course at Michigan State, graduate students serve as 'conversation coaches' for undergrads."[24]

These developments will go a long way to dispel misunderstandings about Chinese language and culture. As a Chinese official said at the announcement of the AP Mandarin course, "Many Americans think that Chinese is difficult to learn, but we have more than a billion people who speak it." Fluency, such as the ability to read a newspaper, can require knowledge of about 4,000 words, or characters. Mandarin, the official national dialect, has four tones, often the most challenging part of learning Chinese for English speakers. One sound, such as *ma*, can be written in many characters (meaning, for instance, "mother," "criticize," or "horse") and each must be correctly pronounced in one of the four tones. Regional dialects, such as the southern Cantonese, involve widely varying pronunciations but share the same characters. (American English isn't that different.)

But in this complexity lies some simplicity and much beauty. Unlike French, Chinese requires no conjugation of verbs and parsing of tenses. The Chinese simply say when an event or action occurred. Chinese characters have their own system of roots, called "radicals," giving clues to their meanings. For instance, words related to water all share the same three "droplets" on the left side of the character. Mastering the writing of characters opens a window on the beautiful and graceful world of Chinese calligraphy, regarded as one of the highest art forms, traditional and modern. Chris Livaccari, associate director for education and Chinese language initiatives at the Asia Society, himself fluent in Chinese and Japanese, describes cognitive, personal, and professional benefits: "Chinese characters utilize cognitive skills that other writing systems do not and involve a graphic and visual element that is also somewhat unique among world languages. Learning a language as different as Chinese opens students to different communication strategies and cultural practices and goes a long way toward making them globally competent, adaptable, and able to see things from multiple perspectives."

There are many interesting videos of speeches from from Asia Society conferences on their site, including one by U.S. Ambassador to China,

Jon Huntsman. A former governor of Utah, Huntsman is fluent in Chinese and started learning it while on a Mormon mission in Taiwan. He began his talk to laughter in the bilingual audience by saying in Chinese, "I tell you, today the U.S. has only one governor who can speak Chinese and that's me." In another video, *Learning Chinese in American Schools*, College Board president Gaston Caperton, an advocate for creating the AP Mandarin course, says, "Today's students really need to know the world. That kind of understanding, I think, brings not only prosperity to the world, but peace to the world." That, in the end, is the ultimate goal of global learning.

THE LANGUAGE OF IMAGES

One sign of the major disconnect between schools and students' lives is the excitement the film industry generates and how little our schools do to teach how film communicates so powerfully. Among all the ways in which the human species communicates using words, pictures, and sound, the school system overwhelmingly prizes books, text, and writing at the expense of photography, cinema, or music. The curriculum is a verbal curriculum. Yet cinema can unify all media—the written and spoken word, images, and sound—into one transcendent experience.

This ability to communicate through multimedia is often referred to as another key twenty-first-century skill that applies to every field and profession. PowerPoint has become a pervasive medium for communicating and persuading, yet if you compare the typical presentation of too much text and not enough design with the best, most dynamic PowerPoints with images, graphics, and music, you get my point.

Dean Elizabeth Daley at the USC School of Cinematic Arts has made this case for a new conception of "multimedia literacy." Daley wrote:

> To read or write the language of media and understand how it creates meaning within particular contexts, one needs some

understanding of frame composition, color palette, editing techniques, and sound-image relations, as well as...the context of signs and images, sound as a conveyor of meaning, and the effects of typography. Such principles as screen direction, the placement of objects in the frame, color choices, morphing, cuts, and dissolves all do much more than make a screen communication aesthetically pleasing. They are as critical to the creation of meaning as adverbs, adjectives, paragraphs, periods, analogies, and metaphors are to text. Multimedia also requires that attention be paid to design, navigation, and interface construction. The mouse, the click, the link, and the database have already taken their place alongside more traditional screen descriptors.[25]

While the costs of laptops, cameras, and production software now place the digital tools of multimedia production within the reach of most students, merely having the tool in one's hands does not guarantee proficiency, any more than having a pen or a brush confers the status of writer or painter. The right curriculum and skilled teachers are still key, and both are noticeably lacking in today's schools.

Note to policymakers and educators concerned about workforce preparedness: The production and distribution of entertainment is a major global industry, one where the United States still enjoys a major comparative advantage. I meet many students who are excited to hear about George Lucas's vision for education, since they also view themselves as visual and artistic thinkers. They are hungry for information on how they might prepare to work in the entertainment industry, but they don't see a pathway from their interest in the arts and technology to careers in film, TV, animation, or video games. Many in the artistic workforce making creative television, films, music, video games, and theme parks owe their success to talents nurtured outside of school rather than to any intentional school curricula.

Martin Scorsese and George Lucas have been involved with a number of educational organizations advancing the cinematic arts in education.

In a video interview on the Edutopia site, Lucas described today's youth as surrounded by media but with few opportunities to study its forms:

> They know music. They may not know the grammar of music. They know cinema, because they spend a huge amount of time in front of the television. So they know visual communication, they know the moving image. They intuitively know a lot of the rules, but nobody's actually taught them. We go through school and learn the grammar of English—punctuation, capital letters, run-on sentences, what a verb is. But nobody teaches what screen direction is, what perspective is, what color is, what a diagonal line means.... Somehow, in the educational system, these need to be balanced out so that kids can communicate using all the forms of communication, especially in this day and age where the power of multimedia is coming to the children.[26]

Lucas and Scorsese both serve on the board of directors of the Film Foundation in Los Angeles, which has produced a unique and engaging curriculum for aiding teachers and students in the analysis of how films communicate: The Story of Movies.[27] Scorsese played a starring role in its development and is featured in its materials, which are intended for middle school classes but, as with all good curricula, can be aged up or down. Its first curriculum unit, on *To Kill a Mockingbird,* was published in 2005 in partnership with IBM and Turner Classic Movies.

"The Story of Movies was not to be just another curriculum on how to make a movie or how to compare a movie to a book," according to the Film Foundation's Web site. "Rather, the focus was to guide students in learning how to read moving images. Although teachers frequently use films in the classroom, film as language and as historical and cultural documents is not widely taught." Advised by the National Council of Teachers of English, the National Council of Social Studies, the International Reading Association, and other organizations, the curriculum's producers chose three classic films for in-depth study based on their quality, educational value, and student appeal: *To Kill a Mockingbird,* adapted from Harper Lee's novel in 1962, *Mr. Smith Goes to Washington,* the Frank Capra classic from 1939, and *The Day the Earth Stood Still,* directed by Robert Wise in 1951.

When free kits of the *To Kill a Mockingbird* materials were promoted on Turner Classic Movies, more than 10,000 sets were distributed, an encouraging sign that teachers are eager for high-quality materials on multimedia literacy. Now, teachers can use the materials by downloading PDFs of the teacher and student guides at StoryofMovies.org and obtaining a copy of the film for classroom viewing.

These three films address significant periods in American history, include children in major roles, and address middle school standards related to American history, civil rights and racism, and the role of government and the legal system. The Story of Movies is an interdisciplinary curriculum based on these principles:

1. *Film is a language.* Students study the way in which images are framed, sequenced, paced, and combined with sounds. They analyze the purpose of a shot, as well as its suggested meanings.

2. *Film is a cultural document* through which students can explore the historical period in which the film was made and the social issues relative to the film's themes.

3. *Film is a collaborative art,* the result of the collaboration of many professionals and artisans spanning science and cinematography, literature and language arts, music, art and design, and digital technology.

The teacher's guide for *To Kill a Mockingbird* is divided into four chapters, titled "What Is a Movie?," "The Filmmaking Process," "Film Language and Elements of Style," and "Historical and Cultural Contexts," focusing on, for instance, Jim Crow laws and racial violence in the 1930s. Teaching resources provide chapter tests and answer keys, performance-based assessment standards, and the National Film Study Standards, developed by the Film Foundation.

In "Film Language and Elements of Style," students are led to consider composition of the frame, the meaning of camera distances and angles, principles of frame lighting—such as direction, intensity, and quality of light—how the arrangement of shots suggests sequential action, and how the rhythm, dynamics, and pitch of music communicates meaning.

In the instructional DVD included in the kit, two middle school students at Bloomfield Middle School in Bloomfield, Michigan, Nicole Byrne and Herschel Mirabel, recount their understanding of one sequence of scenes. Atticus Finch, the stoic lawyer and widower played by Gregory Peck, is putting his daughter, Scout, to bed. Scout asks Atticus about her mother, whom she doesn't remember. As Scout falls asleep, asking questions about her mother, the camera moves out of her bedroom window to find Atticus sitting pensively on a two-person porch swing with his arm around the back. No words are spoken.

"There's one scene where Atticus is putting Scout to bed and he walks out," Nicole recalls. "And Scout starts talking about her mom. And then, as they're having this sentimental moment, they come out of the window, out of the kids' world, and you see Atticus and he's sitting on the bench. And he has his arm up and you can tell he's just missing his wife. When you see that, you see that he does have feelings and that he's lonely."

Herschel adds, "And he has his arm, like, around the bench so that the audience thinks the mom should be here but she isn't." These students are learning the language of images without words. As Scorsese says, "What you're doing is training the eye, and the heart, of the student to look at film in a different way, by asking questions and pointing to different ideas, different concepts."

Teacher Suzanne Johnson says, "Concepts in the past, some of these literary terms, foreshadowing, symbolism, allusion, were so difficult for students to grasp. But to point to it on a screen and dissect it and understand it in that sense, made everything come alive for them." The DVD includes commentary from Scorsese and Clint Eastwood on their own misconceptions about film when they were boys, that film scenes are shot out of sequence and that tremendous planning goes into each shot.

Schools teaching the "visual grammar" of film represent the beginning stage of this Curriculum Edge involving multimedia literacy. Now that video is becoming the lingua franca of the Internet, these students have a head start in the new art of multimedia communication. They are learning to paint with a fuller palette of digital tools, on a larger canvas that can gain a global audience.

Perhaps in 2020, in place of the required courses currently titled as English and those scattered electives on filmmaking or film history taken by artistically inclined students, there will be one integrated course required for all students, teaching all forms of media, called "Communication." That course could trace its roots to the work of the Film Foundation, which is why I say Martin Scorsese should earn an educational Oscar for the Story of Movies.

EDUCATING HEARTS AND MINDS

> *"Children are not merely vessels into which facts are poured one week and then when it comes time for exams, they turn themselves upside down and let the facts run out. Children bring all of themselves, their feelings, and their experiences to the learning."*
>
> FRED ROGERS

In a more encompassing view, the Curriculum Edge also makes visible the hidden connection between students' minds and their hearts. How students feel about themselves, their peers, and their families greatly affects their ability to learn. A more complete view of curriculum starts with the heart in order to drive the mind.

Walk into any classroom to see this connection in action: some students are engaged and some plainly aren't. Some are trying to concentrate on the lesson at hand and others are chatty, disruptive, or quietly bored. The "learning attitude" is apparent on students' faces and in their postures. It's tempting to bless those who appear interested and shrug off those who aren't, assuming it's a matter of low intelligence, bad temperament, or irredeemable family influence.

Those assumptions are dangerous, especially since the clock of learning is ticking and several straight years of acting out or withdrawing inward can be a ticket to dropping out and sliding down the ladder of life's chances. Or, worst case, being forced to live in a very small room where the doors lock from the outside.

Let's take a closer look at the "disengaged." Some may be sad, angry, or depressed. Some may be shy or aggressive. Some may be living through problems with classmates, siblings, or parents. All students bring their feelings to the classroom, and smart teachers have always acknowledged the social and emotional lives of their students, knowing that when students feel good in their hearts and bodies, their minds will naturally follow.

Harvard psychologist Howard Gardner has documented the "intrapersonal" and "interpersonal" intelligences among the eight "multiple intelligences" that include the verbal, logical-mathematical, musical, and bodily-kinesthetic intelligences. He has also reframed the role of these intelligences for twenty-first-century thinking and behavior.[28] He describes the "intrapersonal intelligence" as the ability to identify and use one's feelings and motivations, to have a deep understanding of oneself. The "interpersonal intelligence" is exercised in relationship with others, in having empathy with the feelings of others and working well in groups.

In one of our most popular films, Joe Hinson, a tenth-grade boy, described the growth in his interpersonal learning, working with two girls on a class project to design a school of the future: "When we finally started on the site model, there were these constant little squabblings.... I did learn how to work with people that didn't think the way I did. Thought non-linear, didn't believe in deadlines. They really think out-of-the box, which is not like me. I'm a completely in-the-box kind of person."[29] Through his best-selling books, *Emotional Intelligence* and *Social Intelligence,* psychologist and author Daniel Goleman has improved our understanding of how these intelligences operate in the workplace and the classroom.

Both Gardner and Goleman make the case that these capacities and skills are not static and ingrained at birth but can be developed and taught. What if all teachers could understand this mind-heart-body connection and could teach their students to make these connections? What if all students could learn to identify and manage their feelings and express them productively? Could students' emotional intelligence, their "EQ," be increased? Could their social relationships and social intelligence be improved? And if students felt better about themselves and their relationships, would their academic learning increase?

The response from a recent analysis of the research is a resounding "Yes!" A research team headed by Joseph Durlak at Loyola University in Chicago and Roger Weissberg at the University of Illinois at Chicago has conducted a meta-analysis of 213 studies of social-emotional curricula in K–12 schools and their connection to student achievement. They found a positive and substantial connection. On average, matched groups of students in these programs outperformed those who had not by 11 percentile points, a larger and more consistent gain across many studies than for nearly all other educational interventions.[30]

Social and Emotional Learning

Anchorage, Alaska, and Louisville, Kentucky

Two of the best districts implementing social and emotional learning (SEL) programs are in Anchorage and Louisville. Edutopia profiled the Anchorage program, led by Superintendent Carol Comeau, in 2007, showing how SEL can help students manage their emotions and improve their communication skills. Alaska, as Comeau points out in the film, has the nation's highest per capita rate of domestic violence and child abuse. "We've got a lot of young people in very great distress," she says. Anchorage is one of the largest 100 districts in the country, with about 50,000 students, a majority-minority district with 9 percent Alaskan Native and American Indian students, where ninety-four languages are spoken, most commonly Spanish, Hmong, Tagalong, Samoan, and Korean.

The district's program, Change of Heart, emphasizes active listening, not only in situations of conflict resolution, on the playground and in the classroom, but in the curriculum, such as mathematics, where students learn to describe how they are thinking about their own thinking. Listening to other students rehearse their thinking can pay benefits to the listener as well as to the speaker. In one scene, a group of fifth-graders surrounds a smaller group of students in a "fishbowl," watching, listening, and taking notes as the smaller group works on a problem of proportions with tiles.

In a high school English class, students interview each other about their families and write essays about a classmate's life with a father who has a drug problem or a brother with a disability. Middle school students learn to take on the roles of Aggressor, Victim, and Bystander in their AVB anti-bullying curriculum. District leaders point to the value of incorporating social and emotional learning across the curriculum, in math, English, and music, reflected in the district's making Adequate Yearly Progress (AYP) on annual exams, where 39 of the 96 schools met AYP and another 15 missed only 1 of 31 targets.

In Louisville, a district of about 100,000 students, Superintendent Sheldon Berman arrived from a smaller district in Hudson, Massachusetts, which had achieved a reputation for creating a social/emotional foundation for students' learning. Louisville's CARE (Community, Autonomy, Relationships, and Empowerment, or Creating a Respectful Environment) for Kids program for its elementary and middle schools was adapted from the Developmental Studies Center's Caring School Community, the Northeast Foundation for Children's Responsive Classroom, and Origins' Developmental Designs for Middle Schools. *Edutopia* writer Grace Rubenstein describes its five key elements:

1. Building community and setting a supportive tone through morning meetings: . . . In these daily sessions, teachers and students agree on how they want their class to feel. . . . They discuss emotional topics, such as bullying, friendship, and family struggles, and play goofy games to get to know each other better. And they laugh a lot.

2. Setting and reinforcing expectations—with kids' input.... Rather than the teacher announcing the rules for behavior, students set the expectations themselves.

3. Directly teaching social and emotional skills: Abilities like empathy, kindness, and self-control . . . can be learned through instruction and practice, just like grammar and arithmetic.

4. Using precise teacher language: . . . The hardest part of CARE for Kids . . . the most subtle and personal for teachers . . . as fine as saying "Walk" instead of "Don't run." . . . Use language that reminds and redirects students, rather than condemns them . . . stressing the deed, not the doer.

5. Practicing developmental discipline: consequences for bad behavior must . . . help the child learn how to be responsible for his actions. [When given detention] The student doesn't necessarily learn anything from that. The appropriate consequence may be to write a letter of apology.[31]

The Louisville CARE for Kids program was selected as one of Edutopia's Schools That Work multimedia case studies on successful schools and districts. On the Web site, student outcomes are listed, showing a rise in writing and math scores at one elementary and one middle school. Disciplinary actions, including referrals and suspensions, were dramatically down. The cost? About $500,000 for professional development each year, a miniscule $5 per district student. For a district whose average per-pupil expenditure exceeds $12,000, this may be one of the cheapest and best investments a school system can make, a shining example of how exemplary doesn't have to be expensive.

One of the secret benefits of SEL programs is making teaching more enjoyable for teachers. With less time spent on discipline and meting out punishment and students happier and more willing to learn, teachers are able to focus on why they entered the profession: to teach. SEL programs can enable a rising tide that lifts all boats of students, teachers, parents, and the entire school community. Berman says that the Hudson community passed a bond measure for a new school because voters believed the school would become a center for building a greater sense of community.

Dr. Weissberg heads the Consortium on Academic, Social, and Emotional Learning (CASEL), based in Chicago and chaired by Tim Shriver, who also chairs the Special Olympics. CASEL is spearheading a movement to help educators, researchers, and policymakers understand the importance of social-emotional learning and its integration in the classroom. They are developing a research agenda, including the neuroscience underlying SEL, state standards, and legislation.[32]

Illinois is the first state to promulgate SEL standards and several other states are actively considering them. In 2009, CASEL worked closely with Representatives Dale Kildee, Judy Biggert, and Tim Ryan to propose the Social and Emotional Learning Act, which calls for establishing a federally funded SEL center and providing technical assistance to states and districts implementing SEL curricula. The act is expected to be incorporated into the reauthorization of the Elementary and Secondary Education Act (ESEA), which will redefine provisions of No Child Left Behind.

Some teachers faced with the prospect of incorporating SEL into their teaching may say, "I don't have time to teach another strategy or program. My plate is already full." Roger Weissberg's reply is, "This isn't adding something to your plate. This *is* the plate." SEL programs act as the platform, the foundation, on which all other learning is built. Unless children feel good about themselves as learners, unless they know how to communicate their feelings, unless they're "ready to learn," they won't learn. It's as simple as that. It makes common sense. But as Mark Twain once said, "Common sense ain't all that common."

ASSESSMENT: MISUNDERSTANDING UNDERSTANDING

Not everything that can be counted counts and not everything that counts can be counted.

ALBERT EINSTEIN

One of the biggest barriers to changing our thinking about learning has to do with assessment. Until we get smarter about assessment, we're doomed to mediocrity in our schools. Of all the "big issues" in education today—teacher quality, improved curriculum, the benefits of technology, better school facilities—nothing else matters unless we get assessment right. And for too long, we've only been counting what our outdated tools enable us to count and not measuring those abilities that ought to count for more.

It's almost become a cliché: what gets assessed is what gets taught. If students are assessed via standardized tests, teachers will teach to the test. (This one sentence summarizes the story of No Child Left Behind.) Students themselves shrewdly "sess out" how they'll be measured. What is another of students' most frequently asked questions? Not "How can I become a critical thinker and prepare for the twenty-first-century economy?" Not "Can I go beyond the textbook and look for additional sources to expand my knowledge?" It's "Will this be on the test?" Neither teachers nor students want to waste their time on teaching and learning beyond what they're assessed on. So it's high time to broaden our view of the nature of assessment and what teaching for understanding is about.

In one of my favorite articles on Edutopia.org, "Appropriate Assessments for Reinvigorating Science Education," Dr. Bruce Alberts, former president of the National Academy of Sciences and now professor emeritus in biochemistry at the University of California at San Francisco (UCSF), wrote about how UCSF medical students were experts at playing the assessment game. While one might hope that our nation's best students might exhibit more intellectual curiosity, they also knew they would be judged by multiple-choice exams graded by a Scantron machine. It wasn't until the faculty started including open-ended questions requiring short essays that the students started asking deeper questions. As Alberts wrote, "It was my first encounter with the real power of tests and how important it is to get the test right if we want to get the learning right."[33]

Three essential activities occur in a learning environment: curriculum, instruction, and assessment. Each of these three legs of the classroom stool must be strong and stand on its own for the stool to be well balanced. Curriculum, as I've discussed in this chapter, refers to the educational goals of what is to be taught. These days, it is often paired with standards to communicate school district and state consensus on curriculum goals. But the "standards movement" has led to inconsistency between state and district standards and standards that are "too low, too broad, and too many." The current move to common "core standards" across states that are "fewer, deeper, and higher" will help create a more stable stool.

Instruction refers to the role of the teacher and instructional tools and strategies in delivering the curriculum. As I also discuss throughout this book, we need to overhaul instructional methods for project-based learning and Internet-based resources. In a project-based classroom, the implications for teachers and instruction are clear: the teacher becomes more a manager of students' projects and learning processes than a direct instructor. Students bear more of the responsibility of instructing themselves and others as they work in project-based teams.

Testing ≠ Assessment

Assessment remains the least understood of the three. History and policy have limited our understanding of its possibilities. The default understanding of assessment equates it with tests, especially the multiple-choice kind. But in a broader sense, assessment encompasses all those activities related to how well the curriculum and instruction result in learning outcomes. While tests have been used to assess district and school performance, the primary purpose of assessment should be to give ongoing feedback at the classroom level to teachers and learners on how to improve learning. If we truly believe learners learn in different ways and at different paces, curriculum, instruction, and assessment need to be much more flexible than the wooden approach of "Read the chapter. Take notes on the lecture. Answer the odd-numbered questions at the end of the chapter. Quiz on Friday."

New approaches to assessment remain somewhat of a mystery, because we have few models of assessment systems that match with project-based curricula and student-centered instruction. Edutopia's core concepts advocate for a full-spectrum view of assessment and a child's abilities, what we call "comprehensive assessment."[34] Such a system would measure students' core skills, such as reading, writing, and math, in the context of deeper investigations that integrate across the traditional subject areas, as seen in the courses offered by the Illinois Mathematics and Science Academy. Students would express their knowledge through multiple media and methods, including presentations and Web content for audiences beyond the teacher and the classroom. And their social skills, such as ability to work in groups, effort, and persistence would also be assessed.

Learning = Driving?

What would a system look like that combines the ease of administering hundred of thousands of multiple-choice tests with the higher costs of individualized feedback on performance? We're all familiar with one such system: driving licensure. As with most states, the California driving exam has both a written component and a road component. The written test comes first, to make sure prospective drivers are familiar with the rules of the road such as signs, signals, and safe driving practices. However, the state recognizes that just knowing the rules doesn't make for a good driver. Would any of us get in a car with a sixteen-year-old who had just passed the written test and head out onto the freeway during rush hour? Trust me, when my daughter was sixteen, I wouldn't and didn't.

In driving, we recognize that *performance is what counts.* The act of driving assumes knowledge of its rules, but the application of those rules in performance is where the rubber really meets the road. We're familiar with this type of performance-based assessment in other areas of human endeavor, notably sports and the arts. Athletes and actors know the basic rules and conventions of their professions, but it's how those rules are applied in performance that matters. Professional football teams and acting companies have a common form of assessment when bringing in new members. It's called a tryout or an audition, in which new recruits are asked to perform under real-life circumstances, with their teammates or fellow actors.

Authentic Assessment

Note one important point: the assessment of the activity looks very much like the activity itself. To apply a term used by some assessment experts, *assessment becomes authentic*. The difference between instruction and the assessment of instruction vanishes.

Direct analogies to schools exist. Just because a student can recite grammar rules or the names of Civil War battles or the elements in the Periodic Table doesn't mean they can write well, understand the significance of those battles, or discuss how carbon or chlorine relate to our daily lives. When my daughter was a college sophomore, she reported that the Periodic Table she struggled so mightily to memorize in high school was routinely distributed in her chemistry exams as a reference, a sign that her professor understood that memorization does not equate to learning.

The United States urgently needs assessment systems that measure student understanding and performance at much deeper levels. It will be a critical prerequisite if we are to achieve the status of an Education Nation.

ASSESSMENT 2.0

During the first decade of the twenty-first century, while the United States moved away from assessments that measure performance, other nations forged ahead. It's common for American educators and policymakers to cite with apprehension that "the world is flat," the economy is now global, jobs are changing and migrating overseas, and new knowledge and skills are needed to preserve jobs at home. Tom Friedman, *New York Times* columnist and author of *The World Is Flat*, has mentioned in his speeches, "When I was a boy, my parents used to tell me, 'Finish your dinner. There are children in China starving for your food.' Now I tell my girls, 'Finish your homework. There are children in China and India starving for your jobs.'"

But while the United States pursued a "back to basics" course of education reform under No Child Left Behind, other nations saw the "flat world" as an opportunity to steer a different education course focused on deeper and more authentic teaching and learning. They also foresaw that getting the right kinds of assessments in place would be a driver of this change and organized funding, political will, and teacher development to support a new approach to assessment. Call it Assessment 2.0 Now the United States is trying to catch up.

England, Australia, Singapore, Hong Kong, and others have put in place systems of performance-based assessments. The fact that these are all English-speaking nations should make the translation of their systems easier to ours. A major barrier, however, is the American ego. We, the world's remaining superpower, don't learn easily from other nations. We're very good at coming up with excuses for why innovations abroad won't work here. "They're smaller than we are." "They don't have the diversity we do." "They have a national educational system run by a centralized ministry." And my personal favorite, about Singapore, Hong Kong, and China: "Ummm, they're Chinese. They just work so damn hard. And they're naturally good at math."

 Two Sample Assessments

Alberta, Canada, and England

In 2009 Dr. Linda Darling-Hammond of Stanford summarized approaches from these nations in an Edutopia webinar entitled "Lessons from Abroad: International Standards and Assessments."[35] What do these assessments look like? Here are two examples, one from Alberta, Canada's twelfth-grade biology assessment and one from England's

General Certificate of Secondary Education (GCSE), one of four programs of study for high school students.

> A Twelfth-Grade Biology Assessment (Alberta)

Autism is a complex behavioral disorder. The symptoms of autism vary greatly and occur in different combinations. Symptoms include a reduced ability to communicate . . . to develop relationships, difficulty coordinating facial muscles, and difficulty interpreting social cues.

In the late 1950s and early 1960s, the drug thalidomide was prescribed to pregnant women to combat morning sickness. Thalidomide was found to cause birth defects, such as stunted growth of the arms and legs. Some children also developed autism. . . . The frequency of autism is many times higher in people with birth defects caused by thalidomide, which suggests that autism may originate early in embryonic development.

Scientists have genetically engineered mice that have symptoms similar to those of autism. These mice have a defective copy of the Hoxal gene, which is also present in humans, [and] is normally active only during very early embryonic development. Although people affected with autism are more likely to have the defective Hoxal gene, the presence of the effective gene does not insure the development of autism. Further investigation is required to determine whether environmental factors work in conjunction with genes to produce autism.

PATRICIA RODIER, 2000 THE EARLY ORIGINS OF AUTISM
Scientific American, FEBRUARY, 56–63

Identify two areas of the brain that can be affected in an individual with autism.

Explain the relationship between the areas of the brain identified and the symptoms of autism.

Identify one germ layer in which development could be disrupted by thalidomide and identify one structure that develops from this germ layer. Hypothesize how a person who has autism as a result of in utero exposure to thalidomide can have abnormal ear development but no malformations of the arms and legs.

Describe how the defective Hoxal protein is synthesized in the cytoplasm of a cell.

Explain how the defective Hoxal protein influences brain development and can lead to autism.

Identify and describe two technologies that can be used by scientists to replace an active Hoxal gene with a defective copy of the gene.

Describe three difficulties that researchers could encounter when they attempt to determine the cause of autism in humans.

These challenging items ask twelfth-graders to draw upon in-depth knowledge of human biology, neuroscience, biotechnology, and ethical dimensions of scientific research. The Illinois Mathematics and Science Academy, one school serving elite science students, teaches this revised, contemporary STEM curriculum, but the *entire province* of Alberta does so. They have cleared the hurdles we Americans still wring our hands about—getting to scale and providing a college-ready curriculum during high school.

> ➤ *A GSCE Assessment Task (England)*

Litchfield Promotions works with over 40 bands and artists to promote their music and put on performances in England. The number of bands . . . is gradually expanding. Litchfield Promotions needs to be sure that each performance will make enough money to cover all the staffing costs and overheads as well as make a profit. Many people need to be paid: the bands; sound engineers; and lighting technicians. There is also the cost of hiring the venue. Litchfield Promotions needs to create an ICT solution to ensure that they have all the necessary information. . . .

Candidates will need to: 1) Work with others to plan and carry out research to investigate how similar companies have produced a solution. The company does not necessarily have to work with bands.... 2) Clearly record and display your findings. 3) Recommend a solution.... 4) Produce a design brief, incorporating timescales, purpose, and target audience.

Produce a solution ensuring that ... 1) It can be modified to be used in a variety of situations. 2) It has a friendly user-interface. 3) It is suitable for the target audience. 4) It has been fully tested.

This task asks students to research real examples of event planning, figure out all of the various cost factors and contingencies, create a spreadsheet accurately modeling revenue and expense, test it with potential customers, and be able to present it convincingly to clients. The fact that both of these assessments address subjects that may relate to high school students' lives—autism and managing bands—is a plus.

Note some common themes from these assessments:

- They look and sound like curriculum. These assessments are not artificial exercises that bear no resemblance to what students do during the year but are, in fact, just like the challenging work they should be doing all year long. The hard line between good curriculum and assessment evaporates. It's the road test to evaluate that students really know how to drive, under actual driving conditions.

- Students and teachers are given feedback during the course of the year so performance can be improved on subsequent curriculum units and assessments. Assessment is not tacked on as a final, year-end, high-stakes, anxiety-raising spectacle at the end of the year, with results reported back too late to help students improve.

In a related paper, Dr. Darling-Hammond and her doctoral student, Laura Wentworth, note other traits of modern performance-based assessment systems:

- *Deeper knowledge, more subject areas. Instead of students being exposed to a long list of content knowledge, students experience fewer topics with more depth to the content they do cover. Even so, these assessment systems assess students in more subject areas than . . . in the U. S. [such as] two languages and topics like social studies or technological knowledge.*

- *Students learn how to learn. The nations studied emphasize students' metacognition, reflection, and self-efficacy during learning. They are asked to show their thinking and explain their rationale behind their answers. They are asked to reflect on their own thinking and continue to improve it.*

- *Increases in teacher capacity positively influence student outcomes. The assessment systems of these high-achieving nations all value teachers' capacity. They put resources into training teachers and create structures that rely on their professional judgement. . . . In return, this training and culture of trust among teachers breeds a positive influence on instruction leading to increased student achievement.*[36]

By developing these systems of performance-based assessments, these nations have also changed their curricula and improved the capabilities of their teachers. They recognize that improving assessments improves everything that happens in classrooms. The United States would do well to set its sights on this critical wedge into system reform. In order for the types of rigorous, project-based curricula described in this chapter to get to scale, for districts and states to implement them broadly, Assessment 2.0 is Job #1.

In the next chapter, we'll see how the Technology Edge makes these new approaches to curriculum and assessment possible. They rely on schools and districts, teachers and students, organizing, analyzing, presenting, and producing information from many sources. That's what technology was meant to do.

3

THE TECHNOLOGY EDGE
PUTTING MODERN TOOLS IN YOUNG HANDS

Technology provides wheels for the mind.

SEYMOUR PAPERT, MIT MEDIA LAB

WHEN CONSIDERING THE importance of equipping every student with a computer, many "*buts*" enter into the discussion. But it's expensive. But technology doesn't work. But teachers don't know how to use them. To those doubters, I pose three simple questions:

1. Do you use a computer?

2. Would you give up your computer?

3. Would you share your computer with three other people?

If you answered "Yes" to the first and "No" to the last two, why do we deny students the same tool we rely on? Question 3 is based on the current student-to-computer ratio in U.S. classrooms. A key point often overlooked in discussions about the effectiveness of computers in schools is that until every student has his or her own computer, the benefits of using them on a regular, ongoing basis are undercut.

WEAPONS OF MASS INSTRUCTION: ONE STUDENT, ONE COMPUTER

Imagine classrooms of the past, when four students may have had to share a textbook. Eventually, some smart people knew that the textbook should be a 1:1 "device." I wonder if school board members a century ago debated whether classrooms could get by with eight textbooks for a class of thirty students?

Providing 1:1 access in classrooms doesn't address the larger issue of 24/7 use. Students, as "knowledge workers," need to work and learn around the clock, including afternoons, evenings, weekends, and summers. Some laptop programs allow students to take their computers home; others don't, for reasons of theft and damage. One school I visited, VOISE (Virtual Opportunities Inside a School Environment) Academy on the north side of Chicago, provides two computers per student, one for the student's home use and one for school. And if a family cannot afford Internet access for their home, the school helps pay for it. Students take technology-enabled classes at school, accessing online science simulations, and can enroll in more than 100 online courses offered by the Chicago Public Schools Virtual High School.

These are the "weapons of mass instruction" we need to deploy in the war on illiteracy and "innumeracy." None of our hopes for education—for closing the achievement gap, for getting all students to college, for educating a modern workforce of teachers—will be realized until every student, teacher, and administrator has a computer and access to the Internet. One-to-one access is now the digital civil right of every student to fully participate in his or her own education.

The first 1:1 program can be traced back twenty years, to 1990 and the Methodist Ladies College in Melbourne, which began a program for girls in grades 5 through 12. On the cover of the book documenting this story, *Never Mind the Laptops* by Bruce Johnstone, the laptops look bigger than some of the girls.

As I travel around the country and talk to education groups, I am incredulous that, in the year 2010, there is only one state where every student (albeit only in two grades) has a laptop computer. That is the small but courageous state of Maine. The Maine story is known to many in field of educational technology, but is still not widely known among policymakers, teachers, and parents outside the state.

The story starts in 2000 with an intrepid governor, Angus King, who ran as an independent and was elected to two terms. Since laptop

programs continue to be controversial, it takes true leaders—governors
and superintendents—who understand the catalyzing impact of 1
student:1 computer to bet their students' futures on what critics still
describe as technological folly. King consulted with MIT's Seymour
Papert, who insists that every student should have his or her own
computer, that shared technology dissipates the learning rewards. Papert
believes, "It only turns magic when it's one-to-one."

I like Governor King's answer to the skeptical question: Why laptops
for students? If Maine has funds for computers, why not spend that
money instead on roads and bridges, tax incentives for companies,
health care, any other pressing priorities in the state budget? In a state
where hockey is the closest thing to a state sport, Governor King quoted
Wayne Gretzky's answer to "How did you get to be the best hockey
player of all time? You're not the biggest guy out there, you're not the
fastest." Gretzky said, "Most players skate to where the puck is. I skate
to where the puck is going to be." With industries such as logging in
decline, Angus King saw where Maine's future could be—in a digital,
scientifically literate workforce—and wanted to move Maine there.

The Maine Learning Technology Initiative was established in 2002
to provide "the tools and training necessary to ensure that Maine's
students become the most technologically savvy students in the world."
An important feature of Maine's implementation was enlisting statewide
support of educators at all levels as well as the larger community. A
key leadership role was played by Bette Manchester at the Maine
Department of Education who, along with others, including Mike Muir
of the Maine Center for Meaningful Engaged Learning, advocated
for teacher training and support for the new forms of project-based,
collaborative, and community-based learning. Manchester and others
in Maine understood that the teachers, not the technology, held the key
to success and that simply dropping machines into schools was a recipe
for disaster.

The largest laptop implementation in the United States began in
the 2002–2003 school year, when Apple laptops were distributed to
all seventh-graders and their teachers. The next year, the program

expanded to all 36,000 seventh- and eighth-graders and their 4,000 teachers. Our Edutopia film crew visited King Middle School in 2005 and depicted Maine students, through a partnership with the Maine Lakes Conservancy, going out onto the Maine lakes to analyze water quality and marine species. In one scene, students on Conservancy boats attach a digital microscope to their laptops, viewing daphnia and other microorganisms just collected from water samples. At King, students produced a book on Maine wildlife, and our film showed their presentations to their community. As principal Mike McCarthy said in the film, "Our whole goal is that every student here can have access to high quality learning and produce high quality products. One kid said, 'Nobody feels stupid around here anymore.' And I think that was one of our highest achievements."[1]

In an e-mail interview, Susan Gendron, Maine's chief state school officer, summarized the outcomes:

> Overall, our findings thus far demonstrate that the laptops have helped to improve middle school writing skills, mathematics and science skills if teachers are given comprehensive professional development. Our most successful implementations are in classrooms where we have significantly changed teacher behavior through the integration of technology and the rich digital resources available to them. One study was conducted comparing our students to high school seniors and entering [college] freshmen using a tool that ETS developed to measure twenty-first-century skills. Our students did as well and in some cases better than these students.

In Edutopia's coverage of innovative schools and programs, we have witnessed this phenomenon: typical public school students can perform at three grades above current standards. In an earlier laptop program in Harlem, eighth-grade Latino girls were studying the effects of ozone depletion on microorganisms in the coral reef ecosystem, doing lab research through a partnership at the City College of New York.[2]

(Note to humans: As the coral reefs go, so go the rest of us.) They were eighth-graders who had been given the right conditions to accelerate their learning beyond what high school students know. Maine's 1:1 program is providing similar evidence.

Evidence of Outcomes: The Maine Learning Technology Initiative

The Center for Education Policy, Applied Research, and Evaluation (CEPARE) at the University of Southern Maine has been a research partner with the program. Excerpts from their studies include:

> **Mathematics**

This randomized control trial (RCT) study was designed to determine the impacts of a professional development program.... Middle school teachers in 24 Maine schools participated in a two-year professional development program of over 200 hours designed to improve their ability to effectively use laptop technology in teaching mathematics. Results of the experimental study revealed that this type of professional development was effective in changing teaching and technology practices, which in turn led to improved student performance on standardized mathematics tests. The research also highlights the importance of maintaining high levels of implementation fidelity for improved student performance.

> **Science**

The post-assessment and the student interviews revealed that many of the students found the technology-rich project to be more challenging and time-consuming; however, many of the students also agreed that the project was more fun and engaging. These statements are illustrative of Seymour Papert's concept of "hard fun," by which Papert describes the idea that children enjoy being challenged and that they have greater learning outcomes when they are given the opportunity to actively construct new knowledge in an exciting way.

> **Writing**

... the evidence indicates that implementation of Maine's one-to-one ubiquitous laptop program has had a positive impact on middle school students' writing. Five years after the initial implementation of the laptop program, students' writing scores on Maine's statewide test had significantly improved. Furthermore, students scored better the more extensively they used their laptops in developing and producing their writing. And finally, the evidence indicated that using their laptops in this fashion helped them to become better writers in general, not just better writers using laptops.[3]

As these middle schoolers graduated and entered high school, Maine has looked for ways to continue 1:1 learning. In the face of tougher budget times, about 20 of the state's 150 high schools have continued the program. Five years later, our film crew and editors returned to update the story, which launched as part of our Schools That Work series in 2010.[4] This new coverage will be valuable for other districts and states considering or implementing 1:1 programs. Extensive documentaries, resources, and interviews have been produced, including one with Governor King, who now says, "We thought it was a good idea back in 2002. I realized about the second year in that it was really a radical idea because of the changes to pedagogy and the changes to education. It's a different kind of teaching and learning. Now, as I look around the world and seeing what's happening with globalization and the hollowing out of the American economy, I think it's a necessary idea."

Since Maine made its investment in 2002 and other individual districts have followed, Gordon Moore's law of technology has continued apace. The speed and power of today's computers have doubled every two years, with dramatic declines in cost. Former governor King estimates the total cost of the program, hardware, software, broadband access, tech support, and teacher development for all seventh- and eighth-graders, at $9 million per year for the entire state, less than half of 1 percent of the annual school budget of $2 billion. That's $225 per year for every middle school student and teacher, when a single textbook can cost $150. Larger states would benefit from greater discounts.

Remember Edge 1: The Thinking Edge, when I discussed getting smarter about learning? King puts the argument for 1:1 in terms a school board member or state legislator could understand:

> How long do you have to think about that? If I came to you at the school board and said, 'I'm going to give you something that is going to significantly improve writing scores and also decrease discipline problems, increase attendance, and provide your students with true twenty-first-century skills and it's going to cost about the same as your snowplowing budget,' it seems to me it's pretty hard to say no.

Twenty-First-Century Skills for the Cost of Cleaning Fluids

A sidenote: Susan Gendron is a digital superintendent who also advocates for the efficiencies that technology can bring to the business functions of running schools districts. She instituted an online statewide purchasing portal to aggregate district spending and obtain deeper discounts. Spending on facilities, school buses, lunches, furniture, and every school product and service represents a large percentage of educational spending in every community and state. Gendron told me, "Districts who used it effectively did see reduced costs and allowed them to reinvest these savings into their instructional programs or to reduce local tax obligations. You wouldn't believe how much we spend on cleaning fluids alone."

A number of districts, from Fullerton and Tiburon, California, to Union City, New Jersey, have made the move to 1:1, and states such as Michigan, Illinois, Nebraska, Arizona, and Pennsylvania have considered statewide programs. International interest is also accelerating, with nations as diverse as Australia, Chile, Libya, Mongolia, South Africa, Uruguay, and Venezuela running pilot programs to large-scale implementations. The past three years have shown impressive growth, indicating that 1:1 programs may be at an inflection point, where evidence of student outcomes, together with falling prices, have created a warmer climate for 1:1 programs to thrive. Some schools and districts have put in place 1:1 programs using handheld devices, including the Palm and the iPod.

Today, if I were a parent of a sixth-grader, thinking about moving to a district where my child could receive the tools she needs for a world-class education, I'd move to Maine. The fact that it's a beautiful coastal state should be enough to seal the deal. Angus King says, "If you ask teachers in Maine for one word to describe the project, it's generally *engagement*. Any teacher will tell you, if your students are engaged, you can teach them anything. If they're not engaged, you can be Socrates, and not teach them anything."

More information on 1:1 programs can be found on Web sites of groups such the Maine International Center for Digital Learning, America's Digital Schools, and One Laptop per Child, which focuses on providing a low-cost device in developing countries.[5]

A New State of Assessment: Growing OAKS in Oregon

States are making progress into this digital future in other areas. In the key area of assessment, Oregon is the first state to take its testing program completely online. During 2008–2009, Oregon gave nearly 100 percent of all state tests online. The Oregon Assessment of Knowledge and Skills (OAKS), which began development in 2001, still uses the same multiple-choice format, but offers new benefits made possible through online administration.[6]

Results are reported much more rapidly, so that teachers and students can use the data to improve their teaching and learning. Students have the flexibility to take the test up to three times, during October to May, improve their performance, and use their highest score for the school's accountability data. By varying items given to students during and across test administrations, the online test discourages teaching to specific test items and cheating. Each student's neighbor is answering different items. Tony Alpert, Oregon's testing director, reports one advantage unheard of with paper-and-pencil tests: students seem to like taking the exam on computers and answer more questions rather than guessing randomly or just quitting. Alpert says, "The level of student engagement is higher than on paper."

As the Curriculum Edge continues to make progress in providing a more challenging curriculum that requires thinking and not merely memorization, online assessment will shift to include multimedia simulations. One example is SimScientists, developed at WestEd, the educational research and development organization in San Francisco. Middle school students are presented with a simulated ecosystem and asked to solve problems and provide evidence of their thinking about concepts such as the relationship of nutrients to algae growth.

The unprecedented U.S. Department of Education's 2010 stimulus funds to states and districts are called the "Race to the Top" funds. Here's another race designed by Abilene High School that pits students with technology against those without.

This Web entry is a short and persuasive argument for why schools need to invest more aggressively in technology. It can be read as a race between two American students, but becomes even more compelling when the first student comes from Europe, Asia, or Africa.

Let's have a little competition at school and get ready for the future.

I will use a laptop and you will use paper and pencil. Are you ready?

I will access up-to-date information. You have a textbook that is five years old.

I will immediately know when I misspell a word. You have to wait until it's graded.

I will learn how to care for technology by using it. You will read about it.

I will see math problems in 3-D. You will do the odd problems.

I will create artwork and poetry and share it with the world. You will share yours with the class.

I will have 24/7 access. You have the entire class period.

I will access the most dynamic information. Yours will be printed and photocopied.

I will communicate with leaders and experts using email. You will wait for Friday's speaker.

I will select my learning style. You will use the teacher's favorite learning style.

I will collaborate with my peers from around the world. You will collaborate with peers in your classroom.

I will take my learning as far as I want. You must wait for the rest of the class.

The cost of a laptop per year? $250.

The cost of teacher and student training? Expensive.

The cost of well-educated U.S. citizens and workforce? Priceless.

AUTHOR: ANONYMOUS
SOURCE: ABILENE, KANSAS HIGH SCHOOL
DIALOGUE BUZZ WEB SITE

THE "MISSING MIRROR" IN LANGUAGE LEARNING

I first encountered the importance of listening to one's own speaking in the context of foreign language learning. The Cary Academy in North Carolina, a technology-infused private academy founded by

Jim Goodnight, chairman of SAS, the business intelligence software company, was an early site for Mandarin teaching. When I visited, I asked the teacher what textbook she was using. She said she didn't use a textbook, just her own lessons. She made audio recordings of her readings of lessons and placed them on the school's servers so that students could access them at any time. She also asked students to record their own readings, so she and they could listen to and analyze them.

Just as dancers watch their movements in a mirror and NFL players review films to dissect their performance in key plays, students who listen to themselves read and compare their readings to their teacher's can use the "missing mirror" in language learning. In order for students to analyze their reading aloud, they need to be able to capture their readings, record them, and play them back, repeatedly. That's what technology is good at. It's amazing that the little device that revolutionized the way we use music can provide a solution to the nation's literacy crisis.

iPod, iListen, iRead

Escondido, California, and Canby, Oregon

This classroom innovation grew out of a simple observation by an educator with an entrepreneurial bent. In 2005, Kathy Shirley, technology director for the Escondido Union School District near San Diego, was in one of her schools when a teacher was conducting "fluency assessments" of her students. The assessment involved a full day of individual work with students, taking them into a separate room, listening to them read, and marking on worksheets the pace, accuracy, and expression of each student's reading. The school had to hire a full-day substitute teacher while the regular teacher went through this laborious process.

Shirley, an Apple Distinguished Educator, had been using an iPod to record her own voice memos. The light bulb went off: Why couldn't the student's readings be recorded on an iPod, on their own time, and reviewed by the teacher, on her own time? More important, could the act of students recording and listening to their readings improve their skills? That Escondido is a district with 53 percent Latino English-language learners made the search for a better way even more urgent.

These observations set in motion a remarkable project that adapted the ubiquitous iPod to enable students to record, analyze, and improve their reading. Given the struggles of schools to bring all students to higher literacy levels, the foundation for achievement in all other subjects, there is no more important need.

In 2006, the iREAD (I Record Educational Audio Digitally) project started as a pilot program in Escondido, with six teachers of English language learners working with low-performing readers, content experts, and IT staff. In the second year, thirty-five teachers got involved. This year, more than 100 K–8 classrooms are using 1,300 iPods, and the program has expanded to include readers at all levels.

Students use the iPods with external microphones to record their reading practice and assessments. Some models display text, images, and video. The iPod Touch, with its larger screen, Internet access, and applications, enables a better multimedia experience, as students download audiobooks and songs and read along with the text of stories and lyrics. Teachers are trained to use the iPods, microphones, iTunes, GarageBand for audio production, and other digital tools. Student and teacher recordings are uploaded to iTunes, where teachers create playlists for each student. Students, teachers, and parents can then review progress, creating a powerful learning loop between all three.

As Shirley describes it, "Voice recording using the iPod provides that instant feedback loop, as students can easily record their fluency practice and listen immediately to the voice recording. It's difficult, especially for struggling readers, to 'step outside themselves' during the moment of reading. They are concentrating so hard at the act of reading that they have no idea what they really sound like. The iPod does something that even the teacher cannot do, provide a means for the student to receive feedback by listening to their own recordings. The iPod is very much like 'a mirror' for students."[7]

In 2008, the Canby, Oregon, district also began experimenting with the program. Technology director Joe Morelock is a colleague of Shirley's in the Apple Distinguished Educator community. Canby, a district of nine schools and about 5,000 students, now has about fifty classrooms using iPods of various types and the project has extended into high school, where students are listening to audiobooks and using video cameras to analyze their presentation skills.

‣ Evidence of Student Outcomes

Escondido and Canby classrooms are seeing large gains in the speed of student reading, one part of reading fluency. In a Canby fourth-grade classroom of sixteen students, from the fall to mid-year assessment of reading fluency, when average increase in word count per minute (WCPM) is 12, the average in the iPod classroom was close to 20. (WCPM measures the pace of reading as one component of reading fluency; accuracy is another component.) Most students averaged more than double the average expected.

In an Escondido fourth-grade class of ten students, average increase was 48 WCPM in just six weeks. Two newcomer students improved from 44 to 98 and from 75 to 139 WCPM, respectively, with 130 WCPM the goal at year-end for fourth-graders. At the start of the fourth grade, all of the students lagged behind the 120 WCPM goal for third-grade completion. Within just six weeks, more than half of them had caught up and surpassed the goal for fourth-grade completion, making more than a year's progress in that period.

A pilot study of reading achievement using the Iowa Test of Basic Skills also showed impressive gains. A group of 12 fifth-graders in Escondido using iPod Touches averaged 1.8 years of reading progress in six months, compared with a matched group of students at the same school who averaged .25, a quarter of a year's increase. The students come from a high-achieving school, with most students reading at or above grade level, but the iPod-using students were reading at the eighth- or ninth-grade level. Shirley reported that "The students were using the iPod touch to write on their blogs in response to literature." The teacher said the device caused students to write more and to be much more thoughtful. "They also were motivated to read the material carefully, as they knew their peers would be commenting on their posts."

Both districts are planning larger-scale studies of reading achievement. As word has spread, groups of educators are contacting Escondido and Canby to come by and have a look. When I spoke to Shirley, she had just completed a tour and presentation for fifty educators and said she could do them twice a month to accommodate the requests coming in.

▸ Reading Success Becomes Contagious

These iPod projects create a perfect match between the skills of the digital generation and a piece of technology that specifically supports their learning. The ability to hear their own reading performances, as well as those of their peers, and track their progress excites and motivates students.

In these classrooms, students are leading their own reading. They *want* to practice their speed, accuracy, and comprehension. The iPod makes personal a process that has been painfully public. No struggling reader likes to have his or her weaknesses exposed in a group, in front of the entire class or their reading circle. The iPod enables this process to be much more intimate, between a student and a teacher listening to each other's voices in audio files. This type of relationship is the real benefit of 1:1 technology, allowing a 1:1 relationship between the teacher and each student.

As the students get excited, teachers get excited, too. Success becomes contagious for everyone involved. As Morelock puts it, "This is the secret sauce to all of this: teacher motivation. We have heard teacher after teacher say, 'This has totally transformed my teaching!' 'I'm having more fun and being a better teacher.' 'I'm never gonna retire.' Teachers are empowered to manage their own technology, which they love learning how to do, and seeing their students achieve and have fun." One teacher told Shirley, "Using iPods with microphones has engaged students more than anything I've ever experienced! These tools allow even the softest speaker to be heard and motivate even the most reluctant reader." Another commented, "There's less of me talking and more of them doing."

A classroom set of thirty iPod Touches and a cart costs about $12,000. The iPods can be supplemented with five desktop or laptop computers in the classroom for students to produce media, such as podcasts. It is a less costly model than the 1:1 laptop classroom and right-sized for elementary students, who can hold the key to their literacy in the palm of their hands.

Shirley and Morelock have created a Web site and a wiki for teachers and educational technology staff to manage and share progress from these iPod projects, including videos of classroom scenes and teacher interviews.[8] The videos demonstrate how engaged the students are and how facile young fingers are, typing on that small iPod Touch screen.

 ## Reinventing the U.S. History Class

Tiburon, California

Examples of innovative use of technology in science courses are more common than those in the humanities. A short drive from Edutopia's offices in Marin County, at Del Mar Middle School in Tiburon, is an outstanding example of how a 1:1 classroom is reinventing the teaching of American history. On a campus with a spectacular view of the Golden Gate, Anthony Armstrong, Apple Distinguished Educator, has developed a classroom that harnesses the information-rich world of today's digital learners to enliven a course that they should all come to love: American history.

In 2005, Superintendent Christine Carter of the Reed Union School District in Tiburon, an affluent community, led the bold move to provide Apple laptop computers to every student beginning in the third grade. Armstrong came to the Del Mar school by way of teaching in Texas and South Korea. He developed his model using media and technology in part through his own experience with an online EdM program at Full Sail University, which has a physical campus in Florida but offers primarily online degrees. Armstrong puts a new wrinkle on the old adage that "teachers teach as they were taught," usually cited as a reason why some teachers find it difficult to adapt to new practices. Through an intensive, one-year online program, including eleven monthly courses and a master's thesis, Armstrong experienced the power of online learning himself, including the university's learning management system, and designed the course for his students.

During his studies, Armstrong read books such as *Social Studies for the 21st Century* by Jack Zevin, *Teaching History in the Digital Classroom* by D. Anthony Cantu and Wilson Warren and James and Margaret West's *Using Wikis for Online Collaboration*.[9] He also was inspired by other teachers' use of wikis, such as Vicki Davis's use for Flat World Tales. They and many more teachers are sharing their use of wikis on the Wikispaces site.[10] Vicki Davis, who teaches in Camilla, Georgia, and is known as the Cool Cat Teacher, can be seen in action on Edutopia.org as the teacher of Virginia, an eighth-grader profiled in the Digital Generation project, multimedia profiles of ten digital youth.

➤ The Wiki as Online Collaborative Learning Platform

The desk layout in Armstrong's classroom changes from day to day, depending on whether students are working together, in small or large groups, individually, or presenting their work. Unlike teachers in most American history classes, Armstrong spends relatively little time lecturing, giving shorter talks of 20 to 30 minutes. "I figured that if MIT found it good enough to do away with lectures, I could also do away with lectures," Armstrong says. "The design problem I had to solve both technically and pedagogically was how do I get my students the information they still need to know, without it coming directly from me, the instructor. The solution I found was a wiki." He ensured that his curriculum met the technology and media literacy standards set forth by the National Council for the Social Studies (NCSS).

The platform for his course is a collaborative wiki, where all course materials are contained and students can view their own and their peers' work.[11] The multimedia curriculum includes links to an amazing collection of online materials, including the collections of the American Memory Project of Library of Congress and Digital History, one of the best examples of free, online course materials from the American Revolution to the present. Anyone still involved in the selection of print textbooks should examine it and compare the wealth and depth of resources online versus what a textbook can offer. But, wait, there's more: other references sites include Yale Law School's Avalon Project, with collections of the text of original historic documents organized by century; the National Archives; the History Channel; and videos on the Hippocampus site, typically used by college students.

Students view national and international newsfeeds and tie current events to the history they are studying. Students use a variety of Web tools to organize their Web content, such as Diigo and Delicious, social bookmarking sites to share their links with each other; Zotero and BibMe for organizing and citing references (think of this as the online version of the old 3 × 5 cards you may have used as a student, but much faster and comprehensive). They submit their assignments online and via e-mail to Armstrong, including wiki discussion postings and portfolio samples, which likewise receive online grades and comments from Armstrong. To prepare for exams, students take timed practice quizzes via Quia.com and repeat them as often as they like to make sure they are mastering the content. Multiple-choice tests are also taken via Quia, which provides reports on individual and classroom performance to help focus Armstrong's instruction for struggling students or essential points most students have missed.

› Time for Technology and Time for Talking

On the afternoon I visited, 15 eighth-graders entered the classroom toting their backpacks and their laptops in bright blue carrying cases. But today's class was a 50-minute seminar discussion, with desks arranged in a large circle. The laptops never came out. The school's schedule is organized in three 50-minute periods per week, with 80-minute periods on the other two days to allow for extended individual and group work.

Armstrong led the class discussion in a variety of formats, flashing slides on the whiteboard with discussion questions and images. For a slide showing Thomas Jefferson and Alexander Hamilton, he asked the students to compare their contrasting views of human nature and the role of government. How did they differ in their views on sending 13,000 federal troops to quell the Whiskey Rebellion? What is the balance between allowing the exercise of free speech and ensuring public safety when protests turn violent? What differences in philosophy led to the development of the Federalist versus the Democratic-Republican parties?

The 50-minute period was a series of staccato exchanges between students and Armstrong. Every student participated. In a technique called "think-pair-share," students were given 30 seconds to consider a question and a minute to talk to their neighbors. Two were selected to enter the middle of the classroom and take on the roles of Jefferson and Hamilton in one-minute point/counterpoints. Students were exercising their oral skills and learning to think on their feet, forming opinions and arguments, having a civil discourse. When they agreed with a classmate, they said so, and why. They also felt free to say, "I disagree" with a classmate and why.

Few moments go by without students exchanging views energetically. Armstrong's slides contain his admonition: "Silence is deadly." "The statement," he explained, "is meant to express to students the responsibility they need to take as active learners, not to replicate the typical classroom where they have to sit quietly the entire time. The seminar is meant to put the 'social' back into 'social studies.' It's their time to express their thoughts and, more important, their questions. Ignorance is not bliss." When asked whether Hamilton or Jefferson would find their views of human nature confirmed today, one student cited Bernie Madoff to support Hamilton's view that people act out of their own self-interests. Another said the outpouring of support for Haiti's people after the earthquake was proof that Jefferson was right about the decency and goodness of the common people.

▸ *Anthony Armstrong's Seminar Procedures*

The active discussion with all students participating in Anthony Armstrong's U.S. history class does not just happen naturally. His students have practiced their oral skills each week through explicit "Seminar Procedures," adapted from the Greece Central School District in New York and the Greater Rochester Teacher Center Network.[12] They include:

- Take the initiative in participating. Listen-Respond-Ask Questions. Ask for help to clear up confusion. Silence is deadly for your grade.

- Don't raise your hand to speak. Take turns speaking and do not interrupt another speaker.

- Speak loudly and clearly enough for everyone to hear you. Speak to everyone in the room, not just the teacher.

- Respond to statements made by previous speakers. Help to enlarge the understanding of the group by asking questions that can clarify and deepen discussion ideas.

- Invite others into the conversation by asking to hear their thoughts or opinions.

- Show attentiveness through body language: sit up straight, look at the speaker, and do not belittle or criticize others' comments. Side conversations are not allowed. Doing so will result in the deduction of seminar participation points.

He also gives them some specific scripts:

- You say _____. But _____, because _____. Therefore _____.

- I'm not sure why _____ said _____. Can you reword your comments to help me understand?

- I understand your point but I want to add/disagree/give another side. . . .

Armstrong's students are learning the art of civil discourse, which our democracy requires for exchanging points of view, airing conflicts, and reaching compromise. Perhaps Congress would benefit from practicing these procedures, too.

▸ *"Tell Me Something I Can't Google"*

Armstrong emphasizes to his students the importance of citing sources for information used, in their discussions and their written work. He challenges his students to do original writing and speaking by proclaiming, "Tell me something I can't Google." The group mind of the class is visible on the wiki, and students frequently mentioned the benefits of seeing and hearing how other students think about the issues and being able to work together. For instance, students collaborated to create a wiki page on the causes and consequences of the War of 1812, including original drawings of battles and audio podcasts of songs from the War. Students coauthor scripts for their multimedia presentations and podcasts using Google Docs. Armstrong does something else, both courageous and unusual for a teacher: he asks students to grade him. After each unit, he gives them an online Project Evaluation Survey and invites them to grade his own performance and share ideas about how to make the next units better.

In my discussion with the students, they noted that the computers allow them to access multiple sources from the Internet, far beyond what one textbook claims. They mentioned being able to use Bing and Google to find their own sources, such as the Smithsonian Museum of American History's site. And they noted the value of learning from their peers, in class and online, seeing how their classmates think. The variety and depth of student posts arguing the philosophies of Jefferson and Hamilton can be viewed at the link to their classroom wiki.[13]

Taylor, a student, interviewed for Armstrong's master's thesis, said the course "taught me to question and be suspicious of my sources of information. Similar stories are not always reported the same way and bias exists in the United States and throughout the world. I'm a visual learner so I like to watch the videos best, yet I also use the other resources on the [wiki] page. Since we're writing for an academic audience, there's absolutely no instant messaging language allowed."

When Armstrong presents the online tools and content from his wiki-based classroom to teachers, he reminds them of this stunning fact: "And it's all—free!" His eighth-grade classroom is an example of the move to Open Educational Resources (OER), which began in higher education and is making its way into K–12. MIT's making available the content of 1,700 of its courses for free on the Internet was the landmark event in the short history of OER. These resources can consist of lesson plans, textbooks, videos, library collections, articles, every type of educational material in every medium. OER are supported by communities of content providers willing to create flexible licenses for their intellectual property, allowing them to maintain ownership while publishing them free, online, for educational purposes. The Creative

Commons framework, developed by Stanford law professor Lawrence Lessig, has become the standard for these licenses.

Marshall Smith, formerly of the Hewlett Foundation, a major OER funder, now with the U.S. Department of Education, has written an excellent overview of the history and potential of the OER movement.[14] He gives three opening examples, indicating how the OER movement is democratizing education around the globe:

1. A teacher in a Kenyan secondary school uses a free Web-based interactive simulation designed by a Nobel Prize–winning physicist.

2. In a university in Xian, China, a student having trouble learning linear algebra goes for free help to a translated Web-based collection of course lectures from the Massachusetts Institute of Technology.

3. And, in the United States, thousands of students go to a Web site that provides free homework help aligned with their state standards, for most secondary school academic courses.

While OER faces philosophical, financial, and other challenges as a very different model from the proprietary system of educational publishing, its effectiveness in Armstrong's class is undeniable. As the Internet saying goes, "Information wants to be free."

Research Evidence for Technology-Supported Eighth-Grade American History

Not far from Armstrong's classroom, in a school with greater economic and racial diversity, another eighth-grade American history teacher covered the same curriculum with her four classes using similar inquiry and project-based learning approaches. While students in her school did not have their own laptop computers, the school did have sufficient technology to provide students with the ability to access online archives such as the Library of Congress and History Now, as well as produce culminating multimedia mini-documentaries.

This teacher's classroom was the subject of an experimental study conducted by researchers Pedro Hernández-Ramos and Susan De La Paz at Santa Clara University.[15] The "control classrooms" in a nearby school covered the same six-week unit on American expansion into the Northeast, South, and West during the nineteenth century. The project-based students using multimedia technology outperformed the students in the control condition in greater knowledge of historical content and thinking skills, such as use of supporting evidence for their arguments. The project-based students also ended the unit with more positive attitudes toward the study of social studies and history.

ONLINE LEARNING: LEVELING AND ELEVATING THE PLAYING FIELD

In 1840, Sir Isaac Pitman, the English inventor of shorthand, had the ingenious idea of using the newly invented "Penny Post" service to deliver education to a mass audience: correspondence courses by mail. His innovative use of a new channel, sending learning to where learners were, into their mailboxes, caught on quickly with those without access to Britain's formal institutions—primarily women and those with lower levels of schooling.

By 1892, the University of Chicago was offering the world's first university distance education program, and through the twentieth century, student enrollments at the Open University in the United Kingdom and other distance learning universities from South Africa to China placed them among the largest universities in their nations. Today, online learning in higher education and K–12 is using a new channel to again deliver instruction to learners anytime, anywhere, straight to their e-mailboxes.

Again, this new age of distance learning is leveling the learning playing field for those who do not have access to courses and qualified teachers and who may be homebound or on the move. Online learners are also accessing vast libraries of curriculum and research materials, on-demand delivery of video, images, graphics, and documents, and more frequent interactions with instructors and classmates. Perhaps unexpectedly, some students are finding more success online than in the physical classroom. Online learning is not only leveling but elevating the academic playing field and redefining the course experience.

In this section, I define "online learning" as the provision of courses where teachers and students accomplish most of the coursework, including class meetings, online. Not included in this definition are courses that meet regularly in person and use online resources, such as Anthony Armstrong's U.S. history class. Today, due to phenomenal growth in the past decade, online coursework is more than a growing edge of innovation. It is moving center stage, with thirty states and more than half of the school districts in the United States offering online learning programs. A 2009 survey from the Sloan Consortium, "K–12 Online Learning: A Survey of U.S. School District Administrators," revealed that online learning is growing rapidly, at a rate of 30 percent annually.[16] This trend is moving younger, from higher education to high schools and into the middle school grades. According to the International Association for K–12 Online Learning (iNACOL), more than 40 percent of high school and middle school students have expressed interest in taking an online course.[17]

The Sloan Consortium report documented the growing popularity of courses delivered fully online and through a "blended" or "hybrid" format involving both online and face-to-face classes:

1. Seventy-five percent of public school districts had students enrolled in a fully online or blended course, with 70 percent enrolling students in fully online courses and 41 percent of districts offering blended courses, about 10 percent growth in district participation since 2005–2006.

2. Sixty-six percent of school districts with students enrolled in online or blended courses anticipate their online enrollments will grow.

3. The number of K–12 students engaged in online courses in 2007–2008 was estimated at 1,030,000, representing a 47 percent increase in just two years.

4. The districts reported that online learning was meeting the needs of different types of students, from those needing extra help and credit recovery to those able to take Advanced Placement and other college prep courses.

5. School districts relied on multiple online learning providers, including postsecondary institutions, state virtual schools, and independent for-profit and nonprofit organizations, as well as producing their own online courses.

Florida, Georgia, and Michigan have established statewide online educational programs, while other states allow programs to operate as charter schools. The best resource for staying abreast of this fast-changing field of online learning is iNACOL, which operates the Online Learning Clearinghouse, a comprehensive effort supported by the Bill & Melinda Gates Foundation and WestEd.

Some scholars and policy experts have embraced online learning as the big game-changer in education, capable of delivering a better education at lower cost to the nation's students. Two recent books, *Disrupting Class* by Clayton Christensen, Curtis Johnson, and Michael Horn, and *Liberating Learning* by Terry Moe and John Chubb, herald online learning as the competitive force in K–12 education that finally will challenge the dominance and high cost of bricks-and-mortar schools relying on teachers in physical classrooms. When courses go online, they reason, school budgets should shift, reducing the need for teachers and the cost of building and maintaining school buildings.

I don't buy their entire argument. I still believe in the power of teachers, in George Lucas's words, who "can whisper in the ear of a student and give them a pat on the back." The positive, affirming, human contact between teachers and students is still the most powerful force in education. Virtual environments, when students and teachers can see each other, can go a long ways toward closer and more supportive relationships between teachers and students, but, as we all know, a videoconference is still not the same as being there. So I advocate for the more nuanced view of the benefits of online learning, combining both "high tech" and "high touch."

There are two major ways in which online courses are leveling and elevating the playing field for students: (1) by offering potentially every student the same courses that our best high schools offer and (2) by fully harnessing what technology can do to turn students and the instructor into an interactive, fully engaged "learning community."

Bringing the Curriculum of the Best High Schools to Every Student

The effectiveness of online courses is usually compared to in-person courses. This comparison is appropriate where face-to-face courses exist. Our best high schools offer a world-class education to their students, with a full array of college-prep and Advanced Placement courses. But what if you're a bright student who doesn't live in those communities and your high school doesn't offer the same range of courses you want and need for college admission?

Millions of high school students face this disadvantage, through no fault of their own, but only due to the size of their schools, their geographic location, and the national paucity of qualified teachers in many subject areas, such as science and math. Therefore, in many cases, the more appropriate "compared to what" question is, Are online courses better than nothing? In many states, the answer from many students is a resounding "Yes"! Other students have physical disabilities and injuries or are physically gifted and must travel to compete. In both cases, they are unable to be at school each day. For these growing numbers of students, online courses fill the gap between the courses they should have access to and those their schools can provide. Online learning makes the same playing field of courses available to all students.

One of the most successful areas where online learning has leveled the playing field is in the offering of AP courses. Virtual AP courses enable students to take courses beyond the limits of their high school curriculum. In the Sloan Consortium report, K–12 school district administrators cited "offering courses not otherwise available at the school," "meeting the needs of specific groups of students," and "offering Advanced Placement or college-level courses" as the top three reasons they perceive online and blended courses to be important."

In my state, University of California College Prep (UCCP) was founded ten years ago to use the Internet to help the nearly one million California students whose high schools do not offer enough college prep courses for them to fulfill the course requirements for admission to the UC system. Now, UCCP offers fifteen courses, including AP courses in biology, chemistry, calculus, environmental science, U.S. history, U.S. government and politics, and psychology, as well as other college prep courses in biology, physics, algebra, and Web-based labs. About 76 percent of students who enrolled in a UCCP course and 68 percent of underrepresented students enrolled in a two- or four-year college the year after high school graduation.

Improving the Course Experience

The term "learning community" is now in vogue, expressing the ideal metaphor for students and teachers actively learning with and from each other, or a group of educators with a common purpose focused on their own professional development. A learning community enables each member to share his or her interests and skills and to feel invited and recognized as part of the group. It's participatory and it activates a many-to-many model of learning, rather than the one-to-many, instructor to student "broadcasting" of information. Students learn and teach each other, and the teacher takes on the role of a coach and facilitator rather than the single source of instruction.

Many of the elements of a strong learning community are possible in a face-to-face classroom. Teachers can create small groups in which students share, teach, and learn from each other. They can take on a role as an integral part of the circle of learning rather than the prominent center of it.

However, many aspects of the traditional classroom can frustrate the development of community. Lecture-based classes with 25 to 35 students can often be impersonal. Class time is limited. Only one person can speak at a time, when many may want to. Some students may be less openly verbal especially if English is not their native tongue. And the urge to "cover" the overly broad curriculum of many courses leaves little time for one-to-one attention from teachers.

However, the features of online learning can aid in more fully realizing the power of the group and the assets of the community. Online, the limitations of time are unbound. Students can post comments 24/7. They can take extra time to formulate a written response, can respond in greater depth, and in some courses, can record their oral response or choose to write it. Or create a slide show with music or a podcast with classmates.

Online instructors often remark that the classroom "comes alive" in cyberspace. Students who are less comfortable speaking out in person often write much more articulately in the virtual classroom. Students can review the comments of many more of their fellow classmates and learn from how they are thinking about the issues and problems. The "intellectual capital" of all the students in the course can be activated, moving toward the many-to-many model.

In this way, one of the most ironic and tantalizing advantages of online learning can be its ability to personalize and individualize the learning experience for students. In unexpected ways, online can be more intimate than in-person.

Edutopia's coverage of online learning[18] has included:

⚲ Florida Virtual High School, the largest of the state online systems, offers online courses and Advanced Placement courses for middle and high school students statewide. Florida enrolls 210,000 in K–12 online education through both public and private providers—the largest in the country. If a student decides to take an online class, state funding is directed to the virtual school as long as the student successfully completes the course. This funding model makes sense, yet concerns about oversight and quality assurance continue to constrain growth.

⚲ West Virginia, where Spanish teacher Joyce McClanahan was shown teaching several of her twenty-one classes in fifteen middle schools. She begins her teaching day, as most teachers do, about 7:45 a.m. until 3:30 p.m., working with students in 45-minute periods. But she spends her evenings doing one-to-one tutoring, often until 10 p.m. This work can involve listening to and giving feedback to students' speaking, recorded as an audio file using Wimba. As discussed earlier in this chapter, one advantage of technology for language learning is the ability for students to record their own voices, for review by themselves, their teachers, and even their peers. This is a key component of performance-based assessment: the performance needs to be recorded and sharable for review and improvement.

⚲ Clark County, Nevada, where students take courses not available in their physical schools and where time-shifted online courses enable students to work in the unique economy of Las Vegas casinos. High school students can earn more than $100 per night

parking cars and performing other jobs. The Clark County schools
shifted face-to-face and online classes to start later in the morning.

These examples indicate the promise of online learning. In the coming
decade, these courses, as well as in-person courses using online resources,
will only improve. One exciting area is the rapid publishing of the best
lectures in a field online. On iTunes U and iTunes Beyond Campus,
there are more than 200,000 audio and video files, free, and published
by leading universities, museums, and nonprofits. On one day in
February 2010, there were lectures and commentary, in audio and video,
by leading authorities, from Philosophy for Beginners from Oxford to
The Earthquake in Haiti by the Center for Strategic and International
Studies to Energy Technology from Delft University in the Netherlands.
For Black History Month, lectures by Alice Walker at Emory University
and Cornel West at Southwestern University were available.

While many school districts still block iTunes because of objectionable music, it is only a matter of time before this cyber-barricade
is overthrown to unleash the wealth of online resources to learners
everywhere and provide the highest quality content for online courses.
More than 170 years after Sir Isaac Pitman's innovation, we are still
inventing this new virtual "Penny Post," adapting the Internet to
deliver new and improved courses, a prerequisite to spreading learning
across an Education Nation.

Evidence of Outcomes: Online Learning

Are online courses and programs as effective as face-to-face instruction?
In their 2009 *Summary of Research on the Effectiveness of K–12 Online
Learning*, Susan Patrick and Allison Powell reviewed the research literature
on K–12 online learning. They cited an in-depth review of fifty-one online
learning studies supported by the U.S. Department of Education in 2009.
Of the fifty-one, forty-four of the studies were conducted with students in
higher education.

Remarkably, on average, students in online learning courses performed better than those receiving face-to-face instruction. The study compared both online and blended learning environments with face-to-face classroom instruction. In the studies comparing blended environments with face-to-face courses, "blended instruction has been more effective, providing a rationale for the effort required to design and implement blended approaches."[19]

The study also found that:

- Students who took all or part of their class online performed better, on average, than those taking the same course through traditional face-to-face instruction.

- The "hybrid model" combining online and face-to-face elements was more effective than purely online instruction, when compared with purely face-to-face instruction.

- Studies in which learners in the online condition spent more time on task than students in the face-to-face condition found a greater benefit for online learning.

- Most of the variations in the way in which different studies implemented online learning did not affect student learning outcomes significantly.

- The effectiveness of online learning approaches appears quite broad across different content and learner types.

- Online learning can be enhanced by giving learners control of their interactions with media and prompting learner reflection.

- Providing guidance for learning for groups of students appears less successful than does using such mechanisms with individual learners. (pp. xiv–xv)

In the West Virginia Ed Pace study of the Virtual School, students in the online Spanish I courses learned Spanish I as well as their peers. In Spanish II, Virtual School Spanish students outperformed some peers. Virtual School Spanish students also learned valuable technology skills. The findings suggested that the blended model combining face-to-face sessions with online classes was associated with more successful implementations and improved student outcomes.

In 2007, Florida TaxWatch conducted a comprehensive assessment of the Florida Virtual High School (FVHS).[20] The nonprofit agency is known as the "watchdog" of citizen's tax dollars and conducts independent research on public policies and programs to "increase productivity and accountability of Florida's government." "The study examined student demographics, achievement, and cost-effectiveness, finding that during the 2004–05 and 2005–06 school years, FLVS students consistently outperformed their counterparts in Florida's traditional middle and high schools on such measures as grades, Advanced Placement scores, and FCAT scores. All FLVS teachers are certified, and their pay is tied to student performance, making FLVS the only true performance-based education system in the state."

The study also found that FLVS is a bargain for Florida taxpayers. "Without costs for transportation and physical facilities, FLVS is able to offer computer-delivered instruction at a lower per-student cost than traditional schools."

THE DEATH OF THE LECTURE AS WE KNOW IT

Having attended and taught at Harvard, I am always heartened when this venerable and distinguished institution—America's oldest college dating back to 1636—strikes a blow against dusty academic tradition. Eric Mazur, a Harvard physics professor, has laid siege to one of the most cherished delivery systems of universities and schools: the lecture.

The lecture lies at the heart of the twentieth-century instructional system. We know it well: the instructor has knowledge that he or she needs to impart to the class, usually in one-hour doses, perhaps fielding an occasional question from intrepid students willing to expose their confusion or venture an opinion. The lecture has its roots in centuries-old tradition, when knowledge could only be captured in a textbook or in a faculty member's head and both needed to be opened up and shared with students. The book and the brain were all we had. They were the sources of knowledge and information. They were the first Googles the containers of knowledge in ages past.

But the lecture, like the textbook, is not a very student-friendly way of delivering information. They are one person's—albeit an expert's—version of knowledge. Thanks to Google, Bing, and other search engines, students now know there are multiple versions of knowledge about a topic, with varying lengths, depths, points of view, and media. Thanks to iTunes, YouTube, and other video-sharing sites, students can now watch lectures by expert faculty in every field.

The lecture, which began in an oral tradition, now often carries some visuals, whether text or images or sounds, courtesy of PowerPoint. The design and matching of these visuals to the lecturer's spoken word is also becoming an art form, a communication medium unto itself. (I'm reminded of Fred Allen's line about TV being a medium because it was "neither rare nor well done.") Who among us hasn't been subjected to Death by PowerPoint?

The lecture also carries the liability of delivering its information in a one-way stream. In a chemistry or American history lecture, students who get confused in the first 15 minutes tend to remain lost for the following 45. The ability to ask questions when one has them, to correct misunderstandings or connect information from the last lecture, are inconvenient interruptions once the lecturer gets up a head of steam.

It's worth noting that the appeal of delivering lectures is based not so much on students' enjoyment but on instructors' ego. It's a fundamental part of a faculty member's identity. You're supposed to lecture. It's a great compliment to feel that one has knowledge valued by the institutions—school or university—and students, perhaps not as willingly as an instructor would believe, show up to hear what one has to say. But the lecture has been called a method of transferring a professor's notes to a student's notes without ever passing between either of their brains. Or, as a high school department chair once told me, "I sometimes have to remind my teachers that there are other people in the room besides themselves."

Of course, faculty should share their knowledge with students. The issue is, What is the best way to share an expert's knowledge? What's the best use of valuable face-to-face class time? Professor Mazur has thrown a sledge hammer, in the form of technology, at this ivied form of educational discourse.

 "Farewell, Lecture"

Cambridge, Massachusetts

Faced with evidence that his students had difficulty with mastery of physics concepts, such as analyzing the forces in a collision between a heavy truck and a light car, Professor Mazur decided to up-end the relationship between lecturing time and question-answer time. He places his lecture notes online in a course management system and asks students to review those notes as homework. He structures class time as an interactive mix of short presentations, peer discussions, and interactions to guide students through questions he knows they will have difficulty with.

Through the use of the popular "clicker" devices used with interactive white boards, Mazur asks students to contemplate a multiple-choice question for a few minutes. When he views their responses on his computer, if 35 to 70 percent give wrong answers, he asks them to talk to each other and compare their answers. He and his teaching assistants circulate among the groups and guide their conversations. This peer discussion is vital to improving student knowledge. After the discussion, he re-poses the question. Based on their answers, he gives the correct answer and either poses a related question or, if the class is ready, moves on to the next topic.

Mazur is implementing a principle that technology makes visible: students should play a vital role in assessing their learning and sharing what they know and don't know. As Mazur says, "Instead of teaching by telling, I am teaching by questioning." Socrates would have been proud. Studies of his classes, and others around the world, show *student learning gains of three times* compared with students in traditional lecture classes. Mazur also finds that this interactive class format eliminates gender gaps often found in introductory physics classes.

Mazur is not alone. Many faculty in schools and universities have reached the same conclusion. Closer to the field of education, Mazur's colleague at Harvard, Howard Gardner, the distinguished scholar known for his theory of multiple intelligences, was one of the first education professors to recognize the value of class time for interaction, rather than lecturing, and placed videos of his lectures on a server. Students were asked to watch the lectures before class and come armed with questions.

Nowadays, a faculty member doesn't even need to record his or her own lectures. Thanks to video-sharing on the Internet, there is a growing wealth of lectures on many topics on sites such as YouTube and iTunes U. And most of them are free. Instead of feeling pangs of lecture envy, teachers can view these archived lectures as another form of time-saving course materials. Instructors can assign those lectures, or parts of them, to their students and follow the Mazur Principle: use the valuable and scarce commodity of classroom time to work with your students on their understanding.

Professor Mazur has written a wonderful two-page summary of his experience, entitled "Farewell, Lecture."[21] It begins with a statement we should all take to heart: "Discussions of education are generally predicated on the assumption that we know what education is." It ends with a brutally honest admission: "My only regret is that I love to lecture."

This interactive, segmented form of classroom presentation and discussion is descended from another discovery at another university, nearly thirty years earlier. In 1977, James Gibbons, a Stanford professor of engineering, happened upon a similar finding: that interrupting lectures every 10 or 15 minutes for discussion also led to impressive student gains.

The more startling result was that the Stanford students didn't even attend the lectures on campus. In one of the most impressive demonstrations of early distance learning, the graduate students were working at a Hewlett-Packard campus 75 miles away, watching the lectures on videotape during their lunch hour, stopping the tape with a tutor to discuss key points of misunderstanding. Gibbons called the method called Tutored Videotape Instruction (TVI).[22.] The "remote" students, taking the same course and exams and watching the identical lectures of the same professor, outperformed the students on campus who were present at the live lectures. Imagine that Stanford professor coming to grips with the fact that he was more effective on tape than in person!

INTELLIGENT TEXT

The Holy Grail of technology in education is to personalize instruction, using "intelligent software" to provide powerful, diagnostic support for learners, aiding them in overcoming their mistakes and misconceptions. The best teachers do this, guiding, prompting, and explaining concepts to students when they get confused, stumble, or need to have material presented in a different way. The promise of technology has been to emulate the best teachers and make this type of learning support available to all students.

Before doubt sets in whether computers can take over human functions, consider two examples of how intelligent systems improve your everyday life. One: reservations. Two: maps. In recent years, we've all experienced calling up an airline or a hotel chain and giving basic information about who we are and where we want to go. The intelligent reservation system places this information in our account and enables us to track it online. How does the system understand our various accents and vocal qualities? And how does that friendly voice know how to reply? These magical systems are the result of the revolution in speech technologies that have gone from computer science laboratories into our lives in just the past few years.

Using Google or Yahoo Maps or GPS (global positioning systems) for navigation has also become so commonplace that we may not recognize that these technologies are also intelligent systems. Compare how we used to use printed maps to try to figure out directions with how efficiently online mapping and direction sites do this for us. Think of how much time and fuel has been saved by motorists who haven't gotten lost. These are indeed green technologies.

Educators often talk about "scaffolding," how teachers and materials can build an instructional structure around a learner to help them progress higher and higher. But basic goals of literacy and numeracy can be very difficult to achieve for most students, if their tools are limited to paper and pencil.

Some mathematically inclined students are able to learn in this manner, with some assistance and scaffolding from their teachers. Some who are less inclined are fortunate to have teachers who can spend time on their individual progress and help them climb that ladder. But for many, reading the textbook, listening to the teacher, and making marks (and erasing many of them) on sheets of paper doesn't work. And those activities do little for the all-important, larger goal of stoking their interest in things mathematical. It's not that the students are failing the curriculum; the curriculum is failing them.

The majority of American students struggle to read by staring at text and attempting to make sense of it. According to The Nation's 2009 Report Card from the U.S. Department of Education, only one-third of public school fourth- and eighth-graders read at or above proficiency for their grade levels, even though the goal is to have all students at this level.[23] The old methods aren't working.

But imagine if this text were presented digitally on a computer screen and students could interact with it, asking for help with words they haven't encountered before and words they have seen but need help pronouncing and comprehending. Imagine if the words themselves could give hints, such as partially pronouncing the words, or showing a picture of a noun, or pronouncing the word in another language the student may know, such as Spanish or Russian. The computer's scaffolding makes the text smarter and more able to reveal its pronunciation and meaning to the learner. That's what I mean by intelligent text.

And that's what we now have. A number of computer-based systems are offering this type of assistance to young readers. Among the best known is READ 180 from Scholastic, a system intended to reverse reading declines in grades 4 through 12.[24] Developed by Vanderbilt professor of education Ted Hasselbring and a team of Scholastic producers and academic advisors, READ 180 represents an educational innovation that has achieved scale, now used in more than 15,000 classrooms.[25] The software uses advances in technology for diagnostic teaching, analysis of student reading patterns, and adjusting instruction based on immediate feedback. It also enables students to engage in as much "deliberate practice," in Hasselbring's phrase, as they need on their own, using a technology that meets their learning styles, instead of exposure of their difficulties in front of others.

As Hasselbring explains:

> "If we are to use technology in a meaningful way for intervention in reading and math, we must first understand how we as humans learn and how technology can leverage this learning. Our lack of attention to the human's limited working memory during instruction has caused many students to fail to develop basic skills. Technology offers the best hope of providing students with significant amounts of "'deliberate practice'" and the opportunity to develop fluency and automaticity."[26]

Over twelve years, READ 180 has been evaluated in thirty-seven studies demonstrating improvement in reading achievement, with upper-elementary through high school students, African American, Native American, and Latino students, English language learners, and special education students. A 2008 report by the Johns Hopkins University Center for Data-Driven Reform in Education reviewed high-quality evaluation studies using control groups and named READ 180 as one of four effective programs of the fourteen reviewed.[27] One of these studies in the Los Angeles Unified School District followed 537 eighth-graders who were failing reading and writing. In one year, these students made significant gains compared with a matched control group, who declined in reading, indicating the severe challenge faced by adolescents with low literacy.[28]

READ 180 has also been adapted for use in after-school programs. In another study reviewed by the Hopkins Center, at an ethnically diverse school in Brockton, Massachusetts, recommended 90-minute school periods were shortened to 60 minutes for after-school programs, divided into three segments: small-group direct instruction, independent and modeled reading, and use of the READ 180 software.[29]

The 300 after-school students in grades 4–6 improved in oral reading fluency and word recognition—with some variation by grade level—compared to a control group. The READ 180 students also had more regular attendance and appeared more motivated to participate in the after-school program.

Leapfrog's Tag School Reading System uses a novel type of handheld device in a different type of intelligent text system for pre-K through third grades, making the text of the story interactive and much more engaging. The Tag reader is a penlike instrument that activates audio heard through earphones when students click on various points on pages of specially printed books. The flat page of a book becomes an interactive point-and-click experience. When reading Marc Brown's *Arthur Writes a Story*, young readers can hear the story read, in the voices of Arthur, Francie, Mr. Ratburn, and other characters, click on words and hear definitions, and click on a photo of Marc Brown to hear him describe how he wrote it. A USB cable connects each student's Tag reader holding their audiobooks to the teacher's computer to track student progress.

SERIOUS GAMES

Games and simulations have been one of the most exciting and productive areas in the redesign of learning in the past decade but an example of innovation slowly happening on the edges of the vast majority of schools. Marc Prensky, a noted games designer, speaker, and author who has written several books on games and popular articles on Edutopia.org, likes to ask advocates of games in schools of education or companies if they know of teachers who are using them. He rarely hears of one.

The field of video games has exploded in the past 10 years, aided by increases in computing power and creative advances in both the hardware and software, such as the Nintendo Wii. The industry is estimated to be a $50 billion global business, outpacing even the feature film business. Games designers know that if a game costs $50, compared to a $10 movie ticket, they must deliver five times the entertainment experience. Measured in hours, that's at least ten hours of engagement, and most games are played for much, much longer.

The much smaller field of educational games has nonetheless made similar advances. There are the classics, such as Oregon Trail and SimCity. With support from the National Science Foundation, Dr. Christopher Dede and a team of researchers and designers at the Harvard Graduate School of Education has produced River City, a multiuser virtual environment (MUVE) in which middle school students create avatars to transport themselves back to 1878 and communicate via text chat and virtual gestures with residents and health workers in a town ravaged by a public health epidemic.[30] The simulation is based on authentic historical and geographical situations from the late nineteenth century, utilizing fifty digital objects, such as buildings and street scenes, from the Smithsonian Institution's online collections. River City addresses national science content standards and assessments in biology, ecology, epidemiology, and scientific inquiry.

Students work together in teams to help the town investigate the epidemic, assembling clues on whether the disease is borne through the air, water, or via insects, collecting data, and conducting experiments, learning the scientific method. They examine the higher incidence among low-income families and the potential role of polluted water runoff or insects in swampy areas. As the culmination to this form of project-based learning, students hold a research conference to share their findings and write a letter to the mayor making recommendations.

Studies conducted by the research team indicated that students using the River City interactive environment had higher scores on the biology posttest than students using a paper-and-pencil version and demonstrated greater "thoughtfulness of inquiry," a measure of deeper learning.[31]

Retired Supreme Court Justice Sandra Day O'Connor has also targeted the middle school grades with her concern about the decline of civics and government teaching. As the Justice has commented, "That's the time—sixth, seventh, and eighth grades—when the lightbulb first turns on in the brain that enables them to understand the principles of our Constitution and government. They become curious and open to learning about it, and they're not troubled by the issues often affecting kids in high school or later years."[32]

She observed the popularity of computer games with this age group and created the Our Courts project to produce online games about the law, judges, and the court system, working with legal scholars, teachers, and games designers. In 2007, The George Lucas Educational Foundation helped organize a planning meeting for the project, including producers of games and virtual environments from Electronic Arts, Red Hill Studios, and Second Life. Games available at the Our Courts site include Supreme Decision, where students act as clerks to Justices in deciding a free speech case involving a student's right to wear a T-shirt of his favorite band, and Argument Wars, in which students take opposing sides in landmark cases such as *Brown v. Board of Education* and *Gideon v. Wainwright*.

This movement to create "serious games" represents one of the most creative aspects of the Technology Edge. As with the design of educational TV series that I've worked on, such as *Sesame Street*, *3–2–1 Contact*, or Scholastic's *Magic School Bus*, these projects bring together subject-matter experts with educators and games designers. The results have the potential to reach millions of students with a more engaging way of learning. The structure of game play—having a goal in mind, needing to concentrate and employ different strategies to get to the next level, the chance to cooperate with team members and compete against others—makes this type of learning enjoyable and social.

Dr. Henry Jenkins, professor of journalism, communication, and cinematic arts at the University of Southern California has commented on the new forms of recognition that young people are achieving through computer games: "For those kids who become leaders of guilds in World of Warcraft, that's as much an experience as being the captain of the football team, being the editor of the school newspaper." [33] '

🌐 An Educational Phoenix

Washington, D.C.

What would a school that fully embraced the potential of games for learning—where students designed as well as played games—look like? In the fall of 2009, with support from the MacArthur Foundation, Quest to Learn opened in Manhattan, an entirely new kind of school for digital sixth- through twelfth-graders. Its very name and mission statement use a new vocabulary: "The school has been designed to help students to bridge old and new literacies through learning about the world as a set of interconnected systems. Design and innovation are two big ideas of the school, as is a commitment to deep content learning with a strong focus on learning in engaging, relevant ways. It is a place where digital media meets books and students learn to think like designers, inventors, mathematicians, and more." [34] Its inaugural class of 72 sixth-graders works in teams on missions and simulations in new integrated experiences, such as Codesworlds, combining math and English, and Sports for the Mind, on art and physical education. This is a school worth watching.

Quest to Learn can take inspiration from a high school in Washington, D.C., that is not new, but reborn, an educational phoenix rising from the ashes of its own failure, based on a similar mission to provide technology-rich, immersive experiences for inner-city youth through games and simulations. McKinley Technology High School had closed in 1997 due to violence. It reopened in 2003 with a focus on digital media and preparing students for the field of biotechnology.

In the Edutopia film profiling the school, Principal Daniel Gohl claims:

We want our students not to be consumers of simulation technology, but designers of simulation technology, where they are determining the structure of how that story is told.... By enabling them to have the technical skills, they are able to express individualization and creative skills.... They are able to see why math feeds into video game design, how algebra, physics, and geometry are part of what must be considered when trying to design an engaging and interactive experience.[35]

McKinley students are naturals for helping professional developers of games and simulations improve their products. They have tested and provided feedback to Howard Hughes Medical Institute's Virtual Bacterial ID Lab, a free simulation, which gives students the experience of obtaining DNA sequences and identifying unknown microbes, a lab experience out of reach for most high schools. McKinley students have also helped shape Immune Attack, produced by the Federation of American Scientists, in which students navigate a microscopic nanobot through an environment of blood vessels and tissue to help save a sick patient by retraining her immune cells. They learn about processes such as how white blood cells, or monocytes, fight infections. Preliminary evaluations indicate that students learn about concepts such as how monocytes function and gain confidence in molecular and cell biology.[36]

Our film crew returned to McKinley a few years later to produce a profile on Justin, a senior, for our Digital Generation series.[37] Justin is a gamer, filmmaker, and animator who likes classical music and history and makes machinima (go to the link to learn what it is). As he says on the Edutopia site, "I'm sixteen years old, and I use technology because it allows me to express myself to the fullest extent. When it comes to games or digital media, within those, you create things, and that really resonates with me. The fact that you're making a game, you're creating a world, almost."

In our film, Kurt Squire, associate professor at the University of Wisconsin-Madison, discusses his evaluation of the popular Civilization game with fourth- through sixth-graders. He observes that, by starting without a prescribed curriculum, but just playing the game, students needed to learn about maps and geography and investigate questions such as "How do technology and geography influence how civilizations grow and fade?" After playing challenging games, students often want to go further and design their own games.

Squire notes that educational games may have special impact with adolescent boys labeled as ADHD and given to disrupting class. "We think games are a really powerful way to tap into their interests and channel it into something more positive. The kids certainly love it." In the film, student Ciarra Belle adds, "Just the energy of McKinley is so different, it makes you want to learn. They teach us animation and 3-D modeling and Maya [software for animation and visual effects] and things like that and that's really exciting."

When kids say they "love" learning or something is "exciting" in school, we would all do well to pay closer attention.

ASSISTIVE TECHNOLOGY: "WE ALL HAVE SPECIAL NEEDS"

Those of us who wear glasses are fortunate that our culture doesn't stigmatize using this form of assistive device. At least, as adults. Young children with poor eyesight might get called "Four Eyes" for a few years. I was one of them. Soon after our fourth-grade class photo, I had to move to the front row to see the board and then got glasses. Now I wear bifocal glasses and contact lenses and thank the field of optometry for continually improving this technology. Without it, I would be legally blind.

My form of "disability" is mild, correctable, and widespread, affecting 75 percent of adults, according to the Vision Council of America. It is one end of a spectrum of disabilities that affect physical, emotional, and intellectual function, for which technology is continually innovating new solutions.

The fast-changing field of assistive technology (AT) is one of the most exciting in education today. Still, many educators, policymakers, parents, and funders, remain unaware of its contributions and its role is often left out of discussions of "digital equity." Formally, AT serves students with disabilities, about 6 million or 7.7 percent of the student population. Disability categories include specific learning disabilities; speech or language impairments; hearing and visual impairments; orthopedic impairments; mental retardation; emotional disturbances; autism; and brain injury.

The Individuals with Disabilities Educational Improvement Act (IDEA) mandates that all special education students should have AT "considered" when their individualized education plans (IEP) are written. Based on educational equity alone, everyone seeking to improve schools should advocate for ensuring that special education students receive the best services possible, including use of effective AT devices.

But there's a more fundamental reason why we should all be interested in AT: advances in AT are advances for all of us. The technology tools developed to help students with motoric, sensory, and mental issues are proving valuable to everyone. One example is speech recognition and synthesis, with origins in helping the visually impaired, enabling text to be read in natural language. Remember those phone conversations with the virtual airline or hotel agent? Our speech is being digitized, interpreted, and responded to by a computer. The experience is so seamless, we quickly acclimate to it.

Speech technology research in universities, such as Carnegie-Mellon and Stanford, and companies, such as AT&T and Google, is transforming how we relate to computers, the world, and each other. In the not-too-distant future, we will simply talk to our mobile devices and our communication will be sent as either voice or text. The QWERTY keyboard, amazingly persistent as the primary way in which we produce text, will become one of several ways in which letters are made to appear on a screen.

The field of AT has expanded into a larger movement for the Universal Design of Learning (UDL). CAST, formerly the Center for Accessible Special Technology, near Boston, has been a pioneer in this movement, advocating for the National Instructional Materials Accessibility Standard (NIMAS). With the adoption of NIMAS, publishers are producing digital educational materials that can be converted into many formats for different types of learners, including Braille, audio books, Web sites, large-print versions, and more.

For his leadership in the UDL movement, Dr. David Rose, a cofounder of CAST with Anne Meyer in 1984, was named one of Edutopia's Daring Dozen in 2004.[38] In the early 1970s, David and I had been research assistants together on a project at Harvard to study *The Electric Company* PBS reading series with second- through fourth-graders. Even back then, his passion for using media to help struggling readers was apparent. He is an inspiring example of an educational entrepreneur who has shaped technology to serve all learners.

The National Center for Technology Innovation (NCTI) serves as the national clearinghouse for information, research, and partnerships "to advance learning opportunities for students with disabilities by fostering technology innovation."[39] The NCTI Web site links to the Tech Matrix, a locator for educators and families to match specific disabilities to AT tools and other products. NCTI is a valuable source for tracking this dynamic field and convenes an annual conference bringing together AT leaders, policymakers, and entrepreneurs.

Edutopia's coverage of assistive technology and universal design has included:

- Albano Berberi, a blind high school student in the Boston area who studies computer science and plays violin. He is seen using a note taker with a Braille keyboard that outputs to a speech synthesizer and a screen reader to convert screen text to speech, giving him an edge in his AP computer science class as lines of code are read to him

- Lukas Bratcher, who plays euphonium in his high school marching band from his wheelchair, thanks to a special joystick that electronically signals the valves on his instrument, and

- An article by Elise Brann of the Education Development Center, Tracy Gray and Heidi Silver-Pacuilla of the National Center for Technology Innovation, describing a number of these tools.[40]

I recently attended an event in Berkeley organized by the Center for Accessible Technology, a leading group in the AT movement. There was a demonstration of the new Intel Reader, an ingenious device for blind people that can convert any written text into spoken word. A live demonstration scanned the page on the back of the event program and, within a minute, a friendly male voice read the text flawlessly, with natural language intonation. The presenters mentioned that, in another example of "digital curb cuts," AT advocates use the analogy of "digital curb cuts," that the modified curbs at intersections originally meant to help those disabled in wheelchairs now benefit bikeriders, skateboarders, parents with strollers, and those wheeling luggage. The device could be useful to anyone trying to read a menu in small type in a dimly lit restaurant. On many occasions, I could have used it.

There was one humorous moment, when the voice read "Eighth St." as "Eighth Saint." It was a forgivable error that only made the computer seem more human.

George Lucas has led our foundation to take an inclusive view of the spectrum of ability and disability. In 2000, he wrote in an Edutopia newsletter:

> In filming for our *Learn & Live* documentary [1998], we met Leslie, a girl with cerebral palsy in Fort Worth who used voice

recognition software to dictate feature articles for her school newspaper. The computer eliminated the barrier posed by the need to coordinate the movement of hands and to type at the keyboard. Leslie was liberated to share her innate intelligence and eye for detail in writing.... With the Internet, her story could conceivably be read by people around the world. Readers wouldn't know that the author has cerebral palsy and it wouldn't matter. Students with disabilities are leading us to confront our own disabilities—and to reflect on how technology is helping all of us achieve our true potential.

It seems to me that anyone who is denied full access to information and ideas—or the means to express themselves as individuals—has a type of disability. This can include students with learning disabilities, students in remote areas, and students for whom English is a second language. My hope is that one day, the classroom where students of varying aptitudes and abilities are working together will be the rule and not the exception. The name of a student's "disability" won't matter nearly as much as a student's gifts and aspirations. After all, when you think about it, we all have special needs.[41]

SCOTLAND'S ENLIGHTENED IDEA

Imagine you're a minister of education of some hypothetical nation with fifty different local education authorities (LEAs) or school districts. In the year 2010, you're faced with this complex technological landscape: the fifty districts are each coming up with their own solutions for hardware, software, e-mail, videoconferencing, and Internet connectivity, with varying costs and duplication. What's a national education minister to do? CEOs with fifty different field offices don't tolerate fifty different solutions to their technology needs. They recognize the benefits of creating technology solutions to streamline technology operations for the entire company, cut costs, and save time.

So, now we have Google, YouTube, and a host of leading sites that have indexed the world's information in articles, photos, video, and more and deliver it in a split second to young fingers searching for it. But still, finding what they're looking for can still be a challenge. What are the best sites for learning about science, history, or art? And sometimes, young eyes and ears can find information they're not ready for. Many districts have recoiled from the "dark side" of the Internet by shutting down access to sites with some objectionable content but some very worthwhile material, as well. There is now a tremendous wealth of educational videos on YouTube and iTunes U, from PBS, the Smithsonian, world-class lectures, and documentaries on every subject imaginable. But many districts block YouTube and iTunes due to content that can create legal liability.

Instead of accepting the status quo and walling off very high-quality content, some technology visionaries might ask, "Why don't we built an educational Intranet? Why not create a common technology platform for all of the fifty different LEAs, so that their hardware, software, e-mail, videoconferencing, and discussion groups all talk to each other? Why not build a "gated garden" within the Internet so that when students are working within this Intranet, all the sites are educational and have been authenticated by educators, including students' own teachers?

Most people reading this would say, "That makes so much sense." But no state in the United States has done this, and it will be a cold day in D.C. before there is a national solution. Once again, innovation has come from another nation, and that nation is Scotland. Perhaps it's fitting that the nation that gave rise to so many scientific and technological discoveries during and after the Scottish Enlightenment, from James Watt's steam engine to Lord Kelvin's work in thermodynamics, also illuminated a bold idea to shape the Internet for education.

Glow, The World's First Educational Intranet

Scotland

Shortly after 1999, when control over domestic issues devolved from Westminster in London to the Scottish Parliament in Edinburgh, Scotland looked at this problem among its thirty-two education authorities and wisely said, "Let's build that educational Intranet." In 2001, they invested a princely sum, about $64 million, to build and operate it for three years in a nation of 5.1 million people and 700,000 students. Faced with that amount, most Americans would say, "That's really expensive. It's unaffordable." During his years as chief science officer for Sun Microsystems, John Gage met with numerous ministers of education. Gage, now with the Kleiner Perkins Caufield & Byers venture capital firm, says, "The problem with Americans is we think of education as a cost. But other nations think of it as an investment."

Originally named the Scottish Digital Learning Network and renamed Glow, the system launched in September 2007.[42] As of the fall of 2009, all thirty-two "local authorities," or school districts, had signed up to use Glow. The system has enrolled about 250,000 students, with about 10 percent of them using it as a daily part of instruction. The Scottish government, encouraged by the results, has made a long-term investment in Glow, including plans to upgrade the system and create Glow2, until 2017.

A key to Glow's success, as seen in Maine, is the focus on teacher and principal development. The key was not implanting technology by itself in the schools but demonstrating how it enables better instruction. Glow's cataloguing of lesson plans saves teachers time, their most precious resource. According to Laurie O'Donnell, one of Glow's principal architects as former director of learning and technology for Learning and Teaching Scotland (LTS), the main benefit has been in increased communication of all kinds. Pre-Glow, teachers were often unaware of what their peers, even in their own school and town, were doing.

Glow enables them to search and find lessons from Scotland and abroad. It also enables parents to better track their children's assignments and tests.

For his leadership, O'Donnell was named one of Edutopia's Daring Dozen/Global Six in 2008.[43] To other nations or states considering implementing an educational Intranet, he advises, "The technology is complex but probably easier than the human, political, and cultural issues. You need to be strong on both sides of the equation. You need great technology to support education, because the context is ultra-complex and highly dynamic. But without the human dimension, even the best technology is doomed to provide a very poor return on investment."

Glow has attracted visitors from more than twenty nations, including myself. When I visited one primary classroom in urban Dundee, its teacher and students videoconferenced with a rural classroom as easily as making a phone call. Examples of how Glow is used, especially to encourage collaboration and communication, from the primary grades through high school, can be found on its Web site.[44]

Perhaps the highest praise comes from Jaye Richards, a high school biology teacher from outside Glasgow. Her students studying river pollution looked at local rivers, but also the Yangtze and the Gulf of Mexico. When she compared her students to those in three other classrooms in the same school who used the same biology syllabus but not Glow, her students scored 14 percent better on an end-of-year assessment and other measures. An even better indicator is the students' body language: "I have to drag them out of the classroom at the end of the lesson." They pass Paul Houston's test of a great school: While most students drag themselves to class in the morning and race out at the end of the day, these Scottish students, immersed in a safe and secure Internet connecting them to the world, are slow to leave.

The examples in this chapter demonstrate how teaching and learning are undergoing a wholesale transformation, made possible through new media and technology, in how curriculum is designed and delivered and how groups of learners and instructors communicate and share knowledge. The Technology Edge connects to the Edge 4: The Time/Place Edge in the next chapter, enabling learning wherever and whenever learners are gathered, especially in places beyond the classroom and within their communities.

THE TIME/PLACE EDGE
LEARNING ANYTIME, ANYWHERE

Learning in America is a prisoner of time. For the past 150 years, American public schools have held time constant and let learning vary.

NATIONAL EDUCATION COMMISSION ON TIME
AND LEARNING, 1994

The structure of the day for American children and youth is more than timeworn. It is obsolete. In a new day for learning, there is no final bell.

TIME, LEARNING, AND AFTERSCHOOL TASK FORCE, 2007

TECHNOLOGY, EXEMPLIFIED BY online learning, dramatically changes when and where learning happens. The Time/Place Edge represents the destruction of the old view of education happening within the four walls of the classroom, Monday through Friday, 8 a.m. to 2 p.m., with some homework thrown in after school. Repeat for 180 days, 31 weeks. Take three months off for the summer. Repeat. That's the old but persistent view of when and where learning happens. But when the world's learning resources are always "on," 24/7/365, the institution of "school" is gradually shifting to enable learning "anytime, anywhere."

Technology is not the only force behind this edge. Demographic and societal shifts are also moving this edge to the center. Changing patterns in the workforce have led to the need to create safe places where children can be cared for and learn, for eight or nine hours, not just six. The "achievement gap" has led to efforts to provide more support and enrichment for lower-achieving students during afternoons, weekends, and summers. Urbanization, overuse of technology itself, and concerns about childhood obesity have led to movements to get children out of the buildings and into nature. This "place-based" and "experiential" learning approach connects to the Curriculum Edge, bringing students to the places where they can experience, as Dewey advocated, the real Mississippi River, and not just read about it in their textbooks. Students' communities, states, and the larger nation become their classrooms. Of the six edges, the Time/Place Edge is perhaps the least obvious, but it builds upon many social forces transforming schools today.

One telling example of the Time/Place Edge can be found in an unlikely spot: school buses. Many students spend an extraordinary amount of time on school buses. Students on sports teams also spend many long hours travelling to games. For city kids stuck in traffic and rural students travelling between small towns, this commuting time has been learning "down time" spent playing games, listening to music, talking on cell phones, or, as a *New York Times* article described it, "teasing, texting, flirting, climbing [over seats], and sometimes punching [seats and seatmates]."

That article, titled "Wi-Fi Turns Rowdy School Bus into Rolling Study Hall," described how the Vail, Arizona, district turned its high school buses into mobile Wi-Fi hotspots, enabling students to finish homework, turn in assignments, and search for Internet resources during their 70-minute rides to school.[1] This rural district outside of Tucson, with 18 schools and 10,000 students spread across 425 square miles, already had created Empire High School as a 1:1 laptop school, using textbook funds to pay for the computers. The "Internet buses," as students call them, also transport sports teams to tournaments.

District officials report an increase in "learning time" and a decrease in behavioral problems during these long rides. While some students do use the Internet to play games and e-mail friends, the seriousness with which most students use the connectivity is impressive. Schools and districts in Florida, Missouri, and Washington, D.C., are also implementing Wi-Fi on their buses, for the cost of a $200 router and a monthly service fee of $60. These educators are, pardon the pun, "thinking outside of the bus" and finding creative ways to obtain more learning hours for their students. Cody Bingham, a Vail bus driver, said it best, after driving the soccer team four hours to their game: "That was the quietest ride I've ever had with high schoolers."

One of the more startling scenes in an Edutopia documentary also involved teens and vehicles. In 2002, we filmed two boys from San Fernando High School, near Los Angeles, sitting in a parked car at night; their faces were illuminated by a dim glow. To add to the curiosity, they were parked outside the home of their teacher.

It turns out the students were not lighting up illegal substances. They were illuminating their minds, using the wireless hub inside teacher Marco Torres's home to access the Internet. His students were part of the award-winning San Fernando Educational Technology Team, making films about social issues, from local violence to labor issues in sweatshops.[2] In class, he had let it drop that he had just installed wireless at home. The scene made the point that students know that the world of Internet learning is available 24/7, while their schools operate on a 6/5/180 schedule. Once the high school set up its own wireless network, students sat in their cars in the parking lot, accessing the Internet while the school doors were closed. His students were lighting up the lamp of learning, now a glowing computer screen and always switched "on."

American Youth and Media: The Other Curriculum

We all know that health is a matter of daily and weekly habits of diet and exercise that return benefits over months, years, and a lifetime. Similarly, learning is a matter of how one spends every day, week, month, and year. We can think in terms of "habits of learning" that make productive use of hours spent in and out of the classroom.

In claiming more time for learning, educators and policymakers face stiff competition from entertainment media. The same media and Internet technologies that can be used for education occupy a steadily increasing and dominant share of the lives of American youth.

In my 1994 book, *The Smart Parent's Guide to Kids' TV*, I quoted a shocking statistic: by the time children graduate from high school, they will have spent more time with TV than in the classroom. Do the math: 6 hours a day in school, 31 weeks a year, multiplied by 13 years: 12,000 hours. Back then, kids spent an average of four hours a day watching TV. Four hours a day, over 52 weeks and 13 years, amounts to 18,000 hours. Out-of-school media use was clearly "the other curriculum."[3]

Fifteen years of media proliferation of computers, cell phones, DVDs, Internet TV, and iPods have led to even greater dominance of media in the lives of children. According to a Kaiser Family Foundation study in 2010, *Generation M2: Media in the Lives of 8- to 18-Year-Olds*, children are spending an astonishing 10 hours and 45 minutes with media. That's the average. Some are spending 13 or 15 hours a day. This figure has grown steadily, from an average of 7:29 in 1999 to 8:33 in 2004 to 10:45 in 2009.[4]

You might well ask, How is this possible? There are still only 24 hours in a day. The answer: full-on multitasking. American kids are squeezing 10:45 of media use into 7:38 "human hours." Mobile media have enabled this habit, with cell phone ownership jumping from 39 percent to 66 percent of youth from 2004 to 2009, and MP3 players increasing from only 18 percent to 76 percent in the same period. In one fascinating finding, young people are spending more time listening to music, playing games, and watching TV (49 minutes daily) on mobile devices than they spend talking on them (33 minutes).

In 2007, filmmakers Robert Compton, Chad Heeter, and Adam Raney made a film titled *Two Million Minutes*. It profiles six high school seniors, a boy and a girl, from the United States, India, and China. The title is based on the number of minutes high school students have over four years. The learning "habits" of the students contrast sharply: the American seniors enjoying their video games and time at the mall, while the Indian and Chinese students spend more time in after school cram sessions and Saturday school.

While the film appears critical of how the American seniors spend their time, it's unclear to me whether the American teenagers' lifestyle is more well rounded or frivolous and whether their peers' more intense focus on their studies is narrowing or academically superior. But the film makes the point exceedingly well about how students in different cultures use their two million minutes. And how important and challenging it will be to sequester more learning time for American youth.[5]

LIBERATING SCHOOLS AS "PRISONS OF TIME"

One of my favorite government reports (some might say this is an oxymoron) comes from the 1994 U.S. Department of Education's (USDE) panel with an unusual title: the National Education Commission on Time and Learning, whose staff director was Milt Goldberg, an official at the USDE. The report, titled *Prisoners of Time,* is brief, well designed, and clear. It also has a sense of humor. It began,

> Learning in America is a prisoner of time. For the past 150 years, American public schools have held time constant and let learning vary. Some bright, hardworking students do reasonably well. Everyone else—from the typical student to the dropout—runs into trouble.... As Oliver Hazard Perry said in a famous dispatch from the War of 1812: "We have met the enemy and they are [h]ours".[6]

The problem, according to the commission, is not just the length of the school year but also the lockstep "gridding" of the school day. The report concluded, "Our schools . . . are captives of the school clock and calendar. We have been asking the impossible of our students, that they learn as much as their foreign peers while spending only half as much time in core academic subjects."[7]

The report emphasized that American schools have been operating under the tyranny of time; the length of the typical school period (45–50 minutes), school day (six hours, from morning until early afternoon), and school year (180 days) continues to be remarkably rigid across the nation. Other industrial nations recognize that more time can equal more learning: countries such as Germany and Japan have longer school days and years, with more time spent on core academic subjects.

The 50-minute period of most secondary schools has pigeonholed learning into short episodes interrupted by "passing periods" in which students parade from one classroom to the next, often on the other side of campus. The clock is allowed to set the rhythm of learning. It's *learning interruptus.* Imagine organizing your work day in this way. Every hour, students hop on and off this conveyor belt of the school's assembly-line scheduling, reinforcing the model of the school as factory and students as widgets in production. The hourly ritual where bells still ring prevents students from working in depth on projects in groups and travelling into the community to gather data or talk to local experts.

Even within class periods, "instructional time" is often wasted, compounding the problem. Students' bodies may be in classrooms but their minds are often bored, distracted, or in wait mode while teachers expend valuable class time on disciplining a few unruly students.

If students need to be knowledge workers, why do we impose on them this lockstep schedule for those critical six or seven years, a schedule they have not encountered before and never will after? The schedule reinforces divisions between subjects, where math is taught separately from science and English cannot be connected to history.

Teachers are also isolated in their classrooms by this rigid schedule, denied opportunities to learn from other teachers and focus on student work. Teaching may be the only profession where its members have so little control over how their time is spent.

This assembly-line schedule was born out of the Carnegie Unit, which requires 120 hours of class time for high school courses, based on daily one-hour or 50-minute periods over the course of an academic year, roughly 30 weeks. The Carnegie Unit itself grew out of the early work of the Carnegie Foundation for the Advancement of Teaching, endowed by steel magnate Andrew Carnegie in 1906. Surely it's time for education to abandon this more than a century-old idea. Fortunately, some middle and high schools are moving toward block scheduling in 90-minute and two-hour blocks to allow for deeper engagement, interdisciplinary study, and one innovation that has been around for a long time but is still rarely practiced: team teaching.

More than fifteen years after the *Prisoners of Time* report, the vast majority of American schools are still held captive to an outdated calendar that includes a three-month summer vacation. The seasons of schooling set the schedules for close to 7 million K–12 educators and staff and 55 million students and their families. No other sector of our society—government, business, or nonprofit—considers its year to be composed of six-hour days for 180 days and 30 weeks.

Restructuring time doesn't mean merely adding more of the same kind of hours to a traditional school day. Simply extending the school day with rote memorization and drill and practice will not increase higher levels of student learning and may well decrease motivation. Summer learning should involve more of what the West Philadelphia Automotive Academy (see Edge 2) does and less mind-numbing remedial work for students who are falling behind. Discussions of restructuring time sometimes revert back to these simplistic views. As Milt Goldberg puts it, "A lousy eight-hour day is worse than a lousy six-hour day."

As described in the Curriculum Edge (Edge 2), assessment may drive teaching and learning, but schedules drive how teaching and learning time is spent. It's high time to rethink the learning day and school year. As Ernest Hemingway once said, "Time is all we have."

A NEW DAY FOR LEARNING, BEYOND THE BELL

One of the most encouraging developments in the Time/Place Edge has been the many states and districts moving to redefine the school day beyond its traditional boundaries. Because of the constriction of the curriculum under No Child Left Behind, many districts have responded by forming partnerships to create afterschool programs to support students with homework help, tutoring, recreation and physical activity, and a more creative approach to learning through the arts, science, and technology. These programs are extending the technology resources of schools and keeping the doors to learning open beyond the final bell. Many project-based learning experiences have been moved into the "after-school" hours, which include afternoons, evenings, weekends, and summers.

Around the nation, a new definition of *educator* is emerging as schools work in partnership with community-based groups. These "informal" or community educators come from science centers, art museums, Boys' & Girls' Clubs, local businesses, and many other organizations. Some may be university faculty involved with local schools. They are increasing not only the time students spend learning but also how they are learning.

Edutopia's interest in community partnerships to extend school learning dates back to our 1997 documentary, *Learn & Live*, hosted by Robin Williams, in which we showed the West Des Moines school district's extended use of its school buildings to create centers for its community.[8] A daughter is shown helping her mother learn computer skills. The gymnasium is used by community groups for dance classes. In 2002, we produced a similar story on another national model, the partnership between the Children's Aid Society in New York City and the city's schools, where violin and dance are taught and an Hispanic women's group is seen discussing issues such as domestic violence.[9]

Edutopia's coverage has also included:

The Los Angeles Unified School District's Vaughn Next Century Learning Center, a campus for students in grades pre-K–12. Principal Yvonne Chan grasped the need to extend the school year from 180 days to 200 days to serve the needs of her students, 97 percent from low-income families and 78 percent English-language learners. Vaughn fills each day with a rich array of after-school learning activities and services, including universal preschool, full-day kindergarten, technology integration, arts classes, service learning, and health and counseling services. Over the course of five years, the average scores of its students on the state Academic Performance Index have risen more than 200 points, from 443 to 672 (in a range of 200 to 1,000).

During the 2004–2005 school year, the Alice Carlson Applied Learning Center, in Fort Worth, Texas, scheduled four blocks of nine weeks each and fall and spring intersession workshops, allowing its K–5 students time for hands-on arts, science, and computer projects or sports in addition to language arts and math enrichment.

At the North Kenwood/Oakland Charter School, also in Chicago, middle school students participated in an after-school project making "movie reports" on aspects of Chicago's history. Topics included the African American neighborhood of Bronzeville in the 1930s, the role of the Black Panthers in the civil rights movement, and the redevelopment of the Ida B. Wells housing complex, built in 1941—the first city housing development with a park, playgrounds, and athletic fields.

Mentored by professionals such as National Public Radio producer David Isay, the students used historic photos and footage, digital cameras, editing software, and laptops to produce their documentaries. Some of their work has been honored in student media competitions. The project was documented by former Apple research scientist Kristina Hooper Woolsey as part of an MIT project about today's young digital natives.

At the Global Kids program in Brooklyn, teens channel their enthusiasm for visual entertainment into designing educational video games. Playing for Keeps encourages teens to study topics such as racial profiling in airports, the HIV/AIDS epidemic, or the rural life of a Haitian family as subject matter for their final product.

RECONCEIVING TIME AND LEARNING

In 2005, I joined a Task Force on Time, Learning, and Afterschool convened by the Charles Stuart Mott Foundation of Flint, Michigan, to examine how more "learning time" could be being captured for students during the hours outside of the school day. The committee was chaired by Vince Ferrandino, former executive director of the National Association of Elementary School Principals and included former officials of the U.S. Department of Education, researchers, a superintendent, and leaders of national afterschool groups.

The Mott Foundation has had a long-standing interest in making sure that children have safe and supportive environments in addition to their schools, dating back to when C. S. Mott, a founder of General Motors, asked the Flint schools to stay open longer to accommodate the schedules of parents who were working in his factories. During the Clinton Administration, the Mott Foundation began working with the U.S. Department of Education to create national policy, funding, and technical assistance for the 21st Century Community Learning Centers. Today, the program provides more than $1 billion through the states to support academic and enrichment activities focusing especially on children from low-income families.

In 2007, the Task Force published its report, entitled *A New Day for Learning.*[10] I view it as a companion to the 1994 *Prisoners of Time* report, chronicling progress in schools and communities creating more and better learning time for their youth, but also restating the urgent need to make quicker progress. The title was a double entendre intended to signify the new opportunities now possible for learning and how those opportunities relate to a reconception of time and schedules.

We claimed, "The structure of the day for American children and youth is more than timeworn. It is obsolete.... Quite simply, unless we profoundly change our thinking and policies about when, where, and how children learn and develop, our steady progress as an economy and a society will end." We called for a complete redesign of American schools, unifying disparate policies and funding streams to support children's education and health. We concluded the school day needed to be redesigned to include more learning time beyond the school day, including summers, but also a different kind of learning, anchored in high standards and authentic curricula and utilizing technology, the Internet, and community-based experiences.

We focused especially on the 40 percent of families who are among the working poor or on welfare and the 14 million children, 25 percent of all children, who are "home alone," as well as the millions more whose families are unable to pay for the kinds of experiences, such as science and art classes, that middle-class families can afford. The report also took a broader view of the social costs of not providing a bigger, safer tent for these youth, including the costs of crime and juvenile detention for the 100,000 teenagers in the court system and the millions more who would drop out of high school and enter prison as adults. We cited one study in which law enforcement officials chose the expansion of afterschool programs over hiring more police officers by a 4-to-1 margin to reduce youth-related crime.

We pointed to successful examples and advocated for policies and funding to bring them to scale:

- More than forty Big Picture high schools, originating with the Metropolitan Academy in Providence, whose emphasis on project-based learning and workplace apprenticeships resulted in 81 percent of alumni attending college or graduating
- The PACERS program for high schools in rural Alabama, where every student participating in the aquaculture facility project passed the state high school exam in science
- Rainier Scholars in Seattle, using afterschool and summer periods to provide academic support and enrichment, adding up to more than 120 additional days per year. Sixty Scholars are selected to start the program during the summer before sixth grade. In 2009, 100 percent of the first cohort were admitted to four-year colleges and universities

- Citizen Schools, recently hailed as a model by President Obama, a national network of 2,000 middle school students at 30 campuses, where professionals, fulfilling the definition of active citizens in a democracy, mentor low-income youth, leading to higher student achievement

- Harlem Children's Zone operating in a 60-block district in New York City, directed by Geoffrey Canada, whose strategies involve prenatal classes for young mothers, early childhood education for all four-year-olds, health care, its own charter school, and safe playgrounds, and

- Peekskill, New York, where superintendent and Task Force member Judith Johnson emphasizes a "community as class-room" approach in the district's extended day programs. Youth serve as docents at art museums and volunteers at community health centers, resulting in higher test scores and improved self-discipline.

In 2007, with support from the Mott Foundation, Edutopia produced documentaries and Web content on reconceiving the school day, launched with the Task Force report. We produced an overview documentary and films about high schools in Las Vegas, Nevada, that started morning classes later to allow teens to work in casinos during the evenings; MetWest Academy, one of the Big Picture schools in Oakland, where students experience automotive engineering and work in a veterinary clinic; and John Spry Community School, a pre-K–12 school in a Latino community in Chicago. To relieve overcrowding, the high school started at 11 a.m. and served dinner. Its students committed to a schedule including Saturdays and summers, and nearly 100 percent graduated on a three-year schedule.

Spry also participated in the MIRACLES program, founded by Texas entrepreneur Todd Wagner, which operates twenty computer labs in seven cities. When I visited the lab, students were using Excel spreadsheets and graphs to predict the distribution of colored M&Ms

in a bowl—an interesting and delicious exercise in statistical thinking. Other students were recording their musical compositions for a video.

These films and related content are available on our "New Day for Learning" microsite on the Edutopia Web site.[11]

In 2009, we launched A New Day for Learning, Part II, to respond to users' requests for a deeper learning of information on model afterschool programs. Film segments, schedules, budgets, lesson plans, and technology plans are provided for four exemplary programs:

- Build San Francisco, where students spend afternoons in special design and architecture classes and work in architects' offices.

- Nature Mapping, where fourth-grade students use GPS devices to observe, map, and monitor species, such as the horny toad lizard in rural Washington state. They also train farmers to add their observations to the database.

- Citizen Schools, afterschool programs where professionals learn to teach and mentor middle school students, such as Google engineers teaching robotics.

- Providence Afterschool Alliance (PASA), an ambitious citywide partnership with schools to offer arts, science, and other subjects.

Every year, programs reaching children in the afterschool hours continue to innovate. In 2009–2010, The Afterschool Corporation (TASC) took to heart President Obama's proclamation to the nation's students: "We're going to show you how cool science can be." TASC developed a science curriculum in New York City where third-graders build a telescope, seventh-graders have fun learning about states of matter by making Oobleck, and all of them change their images of who does science.

One project involved drawing pictures of scientists before the program started and again after several months. The initial drawings recalled a 1957 study by Margaret Mead documenting how high school students held a narrow image of scientists as old, white, and male, laboring in isolation in their labs, and a bit mad.[12] In our work developing 3–2–1 Contact, we cited this study and our own formative research showing the persistence of this stereotype. More than fifty years later, the initial drawings of these New York children illustrated this same image of the scientist, as their teacher described it, as "old crazy people." But just a few months later, their drawings showed younger, female, and more diverse individuals, people who looked like them.

Short two-minute videos on the TASC site make the case for how afterschool programs are creating the "new day for learning." Although these activities may be happening at 4 p.m., they are the kinds of inquiry-based science that should be done in school as well. The videos also make the point that, with high-quality science teachers still lacking in many schools, well-trained afterschool educators can fill the gap.

If you don't know what Oobleck is, check out the link.[13] It's based on the title of a Dr. Seuss book and it's sticky.

SUMMER: "THE THIRD SEMESTER"

Summer vacation is a powerful anachronism that dates back to agrarian days, when farm families needed young people home during the summer months to replace the three R's with the two P's—plantin' and pickin'. Today, students need to be harvesting knowledge year-round. Fall should be the time to plant the seeds of learning, and summer should be a time to harvest those crops—students' minds that have grown and developed over an entire year.

In just the past few years, an exciting development in American education has been the growth of summer learning programs. These programs, variously organized by partnerships between school districts, nonprofit organizations, universities, and others provide students with the "third semester" that middle-class and more wealthy families are able to provide for their children, by paying for fee-based summer sessions and a variety of enrichment programs. The "summer slide" for children is well documented. Children from all backgrounds lose their mathematics skills over the summer; in reading, children from low-income backgrounds fall further behind their more affluent peers.

My fourth-grade class photo from Bennett Elementary School, 1961. I'm in the 3rd row with the bowtie, fourth from the right.

The cast and crew of NBC's "Big Bird in China" after filming at the Great Wall, 1982. That's me, a production assistant, standing next to the star.

The staff of The George Lucas Educational Foundation at a staff retreat in San Francisco.

George Lucas and me reviewing Edutopia documentaries and Web content.

Fifth-graders in Anchorage, Alaska, practice social/emotional listening and communication skills in the context of a math lesson.

A class of fifth-graders in Anchorage in a fishbowl arrangement. A larger group listens and takes notes on the mathematical thinking of the smaller group working at the table.

In the daily morning meeting in Darren Atkinson's sixth-grade class in Louisville, students build trust and openly discuss topics such as bullying.

Students at Philadelphia's Academy of Applied Automotive and Mechanical Science, Joseph Pak, Samantha Wright, and Leah Exum (left to right), discuss the placement of the K-1 Attack's front axle and electric motor.

Jeffrey Daniels cuts metal for the award-winning K-1 Attack's drive system.

Teacher Simon Hauger seated in the K-1 Attack with his West Philly EVX team.

High school students in Philadelphia's award-winning West Philly EVX team don't just drive hybrid cars. They build them to use fuel from soybeans, get 55 miles per gallon, and look cool.

In Oakland, California, MetWest High School student Paula Pereira works twice a week at the Broadway Pet Hospital, integrating workplace experience with her project-based classes.

At chef Alice Waters's Edible Schoolyard project in Berkeley, California, students at Martin Luther King, Jr. Middle School grow and cook their own food, a complete "seed-to-table experience."

Middle-school students taste fresh organic figs from their school garden, part of the Edible Schoolyard project.

Opera singers from the Tucson Opera work with teachers to make language come alive and increase reading achievement.

On a visit to a nearby lake, middle-school students in Maine use digital microscopes attached to their laptops to examine water samples.

A teacher, accompanied by a translator (both seated right), visit parents in their homes to discuss student progress in the Sacramento Parent-Teacher Home Visit Program.

YES Prep North Central teacher Bryan Reed (with laptop) meeting with a student and his mother to discuss upholding the commitments they have all signed in the family's contract with the school.

At her school in Camilla, Georgia, eighth-grader Virginia teaches younger students about Internet safety.

Working with his Intel 4-H Tech Wizards team, Luis, a high school senior in Cornelius, Oregon, uses a handheld device and a digital camera to record data for an inventory of trees on city property.

From the Afterword: A Day in the Life of Young Learner: Students in a San Francisco classroom in the year 2020 hold a live videoconference with a National Park Ranger (foreground) while others discuss time-lapse video of lava flows from Mount Kilauea.

At home in the evening, Malia converses with Xiaoyan in China, who helps her learn Chinese vocabulary for soccer. She records her speaking and plays it back to improve her pronunciation.

Middle-class families, with higher levels of education and income, have more books at home, value reading more for their kids, and can take them more frequently on trips where new experiences can lead to new language acquisition.

The National Summer Learning Association (NSLA), a nonprofit chartered in 2009, began as the Center for Summer Learning at Johns Hopkins University in 2001, evolving out of a summer tutoring program called Teach Baltimore. NSLA provides strategic planning, support to the fast-growing number of districts, states, universities, and nonprofits utilizing the summer months, including how to build partnerships, implement, and evaluate. Its Web site provides a wealth of resources, including research on the importance of summer, advice on how to get started, characteristics of effective programs, and descriptions of model programs. It includes a series of downloadable slide presentations that can be used to make the case at faculty, parent, and school board meetings.[14] The NSLA also organizes conferences, works with legislators, and provides professional development.

Since 2005, NSLA has honored the best programs with its Excellence in Summer Learning Awards. Many of the programs provide a continuing connection for their students during the school year. To date, nineteen programs have been recognized,[15] including:

Summer Scholars, Denver: A year-round program partnering with up to twenty Denver elementary schools with a focus on literacy. About 1,750 youth from low-income backgrounds are served each year. The summer program runs for seven-and-a-half hours on weekdays for six weeks. A morning literacy class includes two teachers, a paraprofessional, parent volunteers, and a class assistant, enabling more personalized instruction. English language learners receive special support.

Afternoon activities range from nature and museum visits to bowling, ice skating, swimming, and music lessons, with support from a key partner, Denver Parks and Recreation. An afterschool tutoring and enrichment program is also provided for 1,000 students at twelve schools, and a family literacy program serves

180 Summer Scholars at twelve schools year-round, providing adult education and English language instruction for parents and reading time for parents and children.

Higher Achievement, Washington, D.C., and northern Virginia: Serves fifth- through eighth-graders with an intensive six-week summer program running eight hours each day. In addition, fifteen hours of academic enrichment and mentoring are provided each week during the school year. The program is held on three weekday afternoons and evenings, running 3:30 p.m. until 8 p.m., covering literature, math, and technology, as well as dance, drumming, SSAT prep, and foreign language.

Evidence of Student Outcomes

According to one study, 78 percent of second-grade Summer Scholars and 82 percent of third-graders improved on the Developmental Reading Assessment.

Higher Achievement students showed impressive improvement on school grades. The average GPA of entering students is 2.3 out of 5, about a D+. After four years, as they enter high school, the average GPA of Higher Achievement Scholars is 3.8, about a B-. According to one study of more than 400 children, their DC Scholars improved an average of 20 percent on reading and math scores, while the district average was 3 percent.

Aim High, San Francisco: Historically, private and parochial schools have had little to do with public schools. But some leaders of independent schools see a higher purpose to their missions. Aim High was incubated at Lick-Wilmerding High School, led for twenty-three years by a visionary head of school, Al Adams. It began as an unusual partnership between Lick-Wilmerding and the San Francisco public schools. Independent schools often have excellent facilities, such as labs, computers, sports fields, and theaters that public schools lack due to underinvestment, and strong faculty interested in teaching a more diverse group of students.

Adams and a teacher leader, Alec Lee, now Aim High director, felt that public middle school students could benefit from a "third semester," and their high school students could receive valuable experience teaching and mentoring younger students. Lick-Wilmerding is one of the founding members of a coalition, Private Schools with a Public Purpose (PSPP), whose members include Head Royce in Oakland, the Crossroads School for Arts and Sciences in Los Angeles, and Punahou School in Honolulu, now even better known for its presidential alum.

Starting with fifty students and twelve teachers, Aim High has grown to twelve sites, more than 1,000 students, and 300 teachers. It provides an opportunity for high school and college students to gain exposure to teaching as a career, a "teaching laboratory" within a progressive school environment that includes the core subjects of mathematics, science, humanities. The program includes time to explore personal and social issues and afternoon activities that include excursions to museums sports events, and cultural festivities. Ninth-graders spend a week in a residential environmental education program in a nearby national park site.

PUEO, THE WISE OWL OF HONOLULU

Inspired by Aim High, Partnerships for Unlimited Educational Opportunity (PUEO, Hawaiian for "owl"), started in 2005 with an unusual collaboration between the independent Punahou School and the Honolulu public schools in Honolulu. Middle school students, called PUEO Scholars, commit to spending each summer for three years on the beautiful Punahou campus studying science, engineering, multimedia, and other subjects.

In one class, I observed Douglas Kiang, a Boston-area teacher who enjoyed returning to Honolulu each summer, sharing his passion for flight simulators. Students were using Microsoft Flight Simulator, a software program for adult aviation enthusiasts. Pairs of students used a simulated yoke to practice takeoffs and landings and eventually pilot a plane on a flight path they chart from one Hawaiian airport to another. In another class, students were engaged in Lego Robotics, designing and programming robots to move forward, sideways, backward, and rotate. In one exercise, two Sumo robots were placed in a circle; the robot that pushed the other out of the circle won.

When PUEO has seen a need, it has moved to fill it. One summer, it found funding to buy out leases on the school's Apple laptops, providing PUEO Scholars their own computers. During 2009–2010, when budget cuts led the Honolulu schools to close on Fridays, PUEO stepped in and offered to pay for its students to continue their learning at community centers, such as the YWCA. Four years after its inception, the program received $3 million from the Clarence T. C. Ching Foundation to continue setting its Scholars on the path to college.

There are some common threads interwoven into these programs. Many target the middle school grades as the critical years to prepare students for success in high school and college. For students to be college-ready, high school is often too late, with many ninth-graders arriving with reading and math skills three or more years behind. These programs emphasize the quality of their faculty and professional development. They bring together a blend of educators from both the classroom and youth development programs.

These summer programs also recognize that one summer isn't enough. They require that students and families make a multiyear commitment. Interestingly, some call their students "scholars," a good example of changing the vocabulary of education. Names and labels matter and too many education labels are pejorative—struggling reader, student with a disability, dropout. These programs give students an aspirational label: You're more than a student. You're a scholar. And scholars go on to college and beyond.

As Ron Fairchild, executive director of the National Summer Learning Association told me, "The field of summer learning is at a great inflection point. We have a body of best practices and programs that work. It's incumbent that we use it to leverage increased public investment. It's an agenda that schools and nonprofits can embrace."

Toward a New Learning Year

Can we conceive of a system that encourages learning beyond the standard school day and year, where students are constantly stimulated and want to come to school early and stay late? Perhaps school districts and their community partners will some day envision and fund a new "learning year," where students and teachers are able to engage in learning activities throughout the day and across weeks and months with time off for vacations but without the three-month summer break. In addition to their time in schools, all children would receive the same stimulating mix of visits to museums and libraries, travel experiences, and residential programs in nature that only more affluent families now provide.

Like the workplace, students and families would schedule, say three or four weeks of vacation a year, on their own rather than the school's mandated calendar. The school calendar would become more like the calendar in real life. In the chapter on the Teaching Edge, Cameron McCune, former superintendent in Fullerton, California, advocates for this schedule.

In learning as in life, time is everything. It's about time that schools improve how they use it. There should be greater national urgency about improving the hours that K–12 students have during those vital thirteen years. For policymakers concerned about our nation losing its competitive edge, time is running out.

PLACE-BASED LEARNING: SCHOOL LIFE = REAL LIFE

When schools are freed from the tyranny of time and current schedules, students and teachers are liberated to pursue a much more authentic style of learning. In the most succinct formulation of the six Edges,

School life = real life. Just four words and an equal sign. The artificiality of much of what passes for learning in many schools evaporates. The Time/Place Edge embraces the many places where learning can occur beyond the classroom, identifying with the movement for "place-based learning." These places become the many spokes connected to the hub of the school, going far beyond the typical field trip, already an endangered activity due to budget cutbacks. In this vision of an Education Nation of community-based schools, the school goes out into the community and the community comes into the school.

Place-based learning, and its relative, project-based learning, requires that students go out into many locations to gather information firsthand and speak to local experts. Throughout this book, I describe a number of these settings ranging from the workplace internships in hospitals and companies of the "Linked Learning" model to students in Maine analyzing water quality in lakes on their laptops. Students taken "on location" come to realize how their classroom studies apply to real life. And they are able to meet and be mentored by role models in the professions, whether they are financial analysts, architects, farmers, or park rangers.

Arranging for students to gain consistent exposure to these people and places has important implications for how their "learning time" is organized. The cost of transportation and the logistics in managing young people off site can be obstacles to place-based learning, but educators attest to the tremendous return on these investments. In this section, I focus on opportunities for place-based learning, beginning with a different kind of "learning place" at the school site, requiring no transportation.

In every community, there are places where science, history, and the arts can be studied in their authentic context, including museums, parks, historic sites, universities, and theaters. Beyond the special field trip, new types of partnerships are enabling students to spend more substantial amounts of time in these places. Some communities have gone further, locating schools in and near museums, zoos, and open spaces. School construction and renovation has been a big business this past decade, totaling close to $100 billion in the past five years. As the nation continues to build new schools, a "Zoo School" or a "Museum School" offer new models for thinking about where, when, and how learning can happen.

Place-based learning can be an ally in curing the national epidemic of children with poor nutrition, a lack of exercise, and an addiction to technology. That "A" word might seem unlikely from a technology advocate like me, but I also believe children are spending far too much time in front of screens. Despite the advance of technology and the quickening pace of change, children still only have twenty-four hours in a day. Healthy development and powerful learning require a balance of time spent with family, friends, and schoolmates, in physical as well as mental activity, in and out of school, in nature as well as in buildings. For urban kids, which is most kids, this last requirement is getting hard to come by.

Richard Louv has written an eloquent book, *Last Child in the Woods: Saving Our Children from Nature-Deficit Disorder.* He writes, "Our society is teaching young people to avoid direct experience in nature" by reducing nature preserves, physical education, and field trips. He laments that electronic media are consuming an increasing portion of children's lives. He even points to zoning ordinances that prohibit tree houses. Louv adds that he believes "reducing that deficit—healing the broken bond between our young and nature—is in our self-interest . . . because our mental, physical, and spiritual health depends upon it."[16]

Louv makes the point that some students labeled with attention deficit/hyperactivity disorder (ADHD) may in fact have a form of "nature-deficit disorder." Students who can't pay attention in traditional lecture-bound classrooms come alive when they encounter animals, plants, fresh air, and hands-on activity. "Nature's Ritalin," says Louv, has a restorative effect on children's minds and bodies—without the drugs.

While Louv doesn't acknowledge the role of technology in helping young people understand nature, I agree with his main point: that children need to spend more time in nature, and add the proviso that they should be carrying digital devices to record data and snap photos of plants and animals. Recognizing the value of placing students' minds and bodies in nature, Harvard psychologist Howard Gardner has added the "naturalist intelligence" to his earlier list of the seven multiple intelligences (linguistic, logical-mathematical, spatial, bodily-kinesthetic, musical, interpersonal, and intrapersonal).

Students with high "nature quotients" (NQs) are needed now more than ever. Developing students' NQs provides a valuable pathway for developing the other intelligences. It is also an on-ramp to students' understanding of climate change and preparation for the "green jobs" that will be in demand in the future.

Years ago, a San Francisco educator told me a startling fact: there are children who live in our 49-square-mile city that borders the Pacific Ocean but who have never seen it. I continue to hear this fact. Teachers tell me that some high school students have never put their hands in soil and have never grown a plant. It's very disturbing how narrow the worlds of many children are, and that the adults in their lives have not taken them out to see the wider world.

Before I get too self-righteous about this, my own upbringing had some of the same borders. Just a long bike ride away from my boyhood home on Chicago's South Side lies the historic district of George Pullman's railroad sleeping-car factory and model town built for his workers in the 1880s. In the 1960s, although I rode my bike to a Little League ball field near it, I had no idea it was there. Now, the Pullman District one of my favorite places to visit. Residents are still living in the apartments Pullman built. It's living history that connects with a key period of industrial growth in our past.

The best place to put kids in touch with nature is right where they already are: their own schools. And the best project I know for doing so is a school garden.

![globe icon] **School Gardens: Bringing Students to Their Senses**

Berkeley, California

In 1993, California state superintendent Delaine Eastin announced a "Garden in Every School Initiative" that has gained momentum through legislation and state funding. The California Department of Education provides a free packet of garden start-up information and mini-grants for gardening and nutrition projects and has connected the project to state standards in a publication called "A Child's Garden of Standards."

In 1995, about 1,000 of the state's 8,000 public schools had gardens. By 2003, the school garden movement had grown to 3,000 of the 9,100 schools, mostly in elementary schools. The school across my street, Miraloma Elementary School, has one, demonstrating that when the Time/Place Edge comes to your door, it's really moving to the center. The children are growing kale and lettuce, aided by a water recycling project that channels rain from the small greenhouse's gutters into water tanks. There's even a chicken coop where the students are helping the chickens "grow" their eggs. Their garden, open to anyone walking down the block in front of the school, makes a counterintuitive point: keeping gardens unlocked results in less vandalism and a greater sense of community ownership.

The best school gardens go beyond the growing and harvesting to the cooking and eating. In 2004, Edutopia published its first film and article on school gardens, on one of the earliest and best-known projects, chef Alice Waters's Edible Schoolyard, founded ten years earlier at the Martin Luther King, Jr. Middle School in Berkeley.[17] Waters has created what she calls a "complete seed-to-table experience." The curriculum addresses multiple subject areas, including the science of composting and the water cycle, the mathematics of recipes, and the cultural significance of foods. In using their hands, bodies, and minds, students exercise all of their senses and intelligences. They are also practicing a healthier lifestyle.

As Fritjof Capra, founding director of the Center for Ecoliteracy, says in the documentary, "The kid who is brilliant in math or science or language will not necessarily be brilliant in gardening. Somebody who is not very articulate but is very good with his or her hands will be very happy in the garden and will gain in prestige in the class community."

The film has a special place in my "Best of Edutopia" collection, for showing what engagement really looks like on students' faces, the look of alertness, openness, and vitality as they go about their work in the kitchen and the one-acre garden of fruits, vegetables, flowers, and herbs. When his teacher asks why compost needs to be turned over, Hector explains, so "the FBI, the fungus, bacteria, and insects can breathe." He adds, "We learn the cycle of compost, first it becomes leaves, then it becomes dry, then it becomes kind of soil, then it becomes soil. Then you grow something and then you start all over." He conveys his confidence and interest in this lowly but critical topic of soil quality. When the students make pies from a large pumpkin they've grown, you can almost smell the sweet aroma as they come out of the oven.

Alice Waters makes the clear and simple case: "The kids have been captivated by this experience. You see them looking and smelling and tasting. They don't think that this is school, yet we know what they're learning. . . . They all know what it is to set a table and ask people to come and to sit down and eat together. And talk at the table. They're learning these values of concentration and generosity." She adds, "This is a delicious revolution. . . . This isn't hard to do. If they grow it, they cook it, they want to eat it. There's a whole range of foods that kids love."

Chef-teacher Alice Cook adds, "It's almost a sign of the times that we have a program like this to teach things that are so basic that people used to learn at home from their own families. . . . It's a very dangerous thing to be that cut off from where your food comes from, knowing where it's grown. . . . They get to see that whole cycle, not just see it but make it happen."

When the Edutopia.org site enabled users to start posting comments in 2007, Marcelle Coakley posted this one, four years after our story first published, titled, "Our little garden in outback Australia." It's a perfect example of how Web 2.0 is enabling innovative educators around the world to share their stories:

I am a dedicated follower of Alice Waters.... We have only started our school garden 9 months ago and we put in 20 raised bed tanks.... I am so fiercely proud of this garden and what an impact it has had on our little community, we live 1,500kms from the nearest city.... Our cooking program ... has got the whole town talking.... We have seen the crime rate drop as most of our community especially indigenous were almost suffering from malnutrition.... Children would often break into homes to steal food and loose change.... We are going to ... make one for the general community ... for the elders ... to come and watch there [sic] grandchildren and share their stories with us all.... Thank you for letting us get a glimpse of the wonderful things you are all doing over there it has inspired many and will continue to do so.

Another inspiring example of a school garden is the Verde Garden in Richmond, California, where many languages are spoken and immigrant parents from Asia are able to contribute their farming expertise. The project's award-winning film was produced by Deborah Craig as a master's project at San Francisco State University.[18]

In 2009, the Center for Ecoliteracy in Berkeley published a marvelous book, *Smart by Nature,* a guidebook to its subtitle: *Schooling for Sustainability*.[19] It is an excellent handbook to greening our schools, describing model programs for school gardens and salad bars, sustainable school buildings, and environmental curricula and programs. The Head-Royce School in Oakland, for instance, has a comprehensive fourfold focus on (1) creating a healthy environment, (2) using resources in a sustainable way, (3) developing an educational program, and (4) pursuing a nutritional health program. Its goal is to produce "green graduates."

By working in the garden, nurturing flowers, plants, fruits, and vegetables, children are learning a metaphor for their own development. Each child has the seed of their own growth in their DNA. At birth, they are learning organisms. Cultivating those seeds into a blooming garden requires, as in Sir Ken Robinson's description of a flowering Death Valley, the right conditions and constant attention.

To all those in the nation's capital and state houses wringing their hands over child development gone wrong—obesity, poor eating habits, disconnect with nature, and declining interest in science—look no further. Your answer is right there, in Hector's compost and Rodney Taylor's salad bar.

The Story of the Salad Bar Man, from *Smart by Nature*

This story began with a conversation in 1997 between Santa Monica-Malibu district food service director Rodney Taylor and a parent named Bob Gottlieb, who happened to be an environmental policy professor at Occidental College. Gottlieb noticed his daughter wouldn't eat from her school's salad bar of canned fruit and wilting lettuce. He asked Taylor to create salad bars from fresh produce at local farmers' markets.

"That was the furthest thing from my mind," Taylor now says. "I thought he was just another affluent parent with a little too much time on his hands." . . . Taylor finally gave in and agreed to a two-week trial during a summer child-care class. "I just knew that four-year-olds were not going to eat this food," he recalls. "When I walked in the first day and saw the youngsters grabbing food off the salad bar, I was changed forever. I didn't even need to go back the next day."

The salad bar became a catalyst for place-based learning, as students created school gardens to grow their own food and went on field trips to farms and farmers' markets. Chefs came into classrooms to discuss healthy cooking. Five years later, Taylor moved to the Riverside, California, school district, a less affluent community than Santa Monica-Malibu. His experience there attests to his skills as an educational entrepreneur, transporting an innovation to a larger and more skeptical community:

> When I said I was going to put salad bars in all the elementary schools, people who knew the challenges laughed and said, "This isn't Santa Monica-Malibu." But I knew the salad bar creates a kind of excitement, that once you get it going, it's a vehicle that drives itself. The custodians were talking to each other saying it's not the mess that they think it is. One principal started talking about it, and then it was two, and then three, and now I've got principals jockeying to get up the list for salad bars.

To earn extra revenue, Taylor began providing food services and salad bars to twenty other organizations, such as Meals on Wheels, private schools, and local companies.

> If you ask me, does the salad bar pay for itself? I don't know that it does in and of itself, but that wasn't my intention. My intention was to get your kid at five, and teach her to be a lifelong healthy eater.... I tell my employees we serve more than food. We serve love. I like to think of the salad bars as one of my greatest expressions of love to the kids. There's nothing like walking into a store in your community and having someone say, "I know you. You're the salad bar man."

PLACE-BASED LEARNING IN COMMUNITIES

The Time/Place Edge relies on partnerships between schools and a wide array of community-based partners who can provide the real-world context for student learning. These include science centers and art and history museums; zoos and aquaria; local, state, and national parks;

universities; businesses; medical centers; and many more. Many of these
partners have professionals and provide the tools of modern science or
historical research, such as temperature probes connected to laptops,
global positioning and geographic information systems to track species,
digital cameras and microscopes, and statistical software to analyze data.

A wealth of state and federal agencies, scientific groups, and nonprofit
organizations offer lessons plans, professional development, and Web-
based projects to support place-based learning. The Web sites of two
leading organizations list many of these resources: the Environmental
Protection Agency and the North American Association for Environmental Education. The Place-Based Education Evaluation Collaborative
(PEEC) reports evaluation research on environmental education. One
of the best and most popular sites is the GLOBE (Global Learning
and Observations to Support the Environment) project, supported by
NASA, the National Science Foundation, and others, a global network
of teachers, students, and scientists studying the atmosphere, water
quality, soils, and local flora and fauna.[20]

Edutopia has made films about many inspiring stories of teachers
connecting their students to nature, fostering a sharpened understanding of the ecosystems where they live and making larger connections
to regional and global environmental issues. Some of my favorites
include:

> Journey North, an Annenberg/CPB project, where students track
> the 2,500-mile migration of monarch butterflies from Canada
> to Mexico and upload their observations to an online database.
> Frances Koontz's Maryland third-graders calculate the time from
> egg to caterpillar to chrysalis to butterfly, study the tulips and
> milkweed the larvae feed on, and exchange artwork with students
> in Mexico. The look on one girl's face, as the butterfly emerges
> from its chrysalis, is priceless.

> Louisiana's Wetland Watchers program, directed by teacher Barry
> Guillot, a former bouncer and Army sergeant, whose students
> engage in service learning in the nearby LaBranche Wetlands,

planting trees to prevent erosion and monitoring fecal coliform counts, a threat to the local seafood economy. They could have taught FEMA a thing or two: before Hurricane Katrina, they unfurled a banner from a balcony in downtown New Orleans to illustrate the height of flooding if the levees were to break.

School of Environmental Studies (SES), also known as the "Zoo School," in Apple Valley, Minnesota, where high school students study invasive and native species in a park, monitor oxygen levels in a pond, and work with zookeepers and scientists at the adjacent Minnesota Zoo. The school building itself, designed by Bruce Jilk, is an object of study for its renewable building materials and exposed steel beams and ductwork. The "classrooms" are large, flexible meeting spaces that can be reconfigured for seminars, presentations, and lectures.[21]

THE SCHOOL AS A PLACE OF LEARNING: LOCATION AND DESIGN

A growing number of communities like Apple Valley, faced with the opportunity to build new schools, have located them in or near zoos, museums, medical centers, shopping malls, and even the Louisiana Superdome. Sometimes, costs are shared between these organizations and school districts. In Manhattan, the Museum School enables high school students to take advantage of the city's world-class museums as their classrooms.

In Dearborn, Michigan, the Henry Ford Academy is located within the twelve-acre Henry Ford Museum. Students can walk to Greenfield Village, Ford's collection of eighty-two historic buildings, from Thomas Edison's laboratory to the Wright brothers' bicycle shop. Students use the museum's collections and the village's buildings as their instructional materials, studying, for instance, agricultural methods on a working farm or the engineering in early automobiles. The academy employs 90-minute block periods to enable students to delve deeper into their projects.[22]

As places where students spend most of their learning time, schools themselves could use a makeover. The classrooms most of us attended were, in the architect's vocabulary, "double-loaded" on either side of a main hallway, identical in size and layout. The blueprint for those schools resembled the assembly line, with a main conveyor belt and workers doing repetitive tasks on either side. Architect Trung Le calls this the "cells and bells" model. From the design of the space to the roles of the individuals working within it, the factory metaphor exerted a strong influence on twentieth-century schools. And still does.

Architect Steven Bingler designed the Henry Ford Academy and has been a leader in helping communities think more creatively about the kinds of school buildings they can build. An article about the Ford Academy and one by Bingler can be found on the Edutopia site, along with other commentary by leading school architects.[23] Leading school designers such as Bingler, Bruce Jilk, Anne Taylor, Prakash Nair, and Randy Fielding are part of a movement to redesign school buildings that include flexible meeting rooms, comfortable furniture, wireless broadband, and natural light. In Anne Taylor's phrase, these are "buildings that teach," as students study the design, construction, and energy use of the places where they learn.

Buildings such as the Zoo School also create a new, modern identity for students. Instead of students storing their belongings in a locker and occupying a different desk in each classroom, the student workstation, resembling an office cubicle, becomes the student's home base. Equipped with computers and Internet access, the workstation is the place where students work on their projects when not meeting with a group. Like employees, they personalize their cubicles with photos and favorite items.

With the United States spending between $15 billion and $20 billion each year, school construction and renovation are important opportunities to redesign not only the bricks and mortar of school buildings, but the kind of learning happening within them. As Winston Churchill once said, "First people build buildings. Then buildings build people."

THE NATIONAL PARKS: LEARNING ABOUT "AMERICA'S BEST IDEA"

Through these partnerships between schools and other places of learning, students are connecting in deep and meaningful ways with the rich histories and environments of their communities. School life does become close to real life.

To the many places where students can learn, I would add the national parks. An Education Nation requires a citizenry that understands its history and its values. As 391 of the most significant places in our nation, from Pearl Harbor and Volcanoes National Park in Hawaii to Acadia National Park in Maine, the national parks have a unique role to play in helping students understand their national identity and what it means to be an American. Each year, many students and teachers benefit from visits to national park sites, both in person and online, and as the Internet continues to evolve, richer multimedia online visits will be possible, as well.

Filmmaker Ken Burns adopted novelist Wallace Stegner's phrase as the subtitle of his 2009 series, *The National Parks: America's Best Idea*. The history of the national parks is a lens into the history of America, as Burns's series demonstrates well. Created by Congress, beginning with Yellowstone and Yosemite, the national parks are a truly American institution, preserving our most treasured lands and locations for the enjoyment, learning, and inspiration of all Americans, in contrast to the royal grounds and palaces of monarchs and kings.

Residing in San Francisco, I'm fortunate to live in a national park. The Golden Gate National Parks encompass such landmarks as Muir Woods, Alcatraz Island, and the Presidio, a former Army base, which includes the oldest building in San Francisco, an adobe structure built by Spanish explorers in 1776. I have served as a trustee of the Golden Gate National Parks Conservancy, a leader among park partners that creates civic engagement, develops restoration, renovation, and educational projects, and raises funds to accomplish them.

Educating the next generation to become stewards of the taxpayer-supported property they own has become a central focus. For instance, the Crissy Field Center, an environmental education center on the Presidio, provides year-round programs for Bay Area youth, including an environmental youth leadership program. On a recent visit, I watched young students in its computer lab using Google Earth to compute the distances that Chilean grapes and blueberries have to travel to arrive at their kitchen tables.

The Golden Gate National Parks have also worked with schools of education and school districts on teacher development using park experiences and resources; developed curricula to tell its stories, for instance, of the African American Buffalo Soldiers who served as park rangers before the National Park Service was established; and engaged middle and high school students in native plant nurseries and habitat restoration.

Place-Based Learning in National Parks

During 2008–2009, I was honored to serve on the National Parks Second Century Commission with some distinguished Americans, including retired Supreme Court Justice Sandra Day O'Connor, former NSF director Rita Colwell, and president of the National Geographic Society John Fahey. Organized by the National Parks Conservation Association (NPCA), the commission studied the history and progress of the first century of the national parks and developed recommendations for its next century beginning in 2016. Princeton historian, Civil War expert, and commission member James McPherson gave this compelling rationale for place-based learning in the national parks: "You can read millions of words about the Civil War. Only standing on the battlefields will you really begin to understand it."

During our meetings at the national parks at Gettysburg, Yellowstone, Great Smoky Mountains, Santa Monica Mountains, and Lowell in Massachusetts, we heard from students, teachers, scientists, historians, and education professors about how national parks are helping students engage with the most significant places in our nation. They reported that urban youth came alive in the parks and embraced new interests and career paths. Students often brought their experiences in the parks back to their own communities through activities to reduce pollution and adopt healthier lifestyles. The range of educational activities included:

- Service learning in the parks via groups such as the Student Conservation Association, which places 4,000 student volunteers and interns from high schools and universities at more than 250 parks, providing over 2 million hours of conservation service from tracking grizzlies through the Tetons to restoring desert ecosystems, building trails, and restoring habitats.

- NatureBridge, a residential program in which 40,000 students from the San Francisco and Seattle areas spend a week at Yosemite, the Marin Headlands, and Olympic National Park doing inquiry-based science and environmental studies, learning about native plants, geology, and the ecosystem. For many, it is their first experience spending a night in nature.

- The Tsongas Industrial History Center, where students and teachers who visit the Lowell National Historic Park, 30 miles from Boston, learn about the history of the mills along the Merrimack River that produced cotton cloth during the Industrial Revolution and how Lowell became the largest industrial center in the United States in the mid-1800s.

- Live videoconferencing from the Cabrillo National Monument near San Diego through a partnership between the National Park Service and the California Mediterranean Research Learning Center. Through this videoconference, students around the country view how the Yellow Submarine, a small navigable submarine with a submersible TV camera, helps scientists and students explore the tide pools.

- Education majors at Brooklyn College using the Gateway National Recreation Area, which includes the Statue of Liberty and Ellis Island, as their classroom. They learn to incorporate Gateway's resources into their teaching.

Edutopia.org has published a number of stories and films about education in the national parks, including a film and article about how the Ferryway School in Malden incorporates the nearby Saugus Iron Works National Historic Site into a project-based experience involving the history of the nation's oldest ironworks and the design of a working waterwheel.[24] That Web page also includes interesting commentary on the school's use of technology and its integration of science and history from education students at Arizona State University. Edutopia has also covered how high school students at the Crissy Field Center looked out its windows and saw the aftermath of the November 2008 oil spill just under the Golden Gate Bridge. An experiment with duck feathers in an oil and water mixture quickly showed them the effects on a bird's buoyancy and ability to fly.[25]

Our commission recommended elevating the educational mission for the national parks during coming decades: "National Parks have a distinct role in this [educational] mission, offering place-based learning that promotes a more sustainable environment, encourages the development of lifelong, health-enhancing habits of physical activity and appreciation of nature, and stimulates learners to consider and discuss democratic issues that are central to our civic life." We proposed "that the Park Service and its educational partners ensure access to current and leading-edge technology and media to facilitate park learning. As easily as we now make a phone call, every classroom in American should be able to conduct video conferences with park rangers, natural and cultural resources staff...."[26]

The commission's report, *Advancing the National Park Idea,* is available on the NPCA's Web site at http://www.npca.org/commission. Look for the national parks to play a larger role in how American students can understand the unique history, science, geography, and cultures of our nation.

In this chapter, we saw how issues of time and place intersect, giving students more time to learn in a variety of settings in more productive, authentic ways. In the next chapter, Edge 5: The Co-Teaching Edge, I discuss how teams of adults can work as coeducators to teach and support students in these experiences.

5

THE CO-TEACHING EDGE
TEACHERS, EXPERTS, AND PARENTS
AS COEDUCATORS

I get tears in my eyes when I see children laughing, enjoying their learning. No matter what cultural background, they can connect with the OMA [Opening Minds Through the Arts] program and improve their academics, which is a very exciting thing.

JOYCE DILLON, PRINCIPAL, CORBETT
ELEMENTARY SCHOOL, TUCSON

ALL OF THE edges described in previous chapters rely on the human factor: the capabilities of educators to think differently about their roles (Edge 1); to redesign and implement curricula and assessments (Edge 2); to implement technology (Edge 3); and change how time and place can improve learning (Edge 4). Human capital is paramount in spreading innovation in organizations, whether in businesses or in schools.

At this point, the conversation usually turns to teachers. Yes, teachers, not curriculum or technology, are the most important factor in the educational process. Research supports what parents have long known: high-quality teachers are the keys to a student's success. Yet, for all the lip service we pay to the influence of teachers upon students and the nation's next workforce, the United States still does not pay teachers commensurate with their value, nor do we provide the working conditions, support staff, and professional development they need and deserve.

The students in the classrooms discussed in this book are fortunate to have teachers who represent the new Teaching Edge, who understand and embrace the teaching practices I describe. They come from all teaching backgrounds: some are veteran teachers with more than thirty years of experience, some have only taught for a few years. Some have come through conventional teacher certification routes, others via alternative routes, such as Teach for America. They share a passion for doing "whatever it takes," the motto of YES Prep and the Harlem Children's Zone, to provide a high-quality, twenty-first-century education for their students.

TEACHERS AS PRISONERS OF TIME

In the discussion about how to create more teachers like the ones profiled in this chapter, several points are typically made. One emerges quickly: the educational system simply does not allow teachers enough time to learn about and adopt the new teaching methods possible in the twenty-first century. School budgets are being cut on all fronts, and professional development is among the first to suffer. California, which educates one in eight American students, faces the worst budget crisis in its history. In my city, San Francisco Unified School District has announced $113 million in cutbacks, on top of reductions over the past decade, which will further reduce school staffs and increase class size.

A typical school district might set aside a few days a year for districtwide professional development, hardly enough to sustain real learning. Often the content of those days does not relate to improving classroom practice. There is the long summer vacation, which could offer focused time for teacher development, but school budgets and union contracts do not include, say, an extra month of learning for all teachers. Many enterprising teachers take advantage of summer institutes and conferences, often paying out of their own pockets for additional professional training. The "tyranny of time" that has ruled over schedules for schools and students has constrained learning time for teachers as well.

The discussion also focuses on teacher preparation and the role of schools of education in preparing teachers to teach in new ways. Surely, this focus is a wise and rational one: ensure that new teachers-in-training, eager, younger, and tech savvy, receive instruction in twenty-first-century curricula, teaching, and assessment. This early investment would save costs in retraining further down the line. But the hard reality is that, schools of education, like school districts, have their own barriers to creating the twenty-first-century teaching workforce the nation needs.

The status of teacher education in universities, like the status of teachers in American society, reflects the historical underinvestment in schools and teachers. Of the nation's 1,200 schools of education, only about two-thirds are accredited. About 400 are not. This statistic often comes as a shock to many outside the world of teacher education. Students seeking to enter the professions of medicine, law, architecture, or business would be wary of attending an unaccredited university program. University presidents and boards of trustees would be embarrassed to have such a program in those professions on campus. Yet this situation is tolerated for teacher education.

At the same time, education students typically pay the same tuition as engineering and business majors, yet those programs enjoy greater resources of modern buildings, labs, technology, and staff. In essence, education students subsidize those better-resourced programs. Colleges of education with large enrollments have been called the "cash cow" of their universities. Courses in these programs often emphasize educational theory at the expense of practice.

Consider this tale: A first-year teacher has come up with a successful method for improving her third-graders' reading, having them write and act out their own stories. She rushes back excitedly to her professor, a scholar and senior faculty member, to tell him. The professor leans back in his chair, takes a puff on his pipe, gazes at the ceiling, and says, "Well, now. That might work well in practice. But would it work well in theory?" One superintendent told me, "New teachers graduate having read a lot of theory, but they have never been taught how to teach a third-grader to read."

It's abundantly clear: you can't have a world-class education system without a world-class teacher education system. The barriers in the United States go back to the first step in the teacher pipeline: recruitment. Top-performing nations recruit teachers from the ranks of their best students. In Singapore, teachers come from the top 20 percent of high school graduates and in South Korea, the top 5 percent of college graduates.[1] In contrast, the New Commission on the Skills of the American Workforce reported that most education students in the United States fall in the bottom third of college ranks.[2]

To be sure, there is much good work going on in many of the 1,200 schools of education. In 2008, the Lucas Foundation, together with Dean Patricia Wasley at the University of Washington, hosted a meeting of leading deans of education and faculty from Michigan State, New York University, Stanford, and other universities. Teach for America was also represented, which has filled a real need, especially in hard-to-staff inner-city schools. The group came together to brainstorm a new model for a twenty-first-century college of education, building on digital curricula, tools, and students.

Edutopia has featured many exemplary schools of education and alternate certification routes, including the Curry School of Education at the University of Virginia, a leader in adopting technology; University of Texas's UTeach for preparing science and math teachers; Bank Street College of Education's graduate program, with a K–8 school in the same building; the Boston Teacher Residency, a thirteen-month program leading to a master's degree; and the New Teacher Center in Santa Cruz, California, successfully mentoring new teachers during the critical first years.[3]

Until some of these systemic issues in the teacher development pipeline are addressed, progress to scale these programs will continue to be slow. In this chapter, I discuss a different way forward that involves a new role for all teachers, in service or in training, that they could begin to implement today. This new Co-Teaching Edge is already being enacted in the schools discussed in this book. It places teachers in a much more collaborative role, involving partnerships with other "coeducators"—after-school educators, parents, and many types of professionals—to bring the innovative learning of the other edges to reality for their students.

Just as the world of work has shifted to teams, teachers can also organize their own "teaching teams" in which each member contributes his or her own expertise. Teachers who work in collaboration with others break down the isolation of teachers laboring alone in their classroom, an outdated model still taught in many schools of education today. As Lee Shulman, former president of the Carnegie Foundation for the Advancement of Teaching, says, "Teaching has been an activity done behind closed doors, between moderately consenting individuals."

RETHINKING THE 3 RS: READING, WRITING, AND ROSSINI

As the Edge 1 shift from either/or to both-and thinking suggests, a key to educational innovation is making connections between seemingly unrelated concepts. Either/or ways of thinking have prevented progress by viewing phonics instruction as divorced from using children's literature or the core curriculum as separate from the arts.

Breaking through these barriers involves stretching our own imaginations to see how children can learn in ways that our traditional thinking would have missed or dismissed. One of my pet peeves is hearing how educators think that some subjects—physics, Mandarin, Shakespeare—are too difficult for some students or too advanced for younger students. The real problem is not the subject, but the way it's taught. As Harvard psychologist Jerome Bruner said, "Any subject can be taught effectively in some intellectually honest form to any child at any stage of development."

Teaching reading to primary grade students through opera might strain the credulity of most. Forming a teaching partnership with opera singers would seem unlikely to succeed. For one, isn't opera "really hard"? And isn't it sung in one of those "foreign" languages? How could it possibly help students learn to read and write in English? Most educators, and probably even more policymakers, would dismiss the idea out of hand. In just 8 minutes and 44 seconds, I bet I can change those minds.

🌐 Opening Minds Through the Arts

Tucson, Arizona

This is another case in which it's difficult to describe an educational innovation in words. Watch the Edutopia film we produced on the Opening Minds through the Arts (OMA) program in Tucson, Arizona.[4] You'll see how opera singers and musicians from Tucson's opera, symphony, and the University of Arizona work closely with students and teachers to provide a rich linguistic habitat for K–8 students. The story reveals how the path to fluent reading and writing is not just a matter of staring at pages of text and working on phonics drills but needs to wind its way through kinesthetic, oral, and musical experiences that give meaning to the text on the pages. And make it fun and enjoyable so students *want* to have more of such experiences to fuel their language learning.

OMA musicians and teachers work together in twice-weekly sessions to provide students with experiences listening to expressive, illustrative language, using their bodies to act out feelings and concepts (such as the triangles formed by arms and legs), and writing their own operas over the course of a month. After witnessing the look on one performer's face and the gestures of her body language, first-graders learn to use words such as *thrilled* and *exuberant* to describe her character's feelings, when most reading lessons would place that vocabulary beyond their reach. Second-graders hear a performer sing the words *high* and *low* in different octaves, hear a clarinet player play high and low notes, and observe a line of two adults and two children standing in alternating positions in, as one student perceptively notes, a "high and low pattern." They are using their bodies, as well as their minds, to learn to read and think.

Joan Ashcraft, director of OMA, makes the point that arts educators have been making for many years: the arts—and music and opera in particular—are vital experiences for exercising students' brains during a critical stage of their development. OMA is based on findings in neuroscience that the *corpus collosum*, which connects the left and right hemispheres of the brain, develops between the ages of four and twelve. By using music, as a right brain activity, to support verbal learning, centered in the left brain, the OMA program demonstrates how children benefit from a curriculum that works their entire brains.

At Corbett Elementary School, a Title 1 school, 20 percent of the students are English language learners. OMA has an interesting slant on how to teach them, one that most educators would find baffling. Teach them in a third language, so that both native English speakers and ELL students are playing on a level linguistic field. In the film, you can see Kimberly Chaffin, teaching artist, singing in German and describing why it works.

OMA, now in its tenth year of operation, started in three elementary schools and has grown in impressive scale to 42 schools and 19,000 students in Tucson. It also offers professional development, a program of school visits, and publications to help other educators adapt its work. Research conducted by WestEd demonstrated that all six OMA schools, with high proportions of ELL, low-income, and transient students, outperformed other schools on reading, writing, *and* mathematics. Latino students especially made impressive gains in writing. OMA teachers, not surprisingly, also surpassed other teachers in their lesson-planning abilities and use of a wider range of learning activities.

OMA has benefited from the philanthropy of local businessman Gene Jones, who supported the work ten years ago at the tender age of eighty-four, making the point that it's never too late to donate to public schools.

Cheyenne, a student seen in the film, says it best: "We've learned a lot of things about opera like subtext and how terms of opera are used. You get to use your imagination a lot. It's a really good way of learning because usually when you learn, you just read out of textbooks. When you act out stuff and talk about stuff, it really helps you learn better."

Granted, having opera singers in your local community might seem like a rarefied gift. There are more opera companies than you'd think, 135 in 43 states and the District of Columbia. At Edutopia, we know that educators often interpret these stories quite literally, as in "Well, that's great for Tucson to have an opera company but we don't have one, so we can't do that."

If Rossini isn't your cup of tea, you might try rap. Flocabulary is a small educational publishing company in New York City founded by Blake Harrison and Alex Rappaport that has achieved national media attention for its use of hip-hop to energize student interest in language arts, social studies, math, and science. On their Web site, you can see the clips from the *Today* show, *NBC News*, and MTV showing Harrison and other performers using the rhythm and lyrics of hip-hop to galvanize the enthusiasm of students.[5]

Flocabulary has research to back it up, including one study conducted in six states by Dr. Roger Farr, former president of the International Reading Association, demonstrating reading gains by middle schoolers. This is one curriculum that you have to hear in order to believe it. Check out the "Shakespeare Is Hip-Hop" materials on their Web site to hear the scene between Puck and the fairy from *Midsummer Night's Dream*. Edutopia has also covered students writing Shakespearean raps and producing movie trailers based on the Bard's plays.[6]

The larger point is that anyone can bring in community experts on any topic, to share their experiences and connect the world outside the classroom to the students within it. Every community has artists and writers, musicians and dancers, gardeners and chefs, and scientists and engineers who can contribute to the learning of its students.

Edutopia has profiled many such programs, such as Aviation High School near Seattle, where a partnership with Boeing strengthens the school's STEM (science, technology, math, and engineering) curriculum. In our documentary, the co-teaching team consists of teacher Scott McComb, subject matter expert Doug Gross, a structural engineer, and Eeva Reeder, a project-based learning coach. (Reeder's own geometry teaching, in which she worked with Seattle architects to design a six-week project for her tenth-graders to design a school of the future, is the subject of one of Edutopia's perennially most-watched videos.)[7]

The Aviation High project organizes ninth-graders in teams of three in an ambitious six-month project competition to design and test a lightweight wing structure, simulating the design of an airplane wing. Gross, along with other aeronautical engineers, is seen sharing the teaching duties, showing slides of airplanes with various structural designs, and bringing his real-life experience into the classroom. The student teams present their work to their parents, peers, and a panel of engineers. The link to the Aviation High film includes resources, including sample student work, for teachers, including sample student work, who might want to try out this project.

This concept of co-teaching teams is evident in numerous other Edutopia stories, such as the Build SF architecture program or the MetWest project-based high schools, discussed in Chapter Four, where professionals in the workplace share the teaching with instructors in the classroom. The Acme Animation program, based in Los Angeles and founded by animation teacher Dave Master, uses videoconferencing and an online platform to bring professional animators to students as distant as Birmingham, Alabama.[8]

My family experienced the value of co-teaching through the California Poets in the Schools (CPITS), which sends more than 100 poets into the state's schools each year, the largest authors-in-schools program in the country. My daughter benefited from working with poet Grace

Grafton during her grade school years. Poets, like opera singers, can help teachers communicate how literacy is about using all of one's senses. They are important but undervalued allies in the war on illiteracy and are especially needed in the primary grades, to help all students leap over that first critical hurdle they'll face at the tender age of nine: reading at the fourth-grade level.

It would be marvelous if all fourth-graders could use all of their senses to write a poem like Elizabeth Klimov, a fourth-grader in Santa Barbara County, California, who worked with her teacher, Mrs. Talley and poet-teacher Lois Klein. Elizabeth's poem was published in a California Poets in the Schools statewide anthology called *What the World Hears.*[9]

Different and the Same
I am the one with the dirty blonde hair
Like the Hawaiian sandy shore.
My eyes are the color of ripples
In the pond, but sometimes
Green like the grass on the front lawn.
My skin is the color of butterscotch.
I'm good at playing the violin.
My friend has deep dark hair
Like a crow flying through the night sky.
Her eyes are the color of coffee.
Her skin is the color of milk chocolate.
She has parents from Jordan
While my parents are from Russia.
She's good at dancing.
We are the ones who have parents
From far-away places.
We both like rice with chicken.
Together we love our families.

In case you think this is a rare fourth-grader who plays the violin, think again. With the help of some violinists, Corbett Elementary is doing that, too.

PARENTS AS PARTNERS: THE HOME-SCHOOL CONNECTION

If there's one tenet of education reform, it's that parents are the vital third leg of the three-legged stool of teachers, parents, and students. When all three are stable, aligned, and working together, that stool becomes a driver's seat in a race car for learning that can accelerate a student to success in school and beyond.

Whenever the topic of involving parents comes up at conferences, heads nod. Most involved in education—from the school house to the state house—knows that what happens outside of the classroom, especially in the home, can do more to determine a student's success than anything else, in many cases, more than what schools themselves can contribute.

Yet, parental involvement remains one of the most nettlesome problems in schooling. Historically, it has not been part of the training of principals and teachers. In the old days, parents were supposed to deposit their children with their teachers at the schoolhouse door and "leave the learning to us." We should now acknowledge that parental involvement is probably the most important and least addressed factor in children's learning. Once, before giving a talk to parents, I asked a grade-school teacher for the one thing I should tell them. She said, "Tell them they do more to affect their children's learning before they set foot in kindergarten than we do after."

Endless barriers abound and fingers point blame in many directions: Parents are too busy. Parents are too lazy. Parents are too demanding. Schools are fortresses. Parents aren't welcome. Language is a barrier. Some parents don't speak English. Teachers don't understand other languages. Suspicion mounts. The gulf widens.

The Parent-Teacher Home Visit Project

Sacramento, California

In 2001, Edutopia profiled a new partnership in Sacramento, California, that brought fresh thinking to this problem. The teachers' union, school district, and an unusual partner—an interfaith community organizing group called Sacramento ACT (Area Congregations Together)—had worked together to reframe the issues.[10]

A basic principle is that parents and teachers should be partners, in the word that I like, *coeducators*, for students and that home visits should be part of an overall partnership and not happen only when a student is in trouble. Every student and every family, not just those whose kids are misbehaving or failing academically, is involved in the project. And the project gives equal status to parents and teachers and to communicating in the native languages of some families. Interpreters are provided and accompany teachers on their visits. Two visits are made each year, in the fall and spring. All this takes extra time of teachers, for which they are compensated.

Our film and article about the Sacramento program focused on the Susan B. Anthony School, an elementary school with 450 students, two-thirds from immigrant families from Southeast Asia, Laos, Thailand, and Vietnam and 100 percent low-income. Susan B. Anthony was one of nine Sacramento schools that started home visits in the fall of 1998; by 2001, when we covered it, the program had shown remarkable results in parent participation, fewer behavior problems, and improved test scores. In just a few months, the school went from few parents attending school functions to 600 parents coming to a potluck dinner to hear about the school's new improvement plan. The district had expanded the program to include every school in the district. The California Department of Education had taken notice and provided $15 million in grants to other districts to adopt the program.

When the Edutopia Web site opened a commenting function for users in 2008, a number of revealing comments were posted:

"I think that making parents feel comfortable enough with you to ask a question or for help is important. If they don't know and don't ask, then help at home will be unproductive."

"I think this is one of the hardest things for me to do. I find myself only contacting the parent when there is a problem. Not just because their child has done something good or correct."

"This is so important in helping students achieve success. Negative issues can be cleared up and positive ones reinforced. . . . Many parents are misinformed or believe that no news is good news. Many times as educators we need to take the first step."

"One thing I've found to be helpful is contacting them early if you start to observe issues. Many comments from parents are they want to know why they weren't contacted earlier. If they are communicated with early, many times the situation improves because they get involved."

The Parent-Teacher Home Visit Program (PTHVP) has expanded into other states, including Colorado, Massachusetts, Montana, and Ohio.

YES Prep Public Schools: Commitment to College Completion

Edutopia's 2009 Schools That Work case study of Houston's YES Prep North Central's approach to fostering the home-school connection illustrates a related approach. The YES Prep cluster of schools set the goal of having 100 percent of their students, the vast majority from low-income backgrounds, gain admission to four-year colleges. YES Prep North Central believes this is a seven-year process and must begin in the sixth grade. Once students are admitted at the end of fifth grade, the teachers make home visits and meet with each student's family to explain the contract that students and parents sign that day. Posted a copy of it, which includes student commitments to arrive on time and stay all day; attend on appropriate Saturdays and for the mandatory summer program. Parents/guardians agree to make sure their child attends, provide a quiet place for him or her to study, and attend all meetings and student exhibitions.[11]

LINKING HOME AND SCHOOL VIA THE INTERNET

Making communication pervasive is what technology is meant to do. In recent years, technology platforms that bring parents virtually through the school's doors have increased in popularity. These systems extend the typical school Web site, listing basic information such as courses, staff, and school activities and personalize the information for each family. Parents can see accounts of what happened in their child's class that day and view homework assignments. As any parent knows, children can be "the weakest link" in teacher-parent communication. The most common answer to parents' daily question, "What did you do in school today?," is "Nuthin.'"

These home-school Intranets create channels of communication where there were none and expand the flow of information that had only been a trickle, allowing parents to receive detailed information about their child's progress. Some classrooms even have Web cameras for parents to literally "see" what's going on.

Mark Gross of San Jose, a former high school teacher and Edutopia author, has founded a company called School Loop to provide these types of systems.[12] School Loop Standard is a simple Web platform enabling administrators and teachers to publish to the community information about the school, including school news, calendar, and special events, a one-to-many solution. Its system is in use in more than 2,000 schools in 120 districts and 25 states. Pearson's PowerSchool, a similar platform, is popular in the United States as well as abroad; it is used for more than 8 million students in 49 states and more than 50 countries.

School Loop Plus enables the interactivity of a many-to-many model for a district or a school, enabling "education teams" to form around each student. Its goal is to "make all schools feel like small schools." Parents, teachers, counselors, and students share the same information about the student's courses, schedule, attendance, assignments and homework, grades, and other course content. Parents can e-mail school administrators and teachers individually or as a group. Students can post their assignments and upload files in a digital locker. Groups can be formed among a district, school, or student team to conduct and discuss their work. A course can have its own Web site. A principal can have a bird's-eye view of the entire school, from curriculum and assessment data by classroom to individual student folders.

The system includes a multilingual voicemail system named with an obvious double entendre, TeleParent, which solves the barrier of teachers having to dial 30 or 150 different phone numbers to leave messages for parents. TeleParent enables more than 700 different voice messages to be sent in 23 languages to students' homes. Messages informing parents of a test tomorrow or if a student's grades are rising or falling are sent out daily at 5 p.m. so that time at home can be used efficiently for conversation or focusing on homework. Messages can address problems, such as lack of attendance or declining grades, and offer positive reinforcement as well. In one survey conducted in an Anaheim, California, high school and middle school, teachers and parents overwhelmingly reported that the system aided communication and improved student behavior and academic performance. Teachers also appreciated being able to communicate in parents' multiple languages.

Student results were telling. While most of the high school students reported mostly positive experiences with TeleParent, "many students indicated that they did not like the system because they would be held accountable now that parents are aware of what is going on at school."

The Power of Praise from Teachers and Parents

Adults wield enormous power in students' learning. I've always been impressed by how a single remark from one teacher can make or break a student's spirit. Everyone has a story about that one favorite teacher who took an interest in them, told them they were smart, or encouraged them to pursue a subject or a sport. As parents, teachers, and others work as co-educators for children, they can jointly wield the power of praise.

Delaine Eastin, a former California state superintendent of public instruction, often tells the story of being a shy girl until a drama teacher told her she ought to try out for a play. Eastin learned that she loved performing onstage. She became a riveting speaker, a popular state legislator, and the highest elected education official in the nation—all sparked by one comment from a compassionate teacher.

Research confirms the power of positive affirmation for children. A 1995 study by University of Kansas researchers Betty Hart and Todd Risley studied forty-two families in Kansas City, documenting the quantity and quality of parent-children communication from birth until the age of three.[13] They discovered that higher-income parents spoke about 500,000 encouragements and 80,000 discouragements to their infants and toddlers. Parents with lower incomes encouraged and praised their children only 75,000 times, but spoke discouraging words much more frequently, about 200,000 times. That constant stream of half a million encouragements by the "positive parents" included not only more words but more complex words and sentences, leading their children to describe feelings, causality, and abstractions, connecting language to thinking.

Can affection "cause" intelligence? Can kind words from a teacher's or a parent's heart stimulate a child's brain? By age three, the preschoolers with greater verbal stimulation had average vocabularies of 1,100 words and IQs of 117. Children who experienced greater verbal punishment had vocabularies of 525 words and IQs of 79.

The key factor is not so much parents' social class or economic background but their understanding of how to talk to children. Consider the childhood of one of our nation's most distinguished educators, Dr. James Comer, Falk Professor of Child Psychiatry and director at the Yale Child Study Center, and founder of the Comer School Development Project. In his book, *Maggie's American Dream*, Comer described the parenting style of his mother, who cleaned houses for a living near Gary, Indiana.[14]

During their bus rides together, Maggie would point out and explain the ads on the ceiling of the bus and places along the route to young Jim. She was continually taking her children to places of interest, asking them questions, answering theirs, and setting a positive climate for learning. Without a formal education, Maggie raised five children who went on to earn thirteen college and advanced degrees among them. In the 1930s, she naturally understood what educational research took decades to prove.

The 2005 National Teacher of the Year, Jason Kamras, carried that supportive spirit into his middle school math classroom in Washington, D.C. He used a pervasive tool, the cell phone, to call parents and praise their children for jobs well done, in front of the entire class. In contrast to the vast majority of students, those students *wanted* Mr. Kamras to call their parents.

What students really crave is a pat on the back for learning a difficult concept or a word of encouragement to try something new. Teachers could use some affection, too. They are underappreciated, underpaid, and under a lot of undeserved pressure. Back in 1992, George Lucas stood on the world's stage at the Oscars and received the Irving G. Thalberg Memorial Award for lifetime achievement. It sits in a glass case near our offices.

When I point out the award to visiting educators, they still recall that moment, more than 18 years ago, when he thanked his teachers (which, they note, today's Oscar winners rarely do). Lucas said, "All of us who make motion pictures are teachers, teachers with very loud voices. But we will never match the power of the teacher who is able to whisper in a student's ear."

A little praise can go a long way. Let's resolve to compliment teachers more and express our appreciation for the important national service they're providing. It's a gift that will keep on giving as they pass on that warmth to their students. And it won't require a federal appropriation or a board of education vote. Praise should be one of our nation's abundant renewable resources for fueling the success of our students and teachers.

GROUP EXERCISE: WRITE THE TWENTY-FIRST-CENTURY TEACHER'S JOB DESCRIPTION

The twenty-first-century teacher should be a manager of learning for students rather than their sole instructor. The knowledge that students need to master is now on the Internet rather than contained inside the teacher's head and between the covers of a single textbook. A teacher's knowledge of subject matter is still very important, but it's more important that she or he understands that students need to arrive at their own understanding. Today's teacher also values working with other coeducators to bring in expertise from the outside world and strengthen the parent-teacher-student bond.

At your next school staff or parents' meeting, consider brainstorming and writing the Twenty-First-Century Teacher's Job Description. This exercise can be done in conjunction with the one at the end of Edge Six: writing the Twenty-First-Century Student's Job Description. Following are some skills and qualifications to discuss and help you get started.

Required Skills

Knowledge of how rigorous project-based learning can lead to deeper understanding that lasts.

Ability to organize the classroom for collaborative group work, rather than individual work.

Knowledge of how technologies can support learning; this doesn't mean a teacher needs to know everything about how to implement such technology, as discussed in Edge Six.

Ability to work in co-teaching teams with other experts, parents, and teachers, in person, and online.

Record as a self-starter who seeks out new resources to enliven the classroom, including online materials, local places of learning (museums, companies, theaters, universities), others in the community.

Initiative in seeking out opportunities for professional development, given more flexibility of choice and resources of time and money from states and districts.

Ability to enlist others, including students themselves, in creating technology-based learning experiences for students.

An understanding that connecting with students' social-emotional issues is essential to their learning of academic content.

Qualifications

BA or BS degree in a subject matter discipline; experience and practice in the observation and teaching of children, including acting as a teaching intern to an experienced teacher.

For advancement: EdM or other master's degree that allows for a fifth year of graduate study and practice teaching.

Passion for teaching children or adolescents and for working with them in caring, supportive relationships.

A DIGITAL SUPERINTENDENT'S VIEW OF TWENTY-FIRST-CENTURY TEACHERS AND CLASSROOMS

The best superintendents, as the chief executive officers of school districts, are the true leaders of our school systems, yet few of them are well known beyond their communities. Many of them share a forward-looking vision for their districts but are hampered by the politics of school boards, union regulations, trivial lawsuits, and bureaucracy. In order for innovations such as the Co-Teaching Edge to spread to the center of school systems, superintendents who understand the value of teaching partnerships and closer connections to families are critical. Superintendent leadership is also needed to persuade school boards to allocate the resources for these practices.

Cameron McCune was superintendent of the Fullerton School District, a district of 14,000 students in Southern California, and, like Governor Angus King of Maine, staked his political capital and educational reputation on providing each student and teacher with a laptop, seeking to bring the benefits of digital learning to all students in his district. For his efforts, he was rewarded with public controversy and a lawsuit from the American Civil Liberties Union. In my interview with him, he articulated a radical new vision for schools.

Milton Chen: What is your vision for school districts in the twenty-first century?
Cameron McCune: Schools must change to match the needs of the digital learner and the needs of the world in which we now live. The purpose of school needs to be reinvented, not just modified. Specifically, we need to redefine the role of the teacher, the academic year and school day, and the content and delivery of curriculum.

The ideal school of the twenty-first century will focus on small groups of learners and coaches. This model facilitates learning and creates the bond between teacher and student that keeps both engaged. Thus, the role of the teacher needs to follow the coach model more than the lecturer model.

_____

MC: What changes need to occur in terms of school schedules?

CM: The classic agrarian-based school year also does not support the needs of today's students or society. The typical school day of 8 a.m. to 2:30 p.m. does not address the facts that the majority of households have two working parents and that many students, particularly those in junior high school, do not perform their best at 8 o'clock in the morning. Three-month summers were too long for me, and they are too long for my thirteen-year-old daughter.

_____

MC: Why are we not adjusting academic calendars to accommodate the needs of students and families?

CM: Instead of forcing schools to account for students' whereabouts, much like jailers, they should be an open, year-round environment. Students should be free to schedule vacations just like employees of businesses. Students should be able to take advantage of family trips and other opportunities throughout the year, as long as they maintain a minimum number of days of active classroom attendance and participation.

_____

MC: What can we do to make learning more relevant?

CM: Research and information retrieval skills have replaced memorization. There are several areas in which all students should be proficient to be successful. Every child needs good communication and collaboration skills. Critical thinking, problem solving, and savvy decision making are also vital. Being comfortable with technology and its use are critical. Having a global perspective, particularly an understanding of the world's cultures, is becoming increasingly important, too.

These skills are best acquired through project-based curriculum, which is meaningful and motivating to students and teachers because the activities have a purpose and a result that can be shared with others. Similar to what occurs in the working world today, good academic projects are undertaken by a team of learners with a coach.

Communication skills develop while working with others. Students should be able to select projects that interest them and change working groups based on common interests, regardless of the classroom or the teacher. Projects should be categorized so students choose work that ensures they are being exposed to pertinent curriculum. Their work and schedule should be evaluated and modified regularly.

MC: How can we take better advantage of technology to help manage learning?

CM: Technology is a tool, and its use should be ubiquitous and transparent. We need to make the acquisition of knowledge, skills, and culture fun, engaging, and meaningful. This is best done using simulations, projects, and teams led by students and monitored by learning coaches. In traditional grade configurations, such as K–2, 3–5, 6–8, 9–11, and 12, students should systematically and incrementally be given more responsibility for leading projects. The groups should be fluid and change based on the project and student interests.

The idea is that students would move at a challenging pace with their coach, and parents would constantly monitor and counsel kids for success. Programs such as PowerSchool can facilitate this communication by sending automatic notifications to students and parents, alerting them of progress, attendance, and upcoming opportunities. Parents and students can access a student's progress 24/7 via the Internet and communicate with coaches via e-mail or videoconferencing. The concept of all eighth-graders or twelfth-graders graduating at the same time could become obsolete.

Some learning can also take place outside of traditional classrooms via the Internet. Computer-aided instruction, with appropriate monitoring, works well for attaining basic math skills. New software such as My

Access takes away the drudgery of writing for students and editing for coaches.

MC: What policies are needed to create twenty-first-century school districts at the federal, state, and local levels?

CM: We have developed a rigid system that promotes the status quo instead of a fluid one that adapts to the needs of students, parents, and staff. Employee organizations have become very powerful and are geared toward protecting jobs and structure instead of developing and implementing new standards. Evolutionary change will not work at this point: We need a major revolution in education.

MC: What is the proper balance of power between federal and state governments and districts?

CM: Clearly, there is huge disparity in funding across the United States. State and federal controls need to be withdrawn so communities have more control over funding. When students are meeting standards of achievement, state and federal oversight should be minimal. Outside review is appropriate only when students are not meeting these standards.

MC: How would you write the new job description for a superintendent?

CM: The role of the superintendent is unrealistic and needs to change. The expectation that someone can be the ultimate teacher, principal, business manager, finance expert, facilities expert, and personnel manager for a $100 million-plus-a-year organization is unrealistic. Leadership is critical to the success of an organization, yet, instead of leadership, some boards and superintendents believe the role is to simply be a good manager. In either case, unlike as in the case of most corporations, we don't give them sufficient training.

I believe education would be better served if it were restructured to divide personnel management and business administration, as is common in the medical industry. Hospital CEOs are usually not people who started out as nurses or doctors. They are trained administrators who run the facility. They do not supervise the professional staff.

Applying this model to school districts would require major changes in expectations from communities and from the education professionals, but in the long term it would be better for education. If this model was accepted, superintendents from diverse backgrounds could be successful leaders.

———————

The Co-Teaching Edge is about forming closer partnerships between the adults in children's lives: their teachers, parents, caregivers, and others in the community. The new roles of these adults in creating a modern learning environment must acknowledge a new role for today's students, as digital learners who are already learning in new ways. In the final edge, Edge 6: The Youth Edge, I take up how today's generation of students is different from any previous one.

6
THE YOUTH EDGE
DIGITAL LEARNERS CARRYING
CHANGE IN THEIR POCKETS

Your generation has music in your blood. We have technology in ours.

RURAL HIGH SCHOOL STUDENT TO SUSAN PATRICK,
INTERNATIONAL ASSOCIATION FOR K–12 ONLINE LEARNING

THE YOUTH EDGE represents the biggest edge of all, the 50 million students in schools who are "digital natives," who were "born digital." While the provenance of the term "digital natives" might be hard to trace, Marc Prensky, author of *Don't Bother Me, Mom, I'm Learning,* was one of the first to coin it. Today's students were born in this new land, are fluent in its new language, and are comfortable with its customs and behaviors. They are marching through our schools, carrying a transformational change in their pockets in the form of powerful multimedia handheld devices. Yet this generation, 95 percent of the stakeholders in education and the ones who stand the most to lose from a poor education, are often left out of the conversation about how to change it.

In contrast to the native born, there's the generation of "digital immigrants," those of us over forty. We grew up in another time and place, having learned other habits, customs, and language from the analogue world. You know you're a digital immigrant if you print out your e-mail in order to read it. You're really a Luddite of a digital immigrant if you have your assistant print out your e-mail so you can read it. Or as a friend of mine commented, "That's not a digital immigrant. That's a digital idiot." We remember a time, with some nostalgia, when we actually had to get up off of the sofa to go and change the channel. But we are gratified that we can watch more of what we want, when we want it, Tivoing from 900 channels rather than limited to broadcasts from nine. But we do speak digital with an accent. And kids can tell.

THE MARCH OF THE DIGITAL NATIVES

There have now been two generation of digital natives, who have only used PCs and MP3 players, whose fingers have never touched a typewriter or an audio tape recorder. Unless they're acting out history. A friend of mine told me his son came home one day from middle school and asked if they had a typewriter. He needed one to place on the set for his school play. His father said, "I think we still have one in the garage." Once they scrounged through some boxes and dusted it off, his son observed what must have seemed an ancient writing machine with some pride. "Gee, Dad, that's really cool," he said. "And it even comes with a built-in printer!"

Poet Gary Soto, who has been an active member of California Poets in the Schools, tells the story of showing off his IBM Selectric, a marvelous writing machine for its time, to his fifteen-year-old neighbor.

> A couple of weeks ago my neighbor Sam came to help me with a computer issue. He's fifteen, taller than me and polite enough to . . . help this old guy out. . . . He asked, "Hey, what's that?" . . . He flicked his chin at my IBM Selectric and once top-of-the-line machinery, the mainstay of every poet or writer.
>
> "You mean the typewriter?" I asked. Sam looked at it, a smile building up on his smirking face. "Oh, so that's what they look like." Immediately I felt like Fred Flintstone. . . . So I demonstrated the keyboard action, each letter exploding

black ink on white paper. Sam smirked some more and remarked, "It's loud."[1]

In a retro-twist on new media habits, some teens are experimenting with writing on a typewriter—when they can find one—professing to like a machine "that only does one thing at a time."

My daughter, Maggie, now twenty-three, was in the first generation of digital natives, born in the 1980s, who typed her school reports on a word processor and started using a cell phone in her middle school years in 1998. In 1994, at the age of eight, we bought her her first computer, a lime-colored iMac, primarily to use for writing and playing games, such as Oregon Trail. During her childhood, the Internet was rapidly growing and becoming the repository of the world's knowledge. In her elementary school, there was one computer in the back of the room, for students who had finished their other work to play games.

As parents, we would occasionally point her to the Internet for content related to her homework. For her fifth-grade state report, she was assigned Nebraska and did some Internet research on its cities and their sizes. During her middle school years, when it seems just about every American student reads *Catcher in the Rye*, I pointed out to her the growing number of Web sites devoted to interpretation of J. D. Salinger's novel. But her teachers, in some of the best schools in San Francisco during those years, rarely made Internet research part of their assignments. They were good teachers who viewed their role as teaching their students what they knew, conveying what was in their brains, rather than interpreting what was on the Web.

One day, her fourth-grade class was preparing to go on a field trip to San Francisco's Exploratorium. Her teacher reviewed the rules for the field trip, like staying with the group, and mentioned there would be a demonstration of a cow's eye dissection. She admonished the kids not to give the obligatory "*Eewwhh*" response. My wife, Ruth, happened to be volunteering in class that day and knew that the cow's eye exhibit was on the Exploratorium Web site. She had groups of students come to the computer monitor and look at photos and descriptions of the cow's eye. They also saw a photo with a teen "Explainer" at the exhibit, on the visit, and were excited to meet her in person.

Exploratorium staff say that students who have seen the online exhibit arrive with prior knowledge, quickly get over the squeamish factor, and ask better questions. The Web-based experience supports the in-person experience.

To this day, the Exploratorium Web site is one of the most popular science museum Web sites in the world, with more than 20 million visitors each year. Its Web visitation, if only for a few minutes per visit, exceeds by twentyfold the 500,000 visitors who are fortunate enough to come through its gates in San Francisco.

The second generation of digital native learners can be marked as being born around the turn of this century, when the growth of the Internet was clearly demonstrating its potential for learning. The multimedia Internet was becoming the world's digital library, containing not only print media of books, magazines, and newspapers but collections of photographs, music, and film. In 2000, our Edutopia Web site began presenting our documentaries. We compressed them for what was then high and low bandwidth. Today, only ten years later, as compression technologies and speed of processors on computers have improved, the last decade's high bandwidth is only a fraction of today's wireless broadband.

This second generation of digital students has only known powerful multimedia computers, capable of editing video and storing tens of thousands of photos and thousands of songs. One of my favorite types of Internet-based projects is virtual field trips. The video capabilities of the Web have led to their popularity, as students follow scientists and explorers such as Robert Ballard taking students to national parks, such as Hawaii's Volcanoes, as well as undersea and into space. Groups and agencies such as the National Geographic Society, NASA, National Oceanic and Atmospheric Administration (NOAA), and the National Science Foundation have supported these ventures that present the science and technology in the spirit of exploration, risk, and discovery. What could be more exciting for today's students?

One of these intrepid explorers is a professor of education. With support from the National Science Foundation, University of Minnesota professor Aaron Doering is completing a series of four polar expeditions to the Arctic that he calls "Adventure Learning."[2] For months at a time, Doering explores the Arctic, during 40- degree-below nights, accompanied only by his pack of Alaskan huskies, which I'm sure partially accounts for the affection that students display for his trips. He enlists the students in the villages in measuring the ice core. He interviews village elders for their stories, demonstrating how a learning expedition to investigate climate change can extend into the culture, language, and history of those places.

The digital natives who have grown up with powerful technology and experienced how it enlivens the learning process, are marching through our schools today. They are carrying the reform we seek with them. They are being met by educators, still a minority, who understand how to harness technology for them. These educators can be teachers, after-school educators, or others based in nonprofit and university settings. As we'll see in the next section, the generation "born digital" still needs caring adults who can lead them to the right digital learning experiences.

THE DIGITAL GENERATION SPEAKS

In 2009, Edutopia produced a provocative set of multimedia portraits of digital youth, which we called the Digital Generation.[3] We felt it was important to showcase what American students were doing with digital media, up close and personal. We wanted to put these learners in the foreground and the adults who supported them in the background, a departure from our school-based documentaries that rely more on the principals and teachers for telling the story.

With support from the MacArthur Foundation, we decided to produce extensive portraits of ten American students. We asked several
organizations to put the word out to their youth and have them submit
two-minute YouTube "audition tapes," introducing themselves and
their use of digital media. We received more than sixty submissions
and selected ten, based on what they told us and our interest in having
a diversity of ages (nine to eighteen) and five girls and five boys from
around the country, from urban, rural, and suburban communities.
A brief description of each demonstrates the richness of their digital
lifestyles and learning styles:

> Dana, 9, Maryland: iPhone gamer, iTunes video-watcher, Nin-
> tendo Wii and WebKinz World gamer, University of Maryland
> Kidsteam consultants to children's game and product designers
>
> Cameron, 11, Indiana: video and special effects producer, gamer,
> hockey player using video to analyze his slapshot
>
> Jalen, 12, Chicago: artist and animator, social networker, gamer,
> designed a Nike sneaker
>
> Samantha, 13, DeKalb, Illinois: video producer, World of Warcraft
> gamer
>
> Dylan, 13, New Hampshire: graphic designer, video producer,
> social activist, part of a Thinkquest team of international students
> who developed an award-winning game on animal cruelty
>
> Virginia, 14, Camilla, Georgia: blogger on Digiteen, social net-
> worker, teacher of Internet safety to younger students
>
> Justin, 16, Washington, D.C.: Teacher, educational game developer
>
> Olivia, 17, San Francisco: Uses public access computers for social
> networks
>
> Luis, 18, Cornelius, Oregon: video producer, robotics teacher,
> 4-H citizen scientist producing database on health of city trees,
> technology expert for his family
>
> Nafiza, 18, New York City: video producer, social activist, social
> networker, gamer, used Second Life for a student project on child
> soldiers

In keeping with the spirit of our Digital Generation coverage, I'll let Virginia and Luis speak for themselves.

Virginia: A Facebook Fast

Camilla, Georgia, is a small southern town. We're getting a Walgreen's, and we just got a Burger King. I just love this town, because it's not too big, but it's not too small, either.

› *My Digiteen Life*

First I had a little Game Boy, and I played that. I first started using computers in about the seventh grade. When I first got my cell phone, I didn't text very much. I just used it for calls. And then my friends showed me how to text message and I just got addicted to it. And then I got introduced to IM, where you can instant message people. I use my cell phone as an alarm clock in the morning for prayer breakfast. My math teacher lets us bring out our cell phones and I use it as a calculator, too. Now, I do about one blog a month with people on Digiteen, people all around the world.

The first time I actually made something with digital media was in the eighth grade. We wrote this story about how this person was having trouble with typing correctly. So we got different people to act out skits and then I put them all together. We used Animoto to create that movie.

› *My Friends*

I love to hang out with my friends. We usually come over to my house and play a Wii tennis tournament. Two of the main technologies I use with my friends are texting and my Facebook IM. Kids that I play sports against, I don't really get to see in person. I can talk to them over Facebook and MySpace and ask them, "How did your game go?"

When I get home from basketball, I usually spend about 45 minutes checking my MySpace and Facebook pages. About every other day, I like to go on YouTube and see the top-rated videos and look at them. And then sometimes I'll go to SparkNotes and read up on a couple of the books I'm studying.

▸ *My Digital Learning for School*

I've created so many videos for Miss Vicki in our class. The most recent blog I'm very proud of is the rights-and-responsibilities blog that I did with people from around the world on Digiteen. We've blogged about this man in Australia who got convicted for teaching kids how to blog.

We've recently held an online protest. Google Lively is shutting down and we got all our avatars there and we tried to protest. That's been really effective.

To study, I use ProProfs. You can go in there and create flash cards and it can shuffle them up. I cannot just look at a piece of paper and study. And then Classtools.net has all these games you can play, which are really cool.

For my media projects, we're working on OpenSim, Hippo Open-Sim. You can start from scratch and create something completely new. It is way better than any kind of virtual world I've ever been in. And we're going to use that to teach 7th-grade students digital rights and respon-sibilities. We're going to put real-life scenarios they might encounter on the Internet.

Our literature teacher told us to make a video that recreated the *Romeo and Juliet* story in our own words. Our group wrote a rap song about the different love scenes. I dressed up like Romeo, and my friend was Juliet. We did an intro at the beginning and then we rapped through the whole song. I love to make comedy videos.

▸ *Important People in My Life*

I have three main people who are the biggest influences in my life. One is my mom. She always makes me finish anything I try. Miss Vicki has made me see technology in such a new, different light.

My last one is my basketball coach. She just gets the best out of me, and she pushes me.

› *My Teaching*

I'm teaching young elementary school kids digital citizenship. We're teaching them how to stay safe online, because I've heard so many stories about kids who've given out personal information. I found this Web site called Woogie World, and I said to Miss Vicki, "This would be a great thing to do. We need to do this." The kids have loved Woogie World. My little brother didn't know that people would try and harm you on Web sites.

I got a little bit of a natural teaching gift from my mom. I love to get up there and teach the kids and I love to ask questions and see how their responses compare with mine.

› *My Favorite Hobbies, Books, Music, and Media*

I love to go outside and take pictures, like when we went to Puerto Rico, I went crazy with pictures.

The only series I've ever gotten really into is the Harry Potter series. I've read each of those twice over, and I used to read the Lemony Snicket series, but I never got to finish it.

I do read my Bible every night. That would have to be my favorite book. I just got this new true-life one from my youth pastor.

My favorite type of music would have to be inspirational and my favorite artist would be Matt Nathanson. I recently found him off of Genius on iTunes, and he's amazing. I've bought both his albums.

I bring my iPod to school or I make my friends a CD and I say, "Hey, listen to this song." Sometimes, I spend up to an hour finding new songs on iTunes.

My favorite game is Guitar Hero. Some of the games I like to play on the DS are Mario Kart and all the Mario games. I like to race my little brother in this four-wheeler game. And we get really competitive with the Wii sports, with tennis and bowling.

I like to watch E! News to get the celebrity updates and stuff. I like to watch the news sometimes and see current events. I like to watch

Nickelodeon. I love *Drake & Josh*. My favorite movie that I've seen recently is *Yes Man*.

› *My Own YouTube Channel*

My friend and I have always talked about doing a comedy channel on YouTube. We do funny stuff, and then we're like, "Oh, we should've gotten that on camera. It'd be great." Over the summer, I'd really like to start that and have a series on YouTube.

› *What Adults Need to Know About Technology*

I always hear from adults, "Oh, we didn't grow up with those things. We don't know how they work." And I've grown up with it. I know how it works. My mom was very against cell phones until about two years ago. We finally talked her into getting a cell phone because we could never get in touch with her.

I did a blog about this. I definitely do think there are things adults need to learn and understand. Because of the pace at which technology is growing, they're eventually going to have to learn one way or another. I think that their lives would improve if they started using technology.

› *The Downside of Digital*

People nowadays are surrounding their whole lives with technology. I realized I was being very unhealthy online when I first got my MySpace and Facebook. I would get on for two, three hours a day, and this was over the summer. I started losing the color in my face and I started eating differently. It was really weird, so I was like, "This is not good."

Our church's youth leader was starting a fast, and he said, "Anybody who wants to should give up anything they are really addicted to, just for three weeks. It'll really help your spiritual relationship. Any time you feel the need to, just pray about it." And I joined in and that really helped me. Now, I realize that overusing technology can be very dangerous.

> *My Plans*

My plans are to go to University of Georgia and start my own orthodontist place. I want to bring new technologies into orthodontics, like create a software program so people can schedule their appointments online. That's one thing I plan to do: get rid of the waiting room in orthodontics.

Luis: 4-H Tech Wizard

My name is Luis Chavez. I live in Cornelius, Oregon. What does technology mean to me? It's a better way to connect with families, connect with friends, help me improve my studies, and find out information and use it for the community, not just for myself.

> *My Family*

My mom and my dad are from a state in Mexico by the name of Michoacán. They both came here as rural immigrants looking for jobs. They met at a nursery and actually got married there.

I was born in 1990. My older sister is twenty-nine and came here from Mexico when she was about 11 and took care of me when I was a baby. She works at a home for disabled people. My older brother, Umparo, works in an auto body repair shop. He's taking English classes and learned a lot about computers. Both my mom and my dad have started to learn about computers. My dad recently got a promotion, a management job, and I've offered to teach him how to make Word documents and Excel spreadsheets. So we are all trying to improve on whatever we know as a family.

I've always been the person that goes with my mom for clinic appointments and the bank and there's nobody to translate. My parents said the only time they ever used technology was the ATM. Then I started learning about online banking. I said, "Look, Mom, we can check your bill online, you don't need to go to the bank anymore."

❯ My Digital Life History

In kindergarten, we had these really old computers. All we would use them for were Math Works and Reading Works. I really liked using them. I bought this old Windows 3.1 computer from my uncle. He had just bought it at a garage sale. After that, I went through a lot of older computers that I bought at thrift stores and garage sales. I opened them up to see what was inside, how things were connected. I kept nagging my parents for years to buy me a computer but once they bought it, I started trying to do everything like burning CDs, making small videos, getting on the Internet.

❯ My Work at 4-H Tech Wizards

Recently, we took a group of students to Hillsboro High School where they competed in the Lego tournament. They presented a project relating to climate change and what they can do as young children to help out the environment. They're not just learning about how to build robots but they're learning about working together. If some child wants to make the robot go forward and turn left and the other doesn't, they could compromise and say, "Okay, we'll make it do this first, but you have to let me do this other part that I want to do." In the future, they might be working on something big, building a space shuttle, and those are skills I believe should be learned at an early age.

Tech Wizards has really helped me express myself. I was very quiet, very reserved, but once I got to know the other students, they showed me that it's always a team effort.

❯ The Tech Wizards' Street Tree Inventory

This project is called "Street Tree Inventory Project" and we do it with the partnership with the city of Hillsboro. The students that began the program decided to do a project on the street trees, the conditions of the trees and reporting to the city. When I first started, I was just learning the software involved in creating the maps called ArcGIS. You take geo-reference points, which means points that have the information of where the tree is in relation to a map. I was involved in collecting the data. You have to be very precise because it's difficult to change the data after you already input it into the PDA [personal digital assistant handheld device]. We divided the whole neighborhood into blocks. The information we collected included the species of the trees, its height, its width, the canopy size, and the conditions.

› Learning Digital Video

I started the digital video class when I was a sophomore through my mentor, Cecilia. She taught us about the different types of wide shots, close-ups and mid-shots. We also learned about the different types of cameras, the lenses. We started doing interviews, learning what are good questions, more in-depth questions. Each group did their own project, like a music video or filming the local flea market or the soccer match.

We've been asked by the Red Cross to produce an instructional video on child safety, when they're home alone. Yesterday we watched a video that they had and noticed that it seemed outdated, the phones looked old. We want to make an updated video to show kids how they should use the Internet and cell phones in case of an emergency.

› A Day in My Life

In the morning, I wake up around 5:30. I usually turn on the computer, check e-mail, really quick. Go downstairs, have breakfast. I take my mom to the bus stop. Come back, wake up my brother, we both brush our teeth. He has breakfast. We go out the door around 7:20. I drop him off at school at his middle school, then I go to school, which starts at 7:55.

My first period of class on A days is precalculus, my second class is accounting, third class geometry and fourth class is English. It came as a surprise to me that I'm taking the four AP classes in one day.

On Monday or Thursday, I usually stay after school to do extra work and on Tuesday, I go to the SMILE club, a science, math and engineering club. It's not very technical, but we do get to learn a little bit about different properties of chemicals. Every April, we go to the OSU SMILE Challenge in Corvallis, Western Oregon University and Oregon State University. We do engineering projects relating to the ocean or genetics.

On Wednesdays, I have the Tech Wizards Program. After that, I pick up my brother and my mom at work, we come back and my mom starts dinner.

I go to my room, check my e-mail through Gmail, check the news on Yahoo. I go to technology Web sites to see what new technology is coming out. I check YouTube, watch videos. The most important is Facebook. If I can't go out, at least I know my friends are there and can talk to me. If I need help with homework, they're there. I also can text message them. It's a kind of multitasking task so I can be working on a project, on a paper, and be chatting with them through Facebook.

I come back, help my mom out, set the table. My dad and my older brother arrive and we have dinner. My parents usually watch TV downstairs, I sometimes join them or I'll go upstairs and watch TV. When I'm checking my e-mail, I'm actually doing homework as well. I finish everything up and watch maybe another half hour of television and then go to bed, maybe around 10.

▸ The Important People in My Life

My science teachers. I've known them for four years. Mrs. Jones, Mr. Gray, and Mr. Poff. They usually try to motivate me to stay on top of my homework and make sure I study for tests. My mentors from Tech Wizards, Cecilia Heron, Lisa Conroy. They always try to find opportunities for me to demonstrate how can I help the community. The biggest influence in your life are your parents. They're the ones that teach you your morals, to be active and to actually do something with your life.

› Teaching and Travelling

When I started learning about digital media and about the GIS programs, I realized that they wouldn't just be for me, but I had to teach others. It's because of others that I have opportunities. They just presented them to me and I took advantage of them. I want to show others that they can do the same.

The first major trip I took was to the Dominican Republic. I had never travelled anywhere besides Mexico and the U.S. So that experience was great, I got to definitely learn about the culture. I got to go to San Diego as part of the National GIS team, which includes students from other states. We presented the Street Tree Project at the annual GIS users conference, the biggest conference of GIS users.

The recent trip I took was to Chile. We went to teach at a local school about GIS. A lot of the students had to walk to the school. They decided to create maps to see the distances, mapping the bike routes in the city and how safe they were and what condition they were. That's the part that I really enjoyed, teaching them what the opportunities were for making maps and showing them to the community.

› My Future

Being the first person in my family to go to college, it definitely like excites me. Career-wise, I'm either hoping to go into computer engineering or video editing. I'm still undecided. But it's definitely digital media or electronics.

Based on these ten profiles, we developed three themes to capture how today's youth are using digital media for new forms of learning: creating, collaborating, and teaching.[4] While these categories of behaviors have been possible without technology, digital media enable potentially every student with access to these tools to express a much richer variety of these behaviors—at earlier ages, on a regular, daily basis. This changes everything about learning as we have known it.

Themes from the Digital Generation Project

THEME	DESCRIPTION	EXAMPLES
Creating	Today's youth are active creators and producers who use a wide range of digital tools to express themselves, interpret the world around them, and deepen their understanding of academic content. Their products include original music, animation, video, stories, graphics, presentations, and Web sites. These tools enable young people to create in ways that were not possible for earlier generations. They can become actively engaged in their learning processes rather than passive recipients of knowledge passed down from adults. Favorite tools include: music composition/performance (Garage Band), digital video editing (iMovie), image creation/manipulation (Photoshop), Animoto, and multimedia Web production (Flash).	Cameron produces and edits music videos, short documentaries, school newscasts, special effects, and visual aids for use in math class. Nafiza writes storylines, builds sets in Teen Second Life, and makes virtual films about pressing social and global issues, such as child soldiers.

| Collaborating | Today's youth can actively collaborate in many new ways in the digital, virtual world. They present media they've created for feedback from a large online community. They can be in constant contact with dozens of their friends and participate in multiplayer games online. They can form new friendships with other youth, in the same city or in another country, and can engage in online group work with others. They can find adult experts and mentors to support their interests.

Favorite tools include: social networking (MySpace, Facebook, Ning, Twitter), blogs (blogger.com, wordpress.com), instant messaging, collaborative workspaces (Wikispaces), Google Docs, video- and audioconferencing (Skype, iChat), multiplayer games (World of Warcraft), and game consoles (Xbox, Nintendo Wii). | Jalen posts his creations on Remix World for his peers to critique his work before posting it on YouTube for the public at large.

Justin plays multiplayer online games with youth from around the corner and around the world.

Dylan collaborates with youth from Argentina, Japan, and India to create award-winning Web sites in the Thinkquest competition. |

(continued)

Themes from the Digital Generation Project (*continued*)

THEME	DESCRIPTION	EXAMPLES
Teaching	Given their fluency with digital tools, today's youth can become teachers for younger and older children. They can also teach their parents, teachers, and other adults, a new role for children that reverses traditional authority roles. This teaching role enables youth to gain confidence and reinforce their own learning, since the best way to learn something is to teach it. They maintain content-rich Web sites, share favorite resources, lead workshops and classes, and develop multimedia products designed to share their knowledge with others. Favorite tools include: blogging (Blogger), online course systems (Moodle), presentation software (PowerPoint, Keynote), webinars for group meetings (WebEx), and social networking (Ning).	Virginia uses Woogi World to teach fourth-graders about digital citizenship and online safety. Luis teaches Lego Robotics to younger students and helps his parents learn computer skills. Sam teaches college students about the virtual world, using Open Sim.

Based on a three-year ethnographic study of digital youth, Dr. Mimi Ito of the University of California at San Diego and her research team described three related categories as "hanging out, messing around, and geeking out."

> Online spaces enable youth to connect with peers in new ways... through private communications like instant messaging or mobile phones, as well as in public ways through social network sites like MySpace or Facebook. The majority of youth use new media to "hang out" and extend existing friendships in these new ways.... Young people acquire various forms of technical and media literacy by exploring new interests, tinkering, and "messing around" with new forms of media.... Others "geek out" and dive into a topic or talent. Geeking out is highly social and engaged [in] specialized knowledge groups of both teens and adults from around the country or world. Geeking out... erases the traditional markers of status and authority.[5]

This digital generation is using the Internet, computers, cell phones and smartphones, video games, and many other new tools to learn and socialize in ways that were not possible in previous generations. Many of these tools, such as broadband access enabling video-sharing over the Internet through YouTube and other sites, were not invented even five years ago, as technology has continued to advance. Each year brings new features to previous tools.

The iPhone, introduced in 2007, has redefined the cell phone as a multifunctional mobile computer. In one of my favorite TED talks, Clay Shirky of New York University's Interactive Telecommunications Program brilliantly describes the past 500 years of media dating back to Gutenberg's printing press. He says we are now witnessing "the largest increase in expressive capability in human history. There have only been four periods in the last 500 years where media has changed enough to qualify being called a revolution."

The first was the invention of the printing press in the mid-1400s. The second, about 200 years ago, was the telegraph and the telephone, enabling two-way communication through text, then voice. About 150 years ago, media recorded images and sounds into physical objects, giving us photography and vinyl records. The fourth revolution, starting about a century ago, harnessed the electromagnetic spectrum, giving us radio and TV broadcasting, the revolution my generation knew as children. Few people remember that the early radios were called "the wireless," but today's broadband wireless uses the same airwaves to transmit radio programs and much, much more, notably video. Shirky makes this stunning observation: "As media are digitized, the Internet becomes the mode of carriage for all other media. Phone calls, magazines, and movies. *Every medium is right next door to every other medium.*"[6]

And on a device that fits in your pocket. The iPhone is the latest and smallest incarnation of Shirky's profound statement. Nearly everything that I can do on my desktop or laptop can be done on the iPhone and other smartphones now available. The phenomenal growth in apps for the iPhone gives it a range of functions that far outstrip a normal computer. Some functions are easier and more enabled on my laptop, certainly for older eyes and hands that prefer a bigger screen and full keyboard. But iPhone users can text and call, listen to music, take and view photos, and access e-mail and Internet content.

And they can write essays. In case digital immigrant readers are skeptical of the iPhone as a writing device, talk to some university students. Last year, I got in a taxi in San Francisco and chatted with the twenty-something driver about his iPhone. I said it must be nice to use it both as a phone and a music player. He said, yes, but he uses it to write his papers for college while sitting in a taxi line, which can be hours at the airport. He had just submitted his paper online to his instructor from his cab that morning.

STUDENTS AS TECHNOLOGY TEACHERS

One of the most important new roles for students is to use their technological prowess to help their teachers teach. Why this continues to be a revelation to many teachers is a mystery to me. When teachers' most common criticism of technology is their lack of skill and need for more time and money for professional development, one solution is to enlist those experts right in front of them. Sometimes, the most obvious solutions are right in front of your face.

Of course, the reason why students aren't snapped up for these roles is equally clear: "students" aren't supposed to "teach." And they're certainly not supposed to "teach teachers." For the teachers who see themselves as keepers of adult authority, asking students for help is a sign of weakness. To these teachers, I say, "Get over it!" The days of being the sole source of knowledge and authority in the classroom are over, way over.

There are a few precedents for giving students more responsibility for the operations of the classroom. One is the graduate student acting as TA, or teaching assistant, to university faculty. This role evolved out of the need to give professors help in grading papers, holding small-group discussions, and other matters of administering large classes of college students. It was also thought to be good training for professors-to-be. I was one of them, in my graduate student days at Stanford, teaching a discussion section of Communication 1, a large lecture class on the past, present, and future of radio, TV, and this new machine called the "micro-computer."

The other is the old AV Club, those earnest students, almost all boys, and mostly with eyeglasses, a pocket protector, and a slide rule, who wheeled in the 16-millimeter projector, set it up, and made sure the film was ready for the teacher to present. These teams worked with teachers to identify what content they wanted to present and assembled the mobile technology needed to display it in class.

Generation YES

Olympia, Washington

Take those precedents and fast-forward them through the decades to today's classroom. This is what Generation YES (Youth and Educators Succeeding), founded in 1995 in Olympia, Washington, by Dennis Harper, then technology director for the district, has done.[7] The project benefited from a U.S. Department of Education Technology Challenge grant and was also recognized in 2000 as one of the nation's best educational technology programs by a USDE Technology Expert Panel which I cochaired with Elsie Brumback, then state technology director from North Carolina.

Dennis Harper says, "Teachers don't realize how sharp these kids are, they don't realize that for the first time in history, you have students knowing more than their teachers about something that's really central and important to society."

GenYES students, from fourth- through twelfth-grades, help teachers embed technology in their teaching, by locating the best Web sites on the topic of the day and helping them display Web content or media in the classroom. They also serve as IT support, ensuring that software runs on classroom computers, repairing hardware, and keeping the school network running. Before they are assigned to teachers, they must take a semester-long class on communication and teaching skills. Harper says their surveys show that 98 percent of teachers say they would rather learn from students than other teachers.

GenYES calls this "reverse mentoring," after a management practice instituted by Jack Welch, then chairman and CEO of General Electric, who felt he and his top executives were slow to adapt to new technology. Hundreds of senior managers were paired with younger staff members to tutor them in the "new tools" of e-mail and Internet searching.

In the Edutopia documentary on the project's impact in Washington Middle School in Olympia, you see a rare type of exchange going on: teachers who aren't afraid to admit they need help and students who are patient and confident in explaining what they know.[8] A seventh-grade boy is helping a teacher design her class Web site. "That font is good for the titles," he says, "because it's big, it's big enough you can distinguish the letters." She asks, "Do you see anything you would change?" He replies, "Yeah, there's no home link here. I notice on your previous page, you have one here, but some browsers don't have back buttons so you have to retype the URL, which is really annoying."

In a fourth-grade classroom, two girls are helping their teachers learn how to edit video and explaining "sound tracks" and "transitions." The teacher earnestly asks, "What's a transition?" One girl says, "Transitions are when you can fade in and fade out." One teacher asks, "Are there sound effects we can use?" The girl responds, "Yeah, we'd have to go into a CD and export it to iMovie and then you can use it for the school news." When teachers aren't afraid to ask students about technology and students are given license to help their teachers, it's a beautiful thing to behold.

Deann Barre, media specialist at McKenny Elementary School, said in the film, "It's absolutely joyful to work with these kids. The more power you give them, the more empowered they become. They take responsibility for their own learning. They get very excited about having authentic, purposeful reasons to be at school and authentic ways of helping their teachers. . . . It carries across into all of the disciplines."

Craig Costello, a Washington Middle School counselor and GenYES instructor, added, "The whole culture of our school has changed, in an easy way. It hasn't been teachers feeling like 'I've got to be dragged and pulled into this technology' kind of thing. They've got their students working with them over time on a project and then suddenly they have got the skills. It was kind of a painless way of getting this done."

Over fifteen years, GenYES has been implemented in more than 1,200 schools in the United States and abroad, involving 75,000 students. Generation YES has expanded into other programs, including TechYES, which offers technology certification for students in grades 6–9 and peer mentoring, and TechYES Science, focusing on certifying students' technology skills through science projects. At the Barber Middle School in Cobb County, Georgia, 71 percent for TechYES students passed the state technology literacy test, compared with 51 percent of the students in the rest of the school and 63 percent countywide. TechYes is recommended in the George State Technology Literacy Toolkit as the only project-based learning approach to technology literacy.

The GenYES organization itself practices what it preaches. As Harper describes it, "Most of our organization is kids. Kids do our Web page. Kids answer the phones. They do all of our promotional materials. They monitor all the bulletin boards. We walk the walk."

Of hundreds of Technology Challenge grants given during the 1990s, Generation YES is one of the very few that survives today. For his decades-long efforts, Dennis Harper was selected as one of *Edutopia* magazine's Daring Dozen in 2008. The article about him opens with his blunt statement: "Kids know more than you do." Harper has also launched a new nonprofit, Kijana Voices, to bring technology to the youth of Liberia working with president Ellen Sirleaf, who views GenYES as part of the effort to rebuild her nation.

I've come to know Dennis over the years and admire his passion for making sure the voice of students is heard, loudly and clearly, in education reform. I sat next to him at one conference, several rows from a panel of education experts. As they were being introduced, he wondered, in a stage whisper intended for those on stage and around us, "Why aren't there any students up there?" Harper believes that technology skill can be a student's ticket to a world of equal educational opportunity. "On the Internet, the poorest student in the world has the same resources as Bill Gates's kids. Ready access to technology is an equalizer, a leveler—exactly what Martin Luther King, Jr.'s dream was."

I once asked him, "How did you become such an advocate for students?" He told he had been a student at Berkeley during the activist, antiwar '60s. Suddenly, his dedication to giving power to the young people made a lot more sense.

For schools and districts wanting to implement the Generation YES program, their site has a wealth of information to get you started. Or use an older technology that still works. As Dennis advised one Edutopia user who posted a comment asking how to learn more, "Just call us at 360-528-2345."

Who said changing the culture of schools has to be a long, drawn-out, and painful process? Maybe we've ignored some youthful, energetic allies sitting right in front of us, just waiting to be asked to help.

GROUP EXERCISE: WRITE THE STUDENT'S NEW JOB DESCRIPTION

In the traditional classroom, a student's main job is to sit, listen, take good notes, do the homework, memorize facts, figures, and formulae, and repeat this information back on quizzes and tests. The twenty-first-century student uses technology to actively seek out reliable and high-quality sources of information, analyze these sources, and utilize them in producing a product of his or her knowledge. In the traditional classroom, the teacher works hard and the students rest. In classrooms emulating the modern workplace, the students should be the ones working the hardest.

As the GenYES project illustrates, today's students are eager to be given a job. At your next faculty or school board meeting, devote some time to writing a job description for your twenty-first-century students. Here are some skills and qualifications I'd propose:

Skills

Information literacy. Ability to use technology to find and analyze key information needed. The traditional literacy skills of reading and writing are incorporated into a more complex ability to locate and compare multiple sources of information.

Multimedia production. Ability to select and combine words, images, and sound to communicate a story, a study, or a point of view.

Ability to work with others. In classrooms emulating the modern workplace, teams of students create products of their work that are more ambitious than any one individual can produce. Ability to communicate and make the collaborative process fun and enjoyable. Respectful of differences of opinion and background.

Qualifications

A well-rounded curiosity about the world, an interest in science and how things work and in history, literature, and the arts.

Willingness to come to school and other places of learning on time and ready to learn. As 2005 National Teacher of the Year Jason Kamras says, "I want students to know that they have a job. And that job is to learn."

Persistence and hard work. Resilience in the face of setbacks and ambiguity.

It's fitting to end this discussion of the six edges of innovation in schools with a focus on the student as learner, since these edges have in common the student at each of their centers. The Thinking, Curriculum, Technology, Time/Place, Co-Teaching, and Youth Edges all converge around a redefinition of the student as an active, engaged, curious, and collaborative learner. Perhaps, as these edges continue to grow and move to occupy the center of a new educational system, we will shed the old definitions and vocabulary from the past.

In the Afterword, I look forward to Tomorrow's Edge: what might lie ahead and how societal, technological, and global forces will continue to affect the need for new and more responsive learning environments. In the scenarios that I and others discuss, we are inventing a new vocabulary of education.

In a new Education Nation, perhaps "schools" will change their signage and call themselves "learning centers." "Teachers" might take on new titles as "academic coaches" or "learning mentors." And even the label of "student" might be retired in favor of "team member" or "scholar." Already, some schools are adopting this new vocabulary. Literacy and math coaches for faculty teams are now becoming more common. When school systems finally redefine the word for *student*, we can gain confidence that an Education Nation is coming into being.

AFTERWORD
TOMORROW'S EDGE, A 2020 VISION

It's becoming obvious that no one knows what the world is going to be like when the time comes for the younger to live in it, so perhaps the kindest thing we can do is to try not to burden them with the quaint details of today's beliefs and customs, but just attempt to get across a few principles of how things interact, what is basic in human life, and to acquaint them with as thorough a cross-section as possible of persons, places, and things as they now stand. After this we can only give them a pat on the shoulder and wish them well.

CLARK GESNER, WRITER AND COMPOSER,
PROSPECTUS FOR SESAME WORKSHOP, 1968

The best way to predict the future is to invent it.

ALAN KAY, COMPUTER SCIENTIST AND INVENTOR
OF THE DYNABOOK CONCEPT, 1968

THESE TWO QUOTES about the future were made in the same year by two individuals working on opposite coasts to shape the future for children, one involved with children's television, the other with technology for children. Clark Gesner, based in New York, participated in the early curriculum seminars that led to *Sesame Street,* and was best known for writing and composing the musical, *You're A Good Man, Charlie Brown.*

Alan Kay has had a hand in many of the devices and software we use today, such as the graphical user interface and the portable PC, dating back to his work at the Xerox Palo Alto Research Center (PARC) in the 1970s. As early as 1968, he set forth a vision for an educational Dynabook, "a personal computer for children of all ages," a small, portable, and powerful computer capable of displaying multimedia and a comprehensive collection of learning materials. Their work acts as bookends to my own career, which began in children's TV and, over the decades, have focused on educational technology. In 1968, I don't know that anyone could have foreseen how media technologies would converge onto a single device, carried in our pockets. One wonders about what will be possible just ten years from now.

It's obvious that the world is now changing more rapidly than at any other time in human history. An education based on the world today will not suffice for living and working in the world of tomorrow. We're overdriving our headlamps, travelling so fast that we're unable to see what lies ahead. It's up to all of us who care about creating a better world of tomorrow to do what we can to help invent it today. As this book describes, many education change agents, from thought leaders and policymakers to principals, teachers, and parents, as well as students themselves, are creating the types of schools and other learning environments that will equip today's students to become future leaders, citizens, and lifelong learners. Their work at the edges of the current school system is gradually moving to the center. Yet progress has been slow to achieve scale, especially compared with the pace of technological and global change.

What could be done to move the edges more quickly to the center of the educational system, rather than remain at its fringes? In the decentralized system of the United States, it will take more widespread consensus about what is possible, from policymakers understanding these edges to parents demanding them. Sharing the successes of what's happening at the edges is important to creating this consensus, school by school, district by district and state by state. Edutopia and many other organizations are helping with this effort, on the Web and in the many conferences dedicated to educational innovation.

Finding out about what's possible and what other schools and districts have achieved is a critical part of this change process. Learning how to implement new practices is most likely to occur from one's "near peers," as Professor Everett Rogers named them in his groundbreaking work on the diffusion of innovation.[1] I was fortunate to study with him during my graduate years at Stanford. For one project, we interviewed Kentucky farmers about a new telecommunications system using phone lines for sharing crop disease and pricing information. It was clear that they were most likely to use the new system when they heard about it from other farmers, not from university faculty or USDA agents. Similarly, teachers learn best from other teachers and principals learn best from other principals, those who have stood in their shoes and intimately know what they face, day in and day out.

Another principle from innovation research is that those seeking to change don't adopt new practices wholesale. They *adapt* them to their local needs and experience and often improve the idea they're importing. To that end, it's also important for educators and others in communities to examine their own situations and connect present conditions to future possibilities. So, a complementary strategy engages stakeholders in building future scenarios based on their own experiences and aspirations, addressing local needs and strengths.

In 2002, a number of "educational technologists" were asked by the U.S. Department of Commerce to submit visions of the educational future and what might be possible over the coming decades. The group included Vint Cerf, a founder of the Internet, and Caleb Schutz, president of the JASON Project; Diana Walczak, a computer graphics pioneer and founder of Kleiser-Walczak; Christopher Dede from the Harvard Graduate School of Education; and myself and GLEF cofounder and board member, Steve Arnold. Our projections were published in *Visions 2020: Transforming Education and Training Through Advanced Technologies.*[2] This set of future visions still provides some provocative ideas and models to consider in creating new scenarios. In the following section, you'll see our effort to describe a possible future for San Francisco children.

In creating these scenarios, it's critical to include the voices of youth. As reflected in Edge 6, students represent a powerful force in the reinvention of schools. For too long, students have been excluded from these "adult conversations." But we do so to the peril of creating environments that are still adult-based, as in many past efforts at school reform.

Following up to the *Visions 2020* report, a sequel was produced, which asked students for their views. *Visions 2020.2: Student Views on Transforming Education and Training Through Advanced Technologies* was commissioned by the Commerce Department, U.S. Department of Education, and NetDay and published in 2004.[3] It was based on student responses to the online survey from NetDay Speak Up Day for Students, to which 160,000 U.S. students responded. An open-ended question asked, "Today, you and your fellow students are important users of technology. In the future, you will be the inventors of new technologies. What would you like to see invented that you think will help kids learn in the future?" More than 55,000 students answered, and 8,000 of those responses were analyzed for common themes.

The report synthesized four major themes of the student responses—digital devices, access to computers and the Internet, intelligent tutor-helper, and ways to learn and complete school work—into this scenario:

> Every student would use a small, handheld wireless computer that is voice-activated. The computer would offer high-speed access to a kid-friendly Internet, populated with websites that are safe, designed specifically for use by students, with no pop-up ads. Using this device, students would complete most of their in-school work and homework, as well as take online classes both at school and at home. Students would use the small computer to play mathematics-learning games and read interactive e-textbooks. In completing their schoolwork, students would work closely and routinely with an intelligent digital tutor, and tap a knowledge utility to obtain factual answers to questions they pose. In their history studies, students could participate in 3-D virtual reality-based historic reenactments.

Students clearly want and deserve a digital learning environment. If adults provide it, students are ready and willing to carry more of the responsibility for their own learning.

Two other groups have designed materials to help educators, policymakers, and others plan for a new educational future. The KnowledgeWorks Foundation in Ohio, together with the Institute for the Future, have created a 2020 Forecast summarizing in one graphical map six broad and global drivers of change, societal and technological trends related to each driver, and signals of each driver and trend.[4] For each driver, I include one of several trends:

1. *Altered Bodies:* How advances in neuroscience are revealing a new understanding of the brain and human performance. How external threats from climate change, pollution, war, and urbanization are creating new stresses on bodies and minds. *Trend*: Eco-schools emphasize health, environment, and learning.

2. *Amplified Organization:* Digital natives and technologies of cooperation will amplify human capacity and remake organizations. *Trend*: "Transliteracy" requires skill across multiple media and social platforms.

3. *Platforms for Resilience:* Society will face disruptive shocks in energy, health care, and finance that will impact school systems, which will need to build resilience for adapting through partnerships and networks. *Trend*: Learning Grids of networked resource providers create new kinds of learning infrastructures.

4. *A New Civic Discourse:* Social networks and participatory media, along with population movements, will lead to more "bottom-up" monitoring of learning and the need for schools to engage with the public in new ways. *Trend*: Learning Commons involve education stakeholders in growing collective learning alternatives to public and private schools.

5. *The Maker Economy:* New digital tools and open-source platforms will allow communities to share their knowledge and

new businesses and economies. *Trend*: Community-based manufacturing enables flexible, fast, and customized production.

6. *Pattern Recognition:* Data trails from online interactions and geographic information systems will enable "data pictures" of our lives as citizens, workers, and learners. Organizations that can make sense of data patterns will make better decisions. *Trend*: Visual Literacy tools summarize vast amounts of data.

The Institute for Creative Collaboration at KnowledgeWorks presents workshops to assist groups in creating the new kinds of school and social structures needed to respond to these drivers of change. Their Web site presents updates, blogs, and an online community to continue the discussions.

In 2009, FutureLab in Bristol, England, published the Beyond Current Horizons program to explore the future of education beyond 2025.[5] The program was the result of an eighteen-month planning and consultation process resulting in three "world views" and six future scenarios based on more than sixty white papers. Similar to the KnowledgeWorks's 2020 Forecast, Beyond Current Horizons considered trends such as a denser, deeper, and more diverse information landscape; constant connectivity to knowledge, people, and tools; a changing human-computer relationship as technology assumes more tasks formerly done by people; and the decline of distance as a determining factor in education, work, and social life, while place, physical location, and face-to-face relationships continue to be important.

The worlds and scenarios reflect the British system in which the national government plays a larger role in the provision of education than in the United States. They are described as:

World 1: *Trust Yourself* anticipates a world in which government funding and management of education recedes and individuals are left to craft their own personalized learning paths. Its scenarios are titled as Informed Choice, creating a personal learning plan with mentors, and Independent Consumer, where learners choose from a marketplace of educational offerings.

World 2: *Loyalty Points*, in which government's role is to enable and regulate relationships between institutions and individuals. Two scenarios are Discovery, where individuals assess how they might fit in a variety of organizations, and Diagnosis, in which the schools assess students' potential and place them in careers and organizations.

World 3: *Only Connect*, where citizens act as members of society first and as individuals second. Its scenarios are named as Integrated Experience, in which education is based on authentic experiences in different communities and Service and Citizenship, where service learning and civic participation are valued.

Beyond Current Horizons has also published a free online Future Mapper to support planning for new school facilities and curriculum, including thirteen case studies from schools in England. The materials include slide presentations and activity cards to be used in group meetings.

In the following 2020 scenario, you will hear echoes of many of the six edges in this book: a middle school student's 24/7 access to multimedia information; learning of a second language through online curricula, voice recording, and Internet connections to youth in other countries; the teacher's role as guide, mentor, and manager of learning experiences; integrating the study of sciences and history; and all this happening in the month of July. If Steve Arnold and I were to revise it today, eight years later, we'd include a mobile device that fits in learners' pockets, describe their participation in social networks, and instead of parents who have to ask their children what they learned today, a home-school communication system would keep them informed.

Since writing this vision in 2002, some technologies mentioned have progressed quickly, such as the rise of YouTube, for students to post wikis, and content management systems to share work among classmates. Others have been slower to develop, such as 3-D simulations and human-computer voice interfaces, although current video games and voice recognition software reveal how these technologies will only improve.

We share this story with you to encourage you to write your own "Day in the Life" stories of what learning in the future might look like. Focusing on individual students helps to make these stories more specific. Years ago, Chad Wick, president of KnowledgeWorks Foundation, and I went through a similar process led by a communications firm in which we cut out photos from magazines that captured our hopes for student learning. We were interviewed by the firm, which produced slide shows of our images set to music with a narration based on our words. The results were inspiring, and we learned from each other's ideas.

The seeds of what a 2020 school should look like already exist in many schools today, as the six edges represent. Hopefully, some of the projects and classrooms described in this book can provide ideas. Producing these 2020 scenarios can be creative exercises to share in groups of educators, parents, and community leaders working to envision the future. I've participated in several conferences where small groups brainstormed and presented a future scenario through a short skit or slide presentation. In the spirit of the twenty-first-century multimedia skills, you could produce them in various media forms: as poems, artwork, slide shows with audio and visuals, plays, and movies. LucasArts artist Greg Knight added a lot to our scenario with his illustrations.

Consider enlisting some young people to help you produce your scenarios. Now through video-sharing sites, these short media presentations can be exchanged and even remixed among a much larger audience. By sharing ideas about the future of learning, and connecting them with innovative classrooms today, we can build on the present to create the future for this Education Nation. I'll close with one of my other favorite quotations, from Immanuel Kant: "The actual proves the possible."

A Day in the Life of a Young Learner: A 2020 Vision

With Stephen D. Arnold [6]

Technology helps overcome the two enemies of learning: isolation and abstraction.

GEORGE LUCAS, CHAIRMAN,
THE GEORGE LUCAS EDUCATIONAL FOUNDATION

July 15, 2020: On a foggy summer day in San Francisco, eleven-year-old Malia is hard at work—in school. In 2007, her school district changed from the nine-month school calendar, recognizing that teaching and learning are year-round activities and that the long summer vacation was an anachronism from a time when children were needed to bring in the crops. Her school looks and feels like a cross between a working office, a public library, and a movie set, with individual student cubicles decorated to express each student's personality and interests, and ten large multimedia production and research centers, enough for a whole class. Nearly all of the furniture is on wheels so that work areas can be easily reconfigured to adapt to the needs of particular student activities. The school's design was inspired by Minnesota's School of Environmental Studies, founded in 1995 and a pioneer in its time in new school architecture.

At the start of this school day, the classroom environment is brimming with student teams chatting about last night's online exchanges and organizing to continue their work on the class earth science unit. Malia and two of her classmates, Sahar and Osvaldo, are seated in comfortable task chairs at a multimedia production and communications station. Facing them is a high-resolution, luminescent display screen, viewable from front and back, on which combinations of images, text, and digital video can be summoned by voice command.

Osvaldo, born blind, uses the assistive technology of a digital "visual prosthesis system" to see. The system consists of a minicamera mounted on eyeglasses with signal processors and electrodes stimulating his visual cortex, a technology first pioneered on Patient Alpha in 2002. Unlike blind students of previous generations, Osvaldo is able to participate fully in all activities with sighted students. "Give us our team project on volcanoes," Osvaldo asks the school's server, enabling the team to review its progress from the previous week.

Their research using the Global Learning Network has led them to the Hawaii Volcanoes National Park Web site, where they have witnessed several hours of video footage of volcanic eruptions, observed volcanologists at work tracking and measuring lava flows, and watched interviews with them. The site included a 3-D time-lapse hologram of the 1983 Mount Kilauea eruption on the Big Island. Through the time compression of time-lapse photography, they were able to witness lava flows over the past forty years. They had made a copy of the hologram and left it in the classroom for use by other students.

Yesterday, donning special virtual reality headgear, they had gone on a simulated trip to the lava fields, giving them an on-the-ground sensation of hiking across acres of older lava formations to arrive at a scene of bright orange lava flowing toward the sea. "How cool was that," Malia grins. "You could hear the lava crackling." Last night, from their homes, they had brainstormed some questions in preparation for an interview with a volcano expert scheduled for today. "Last night's interview questions," requests Sahar.

The system promptly displays the students' work on the screen. Their teacher, Kavery Dutta, stops by to observe their discussion as they prepare for their videoconference. "You know," she advises them, "it would be great to also look at what volcanoes meant to the native Hawaiians centuries ago. They believed in a goddess of fire, Pele." She gives them some resources to search and access from the University of Hawaii Digital Library. She also suggests they look up the pioneering work of MIT geologist Thomas Jaggar, who founded the Hawaiian Volcano Observatory in 1912 and persuaded Congress to preserve the area as a national park.

Ms. Dutta strolls over to check in with another group of students. One of them is holding a sample of volcanic rock, while another examines it under a handheld digital microscope, with the magnified image projectable on a large screen behind them. A third student is reviewing the volcano hologram left by Malia's group.

"Okay, we're ready for our appointment with the volcanologist at Hawaii Volcanoes National Park," Malia announces. The face of Harold Levitt, the park's chief of interpretation, appears in the familiar green uniform of a National Park Service Ranger. Responding to their questions, Ranger Levitt leads them through several more screens of images showing video news clips and data sources dating back to the Mount Kilauea eruption; the science and chemistry of volcanoes (including dangers such as the release of sulfuric fumes); and the human impact on local communities, from devastation of homes to increased tourism. Malia and her classmates are also able to observe today's lava flows in real time from cameras trained on the site, enjoying the chance to watch the creation of black sand when hot lava meets the cold ocean water.

Malia asks, "A few weeks ago, we had a small earthquake here. We felt it but it didn't damage anything. How are earthquakes related to volcanoes?" On another screen, Ranger Levitt calls up a simulation of plate tectonics and shows them cross-sections of the Earth, as well as aerial satellite photos from different elevations, with overlaid graphics indicating earthquake fault zones in the Bay Area and then San Francisco. For other experts, he refers them to the U.S. Geological Survey (USGS) offices in the Bay Area. Malia and her classmates make a voicenote in their ongoing project record to ask their teacher about making a field trip and to look up the USGS website.

After their 20-minute interview with Ranger Levitt, recorded on the school's server to become a part of the project archive, the students quickly review the video transcript and earmark some of his comments for possible use in their final multimedia report. At the end of the two-hour session, they make a multimedia summary of their work, calendar next meetings, and assign themselves homework before their next meeting. They each place a copy of today's workfile in their digital backpacks, rugged mobile personal computers and communications consoles "checked out" by each student at the beginning of the school year, the way textbooks used to be issued. Malia's "digipack" allows her to spend some more time on her volcanoes project later in the afternoon after walking a few blocks to her father's office. As she waits for him to finish his work, she uses it to connect to the school's library information system and the widely available wireless network.

Searching links and browsing through references on Hawaiian mythology, she watches a short video clip on the goddess Pele on her viewscreen, recording some voicenotes to share with her project partners at school tomorrow. Later that night at home, Malia is practicing her Chinese in the family room. She hopes to visit China one day and has been using an online language learning system to gain proficiency in basic Chinese conversation, reading, and writing. Her younger sister, Sonia, likes to look on. and she sits by Malia's side as they face a multimedia screen similar to those in their schools. They both hold handheld digital devices serving as Chinese-English dictionaries for looking up words and phrases in both languages, in text and audio. They can also store their own spoken phrases.

Malia requests, "The lesson on soccer, please," which begins with a scene of Chinese soccer star, Chen Mingde, dribbling around a Brazilian defender and scoring with a precise kick into the corner of the net. The play-by-play commentary is heard in Mandarin, with both the romanized phonetic system and Chinese characters shown as legends at the bottom of the screen. The individual words and characters light up as they are spoken. As Malia practices her pronunciation of the scene, the system provides feedback, allowing her to hear her rendition and then a digitally corrected version, ensuring that she improves her pronunciation of the four tones, a typically difficult task for English speakers.

Through this online system, she is also able to converse with students with similar interests in other countries and engage in mutual language tutoring. "I'd like to talk to Xiaoyan," Malia says, asking the system to call her online friend, Xiaoyan Zhao, an eleven-year-old girl who lives in Shanghai and goes by the nickname of "XYZ." XYZ appears on screen at lunchtime in her school cafeteria, speaking in English while Malia practices her Chinese as they help each other with vocabulary and pronunciation. They promise to make short videos introducing their family members to each other and send them in the next week.

Malia mentions she's working on a volcanoes project at school, and XYZ recalls that her geography class had studied Mount Fuji, named after Japan's ancestral fire goddess. Malia captures XYZ's comment as a voicenote and mails it to her classmates as a suggestion for extending their research. As Malia finishes her conversation and logs off, her father enters the room and asks her the age-old question parents have asked their children for generations: "So what did you do at school today?" As Malia enthusiastically recounts her day, and her excitement about returning to school tomorrow, he shakes his head in amazement. "And to think," he recalls, "twenty years ago, all we had was the Internet."

NOTES

PREFACE

1. Davis, M. (2008). *Street gang: The complete history of Sesame Street* (pp. 139–140). New York: Viking.

INTRODUCTION

1. National Center for Education and the Economy. (2006). *Tough choices or tough times.* San Francisco: Jossey-Bass.

2. Barber, M., & Mourshed, M. (2007, September). *How the world's best performing school systems come out on top.* McKinsey & Company. Retrieved from www.mckinsey.com/App_Media/Reports/SSO/Worlds_School_Systems_Final.pdf.

3. John Merrow's documentary can be found at http://learningmatters .tv/blog/documentaries/first-to-worst-the-documentary/651.

4. Hagel, J., & Brown, J. S. (2005). *The only sustainable edge: Why business strategy depends on productive friction and dynamic specialization* (pp. 10–11). Cambridge, MA: Harvard Business School Press.

EDGE ONE: THE THINKING EDGE

1. Dewey, J. (1990). *The school and society and The child and the curriculum.* Chicago: University of Chicago Press.

2. Ibid., 7.

3. Ibid., 7.

4. Duncan, A. (2009, September 6). How parents can support kids. *Parade.* Accessed at www.parade.com/news/2009/09/06-how-parents-can-support-kids.html.

5. Ibid.

6. Dewey, *School and society,* 75–76.

7. Leonard, G. (1987). *Education and ecstasy* (2nd ed.). Berkeley, CA: North Atlantic Books, pp. ix–x.

8. Ibid., 138.

9. Ibid., 14–15, 16.

10. Ibid., x–xi.

11. Ibid., 248–256.

12. Blackwell, L. S., Trzesniewski, K. H., & Dweck, C. S. (2007, January/February). Implicit theories of intelligence predict achievement across an adolescent transition: A longitudinal study and an intervention. *Child Development 78*(1), 246–263.

13. The NPR story can be found at Npr.org/templates/story/story .php?storyId=7406521.

14. Blackwell et al., Implicit theories of intelligence, 254.

15. Dweck, NPR interview.

16. Blackwell et al., Implicit theories of intelligence, 256.

17. Ibid., 259–260.

18. Dweck, C. (2006). *Mindset: The new psychology of success.* New York: Random House.

19. Information on Brainology software is available at www .brainology.us.

20. Original Edutopia coverage of Build SF can be found at www .edutopia.org/learning-design. Subsequently, more detailed interviews, lesson plans, and articles were produced and can be accessed at www.edutopia.org/new-day-for-learning-two.

21. A collection of Ellen Moir's columns can be found at www .edutopia.org/search/node/moir.

22. The American Memory is a free, comprehensive multimedia archive of American history, in text, audio, photography, film, maps, and music, organized in twenty-three collections ranging from

advertising and African American history to law and government, literature, presidents, military war, and women's history. It can be accessed at http://memory.loc.gov/ammem/index.html.

EDGE TWO: THE CURRICULUM EDGE

1. The Buck Institute for Education's project-based learning definition can be found on its Web site at www.bie.org.

2. The Buck Institute's PBL Handbook and PBL Starter Kit can be ordered at www.bie.org/tools. Boss, S., & Krauss, J. (2007).*Reinventing project-based learning: Your field guide to real-world projects in the Digital Age.* Washington, DC: International Society for Technology in Education.

3. Barron, B., & Darling-Hammond, L. (2008). *Powerful learning: Studies show deep understanding derives from collaborative methods.* Accessed at www.edutopia.org/inquiry-project-learning-research. The citation for the book from which it is excerpted is Darling-Hamond L., Barron, B., Pearson, P. D., Schoenfeld, A. H., Stage, E. K., Zimmerman, T. D., Cervetti, G. N., & Tilson, J. L. (2008). *Powerful learning: What we know about teaching for understanding.* San Francisco: Jossey-Bass. Further resources for research on project-based learning can be found at the Buck Institute for Education's Web site, www.bie.org/research, such as articles in a 2009 issue of the Interdisciplinary Journal of Problem-Based Learning.

4. Lederman, L. (2007). *Out with the old, in with new science.* Accessed at www.edutopia.org/out-with-the-old-in-with-new-science.

5. This article can be found at www.edutopia.org/start-pyramid.

6. This film can be viewed at www.edutopia.org/clear-view-charter-elementary-school.

7. I updated the *Learn & Live* story for Edutopia in 2001: www.edutopia.org/bugscope-magnifying-connection-between-students-science-and-scientists. Bugscope project information is available at http://bugscope.beckman.illinois.edu.

8. Steering team members included John Bransford, Susan Mosborg, Walter Parker, Nancy Vye, and John Wilkerson from the University of Washington; John Brill, Adrienne Curtis, Amber Graeber, Marian McDermott, Don Myers, and Katherine Piper from the Bellevue School District; and Steve Arnold and Milton Chen from GLEF.

9. www.edutopia.org/auto-motive-teens-build-award-winning-electric-cars.

10. To see this *Today* segment, go to today.msnbc.msn.com/id/26184891/vp/33394453#33394453.

11. Results of the Progressive Insurance X Prize competition can be viewed at www.progressiveautoxprize.org.

12. Sir Ken Robinson's talk can be accessed at www.edutopia.org/take-chance-let-them-dance. Also see Robinson, K. (2008). *The element: How finding your passion changes everything*. New York: Viking.

13. The National Academy Foundation Web site is at http://naf.org.

14. For more information about ConnectEd, go to www.connected california.org/index.php.

15. Orr, M. T., Bailey, T., Hughes, K. L., Karp, M. M., & Kienzl, G. S. (2004). *The National Academy Foundation's Career Academies: Shaping postsecondary transitions*. New York: Institute on Education and the Economy, Teachers College, Columbia University.

16. www.mdrc.org/publications/482/overview.html.

17. Studier, C. (Ed.). (2008, May). *Evidence from California Partnership Academies: One model of pathway programs*. Berkeley, CA: ConnectEd. Further information is available at www.connected california.org/pathways/evidence.php.

18. For more information on the Partnership for 21st Century Skills, its Framework for 21st Century Learning, and the role of global awareness, go to www.21stcenturyskills.org.

19. The map of the States Network on International Education in the Schools can be found at http://asiasociety.org/node/8740.

20. Links to these stories can be found at www.edutopia.org/global-dimension-walter-payton; www.edutopia.org/ohayo-portland; and www.edutopia.org/digital-generation-profile-dylan-video. Or go to www.edutopia.org and search on the school name. Information on the ThinkQuest competition can be found at www.thinkquest.org/competition.

21. The Asia Society and National Geographic sites can be accessed at www.asiasociety.org/education-learning and www.nationalgeographic.com/foundation/index.html.

22. Edutopia coverage of Eva LaMar's class can be found at www.edutopia.org/geo-literacy-forging-new-ground. Her Geo-Literacy Web site can be accessed at www.geolit.org.

23. Dillon, S. (2010, January 21). Foreign languages fade in class—except Chinese. *New York Times*, p. A20. An executive summary of the Center for Applied Linguistics study can be accessed at www.cal.org/projects/Exec%20Summary_111009.pdf.

24. The Chinese Language Initiatives of the Asia Society can be found at www.asiasociety.org/education-learning/chinese-language-initiatives.

25. Daley, E. (2003). Expanding the concept of literacy. *Educause*, 182–183. The article can be accessed at http://net.educause.edu/ir/library/pdf/ffpiu027.pdf.

26. This video interview with George Lucas can be viewed at www.edutopia.org/george-lucas-teaching-communication.

27. The Story of Movies materials are available at www.storyofmovies.org.

28. Gardner, H. (2000). *Intelligence reframed: Multiple intelligences for the twenty-first century*. New York: Basic Books.

29. The film, *Academics and Architecture*, can be viewed at www.edutopia.org/mountlake-terrace-geometry-design-video.

30. Durlak, J. A., Weissberg, R. P., Dymnicki, A. B., Taylor, R. D., & Schellinger, K. B. (in press). The impact of enhancing students'

social and emotional learning: A meta-analysis of school-based universal interventions. *Child Development.*

31. This article, along with films and other resources for this Schools That Work case study, can be found at www.edutopia.org/louisville-sel-schools-that-work.

32. The CASEL Web site is at casel.org.

33. www.edutopia.org/appropriate-assessments-reinvigorating-science-education.

34. www.edutopia.org/assessment-overview.

35. www.edutopia.org/assessment-linda-darling-hammond-webinar. A community discussion about these issues is available at www.edutopia.org/groups/assessment/8306.

36. Darling-Hammond, L., & Wentworth, L. (2009, September). *Assessing 21st century skills around the world: College and career readiness in four high-achieving nations.* Stanford, CA: Stanford University.

EDGE THREE: THE TECHNOLOGY EDGE

1. Edutopia's 2005 coverage of the Maine laptop initiative can be accessed at www.edutopia.org/leading-laptops.

2. The Mott Hall 1:1 laptop program is profiled at www.edutopia.org/laptops-all.

3. The full studies conducted by the CEPARE at the University of Southern Maine can be found at www.usm.maine.edu/cepare/mlti.htm.

4. The 2010 Maine feature in Edutopia's Schools That Work series can be found at www.edutopia.org/maine-project-learning-schools-that-work.

5. The Maine International Center for Digital Learning's Web site is at www.micdl.org. America's Digital Schools 2008 Web site is www.ads2008.org. The One Laptop Per Child, bringing laptops to developing nations, can be accessed at laptop.org/en.

6. Rothman, R. (2010). Online testing, version 1.0. *Harvard Education Letter, 26*(2), 1–2, 5–6.

7. Shirely, K. E-mail interview, February 10, 2010

8. The Escondido school district iRead Web site can be accessed at https://sites.google.com/a/eusd.org/eusd-iread. The wiki resource site can be found at http://wiki.canby.k12.or.us/groups/poduser group.

9. Zevin, J. (2000). Social Studies for the Twentieth Century. Mahwah, NJ: Erlbaum. Cantu, D. A., & Warren, W. (2003). *Teaching History in the Digital Classroom.* Armonk, NY: Sharpe. West, J., & West, M. (2009). Using Wikis for Online Collaboration. San Francisco: Jossey-Bass.

10. Educationalwikis.wikispaces.com.

11. Anthony Armstrong's classroom wiki can be viewed at web.me .com/aarmstrong/History/Welcome.html and at delmarhistory8 .wikispaces.com/message/list/Rise+of+Political+Parties+Pt.+II.

12. Information on the Greece, New York, school district's Socratic Seminars can be found at www.greece.k12.ny.us/instruction/ela/ socraticseminars/responsibilitiesofparticipants/htm.

13. Educationalwikis.wikispaces.com.

14. Smith, M. S. (2009). Opening education. *Science 323*, 89–93.

15. Hernandez-Ramos, P., & De La Paz, S. (2009). Learning history in middle school by designing multimedia in a project-based learning experience. *Journal of Research on Technology in Education 42*(2), 151–173.

16. Sloan Consortium (2009). *K–12 online learning: A survey of U. S. school district administrators.* The report can be accessed at www .sloanconsortium.org/sites/default/files/k-12_online_learning_ 2008.pdf.

17. www.inacol.org.

18. Edutopia's coverage of online learning can be found at www.edutopia.org/high-school-dot-com; www.edutopia.org/online-learning-florida-virtual-school; and www.edutopia.org/professional-development-through-learning-communities.

19. Patrick, S., & Powell, A. (2009). *A summary of research on the effectiveness of K–12 online learning.* Vienna, VA: International Association for K–12 Online Learning. This report can be accesssed at www.inacol.org/research/docs/NACOL_ResearchEffectiveness-lr.pdf

20. Florida Tax Watch Center for Educational Performance and Accountability. (2007). *A comprehensive assessment of Florida Virtual School.* Tallahassee: Florida Tax Watch Center for Educational Performance and Accountability.

21. Mazur, E. (2009). Farewell, lecture. *Science 323,* 50–51.

22. Gibbons, J., Kincheloe, W. R., & Downs, K. S. (1977). Tutored videotape instruction. *Science 195,* 1139–1146.

23. The Nation's 2009 Report Card and related commentary can be viewed at http://nationsreportcard.gov/reading_2009.

24. http://teacher.scholastic.com/products/read180.

25. Hasselbring, T. (2010, March 18). *Why technology can make a difference.* Presentation at Scholastic 21st Century Learning Summit, Boston.

26. Ibid.

27. Slavin, R. E., Cheung, A., Groff, C., Lake, C. (2008). Effective reading programs for middle and high school students: A best-evidence synthesis. *Reading Research Quarterly 43*(3), 292–322.

28. Papalweis, R. (2004). Struggling middle school readers: Successful, accelerating intervention. *Reading Improvement 41*(1), 24–37.

29. Visher, M., & Hartry, A. (2007). *Can after-school programs boost academic achievement? An impact evaluation of a reading intervention in an after-school program.* Berkeley, CA: MPR Associates.

30. The River City project from the Harvard Graduate School of Education can be accessed at http://muve.gse.harvard.edu/rivercityproject.

31. Clarke, J., & Dede, C. (2009). Design for scalability: A case study of the River City curriculum. *Journal of Science Education and Technology, 18*, 353–365.

32. The Our Courts Web site can be accessed at http://ourcourts.org. Justice O'Connor's quotation was published in "Courting Kids: An Interview with Sandra Day O'Connor," in *NEA Today*, and can be accessed at www.nea.org/home/38146.htm.

33. Henry Jenkins's comment is contained in the overview video for Edutopia's Digital Generation coverage at www.edutopia.org/digital-generation.

34. The Quest to Learn school's Web site is at http://q2l.org.

35. Edutopia's coverage of games and simulations and McKinley Technology High School can be accessed at www.edutopia.org/no-gamer-left-behind and www.edutopia.org/digital-generation-game-design-video.

36. The Immune Attack game can be found at http://fas.org/immune attack.

37. Justin's Digital Generation profile can be viewed at www.edutopia.org/digital-generation-profile-justin.

38. David Rose was one of Edutopia's 2004 Daring Dozen awardees, published at www.edutopia.org/node/1190#rose.

39. The National Center for Technology Innovation Web site can be found at www.nationaltechcenter.org.

40. Links to Edutopia coverage of assistive technology can be found at www.edutopia.org/assistivetechnology; www.edutopia.org/assistive-technology-enhances-learning-all; www.edutopia.org/assistive-technology-albano-berberi-video.

41. Lucas, G. (2000). We all have special needs. *Edutopia* newsletter. San Rafael, CA: The George Lucas Educational Foundation.

42. The Glow network from Scotland can be accessed at Glowscotland.co.uk.

43. Laurie O'Donnell's recognition as a Daring Dozen/Global Six innovator is found on the Edutopia Web site at www.edutopia.org/laurie-odonnell.

44. Stories of "Sharing Practice" from Scottish teachers using Glow can be accessed at www.ltscotland.org.uk/glowscotland/sharingpractice/index.asp.

EDGE FOUR: THE TIME/PLACE EDGE

1. This article on Internet-ready school buses can be accessed at www.nytimes.com/2010/02/12/education/12bus.html.

2. Marco Torres's work with his students can be seen at www.edutopia.org/san-fernando-education-technology-team.

3. Chen, M. (1994). *The Smart Parent's Guide to Kids' TV.* San Francisco: KQED Books.

4. The Generation M2 study and slides can be viewed at www.kff.org/entmedia/mh012010pkg.cfm and http://slides.kff.org/chart.aspx?ch=1351.

5. Information about the Two Million Minutes film can be found at www.2mminutes.com.

6. The *Prisoners of Time* report can be accessed at www2.ed.gov/pubs/PrisonersOfTime/Prisoners.html.

7. Ibid.

8. The West Des Moines school can be viewed at www.edutopia.org/schools-hubs-community-west-des-moines.

9. The Children's Aid Society partnership with a New York middle school can be seen at www.edutopia.org/childrens-aid-society-video.

10. The *New Day for Learning* report can be downloaded at www.newdayforlearning.org/about.html and at www.edutopia.org/new-day-for-learning.

11. These media can also be accessed at www.edutopia.org/new-day-for-learning.

12. Mead, M., & Metraux . R. (1957). Image of the scientist among high school students. *Science 126*, 384–390.

13. More information on TASC's science curriculum and the videos can be found at www.tascorp.org/section/what_we_do/develop_program_models/science.

14. The National Summer Learning Association Web site is www.summerlearning.org.

15. Descriptions of these award-winners can be found at www.summerlearning.org/?page=excellence_finalists.

16. Louv, R. (2005). *Last child in the woods: Saving our children from nature-deficit disorder.* Chapel Hill, NC: Algonquin, 00.

17. Edutopia's coverage of The Edible Schoolyard can be found at www.edutopia.org/edible-schoolyard-video.

18. The Verde Garden film can be viewed at http://vimeo.com/931539.

19. Stone, M. K. (2009). *Smart by nature: Schooling for sustainability.* Healdsburg, CA: Watershed Media.

20. The Web site for the EPA's educational activities is www.epa.gov/Education. The North American Association for Environmental Education can be found at www.naaee.org. The Web site of the Place-Based Education Evaluation Collaborative is www.peecworks.org. The GLOBE project can be found at www.globe.gov.

21. The March of the Monarchs project can be viewed at www.edutopia.org/journey-north. The Nature Mapping project can be accessed at www.edutopia.org/naturemapping. The School of Environmental Studies can be viewed at www.edutopia.org/school-environmental-studies.

22. The Henry Ford Academy is profiled at www.edutopia.org/it-takes-village-and-museum.

23. The article by Steven Bingler can be found at www.edutopia.org/community-based-school-planning-if-not-now-when. Other

resources on school architecture include www.edutopia.org/its-all-happening-zoo-school and www.edutopia.org/prakash-nair.

24. The Ferryway School film can be viewed at www.edutopia.org/ferry way-video.

25. The Edutopia article on students studying the effects of an oil spill can be found at www.edutopia.org/project-wise-environmental-science.

26. National Parks Second Century Commission (2009). *Advancing the national park idea* (p. 24). Washington, DC: National Parks Conservation Association. This report can be accessed at www.npca.org/commission.

EDGE FIVE: THE CO-TEACHING EDGE

1. Barber, M., & Mourshed, M. (2007). *How the world's best-performing school systems come out on top.* McKinsey. This report can be accessed at http://www.mckinsey.com/clientservice/Social_Sector/our_practices/Education/Knowledge_Highlights/Best_performing _school.aspx

2. National Center for Education and the Economy. (2007). *Tough choices or tough times.* San Francisco: Jossey-Bass.

3. Edutopia's coverage of exemplary teacher education programs can be viewed at www.edutopia.org/schools-of-education-boston.

4. The film and article about Opening Minds through the Arts in Tucson can be accessed at www.edutopia.org/arts-opening-minds-integration-video.

5. The Flocabulary Web site can be found at www.flocabulary.com.

6. "Teachers Shake Up Shakespeare with Digital Media" can be accessed at www.edutopia.org/teaching-shakespeare-digital-media.

7. The Aviation High School film and resources can be found at www.edutopia.org/pbl-action-wing-strength-design-project. Eeva Reeder's tenth-grade architectural design projects can be accessed at www.edutopia.org/mountlake-terrace-high-school.

8. These Edutopia examples of co-teaching can be found at Build SF architecture program: www.edutopia.org/learning-design. Metropolitan Academy: www.edutopia.org/learning-one-one. Acme Animation: www.edutopia.org/animation-dreams.

9. McLaughlin, M., Mergen, A., & Singleton, G. (2009). *What the world hears* (p. 34). San Francisco: California Poets in the Schools.

10. The film and article on the Sacramento Parent-Teacher Home Visit Project can be accessed at www.edutopia.org/making-connections-between-home-and-school.

11. The YES Prep video and related materials, including the school-family contract, can be viewed at www.edutopia.org/yes-prep-parent-involvement-video.

12. School Loop's Web site can be found at www.schoolloop.com. Mark Gross's article, "Inside, Looking Out: Students Get the Picture" describes his class's experience creating a Web site to obtain photos from around the world for their classroom without windows. It can be accessed at www.edutopia.org/inside-looking-out.

13. Hart, B., & Risley, T. R. (1995). *Meaningful differences in the everyday experiences of young American children*. Baltimore: Brookes.

14. Comer, J. (1988). *Maggie's American dream: The life and times of a black family*. New York: Penguin.

EDGE SIX: THE CO-TEACHING EDGE

1. McLaughlin, M., Mergen, A., & Singleton, G. (2009). *What the world hears* (p. 15). San Francisco: California Poets in the Schools.

2. The Web site for Aaron Doering's expeditions is http://polarhusky .com.

3. Edutopia's Digital Generation coverage is at http://edutopia.org/ digital-generation.

4. This section of the Digital Generation site is found at www.edutopia.org/digital-generation-themes. Users can click on

links to see the specific scenes of youth engaged in these behaviors of creating, collaborating, and teaching.

5. Ito, M., Horst, H., Bittanti, M., Boyd, D., Herr-Stephenson, B., Lange, P. G., Pascoe, C. J., & Robinson, L. (2008, November). *Living and learning with new media: Summary of findings from the Digital Youth Project*. MacArthur Foundation Reports on Digital Media and Learning. This report can be accessed at http://digitalyouth.ischool.berkeley.edu/report.

6. Clay Shirky's TED talk can be found at www.ted.com/talks/clay_shirky_how_cellphones_twitter_facebook_can_make_history.html.

7. The Web site for Generation YES is http://genyes.org.

8. This film and article can be accessed at http://edutopia.org/generation-yes-technology-training.

AFTERWORD: TOMMORROW'S EDGE, A 2020 VISION

1. Rogers, E. (2003). *Diffusion of innovations* (5th ed.). New York: Free Press.

2. U.S. Department of Commerce, Office of Technology Administration. (2002). *2020 Visions: Transforming education and training through advanced technologies*. Washington, DC: U.S. Department of Commerce.

3. The Visions 2020.2 report on student views can be accessed at www2.ed.gov/about/offices/list/os/technology/plan/2004/site/documents/visions_20202.pdf.

4. The 2020 Forecast site can be found at www.kwfdn.org/future_of_learning.

5. The Beyond Current Horizons Web site can be found at www.beyondcurrenthorizons.org.uk.

6. Chen, M., & Arnold, S. D. (2002). A day in the life of a young learner: A 2020 vision. In *2020 Visions: Transforming education and training through advanced technologies*. Washington, DC: U.S. Department of Commerce.

SELECTED WEB SITES

In this section you'll find a list of resources online that are discussed within the Six Edges. Change is the only constant, so if you find that any of these links no longer work, please try entering the information in a search engine.

EDGE ONE: THE THINKING EDGE

The Brainology® Program

www.brainology.us

"Students' View of Intelligence Can Help Grades" NPR report by Michelle Trudeau

www.npr.org/templates/story/story.php?storyId=7406521

Edutopia coverage of Build SF can be found at

www.edutopia.org/learning-design

Subsequently, more detailed interviews, lesson plans, and articles were produced and can be accessed at

www.edutopia.org/new-day-for-learning-two

A collection of Ellen Moir's columns can be found at

www.edutopia.org/search/node/moir

The American Memory is a free, comprehensive multimedia archive of American history, in text, audio, photography, film, maps, and music, organized in twenty-three collections ranging from advertising and African American history to law and government, literature, presidents, military war, and women's history. It can be accessed at

http://memory.loc.gov/ammem/index.html

EDGE TWO: THE CURRICULUM EDGE

"Out with the Old, In with New Science" article by Leon Lederman

www.edutopia.org/out-with-the-old-in-with-new-science

"Real-World Issues Motivate Students" article by Diane Curtis. This article can be found at

www.edutopia.org/start-pyramid

"*Learn & Live: Clear View Charter Elementary School*" video. This film can be viewed at

www.edutopia.org/clear-view-charter-elementary-school

"Bugscope: Magnifying the Connection Among Students, Science, and Scientists"

www.edutopia.org/bugscope-magnifying-connection-between-students-science-and-scientists

Bugscope project information is available at

http://bugscope.beckman.illinois.edu/

"Auto Motive: Teens Build Award-Winning Electric Cars" article by Ginny Phillips

www.edutopia.org/auto-motive-teens-build-award-winning-electric-cars

Automotive Academy segment aired on *Today*

show.http://today.msnbc.msn.com/id/26184891/vp/33394453#33394453

Results of the Progressive Insurance X Prize competition can be viewed at

www.progressiveautoxprize.org

"Schools Must Validate Artistic Expression" by Sir Ken Robinson. The article and a video of his talk can be accessed at

www.edutopia.org/take-chance-let-them-dance

The National Academy Foundation Web site is at

http://naf.org

For more information about ConnectEd, go to

www.connectedcalifornia.org/index.php

Article on Career Academies

www.mdrc.org/publications/482/overview.html

Evidence from California Partnership Academies. Further information is available at

www.connectedcalifornia.org/pathways/evidence.php

For more information on the Partnership for 21st Century Skills, its Framework for 21st Century Learning, and the role of global awareness, go to

www.21stcenturyskills.org

Links to stories on Walter Payton College, the Portland language immersion program, and Dylan, a New Hampshire teen, can be found at

www.edutopia.org/global-dimension-walter-payton

www.edutopia.org/ohayo-portland

www.edutopia.org/digital-generation-profile-dylan-video

Or go to

edutopia.org and search on the school name.

Information on the ThinkQuest competition can be found at

www.thinkquest.org/competition

The Asia Society and National Geographic sites can be accessed at

www.asiasociety.org/education-learning and www.nationalgeographic.com/ foundation/index.html

Edutopia coverage of Eva LaMar's class can be found at

www.edutopia.org/geo-literacy-forging-new-ground

Her Geo-Literacy Web site can be accessed at

www.geolit.org

The Chinese Language Initiatives of the Asia Society can be found at

www.asiasociety.org/education-learning/chinese-language-initiatives

"Expanding the Concept of Literacy," by Elizabeth Daley. The article can be accessed at

http://net.educause.edu/ir/library/pdf/ffpiu027.pdf

A video interview with George Lucas can be viewed at

www.edutopia.org/george-lucas-teaching-communication

The Story of Movies materials are available at

www.storyofmovies.org

The film, *Academics and Architecture*, can be viewed at

www.edutopia.org/mountlake-terrace-geometry-design-video

This article, along with films and other resources for this Schools That Work case study, can be found at

www.edutopia.org/louisville-sel-schools-that-work

The CASEL Web site is at

casel.org

"Appropriate Assessments for Reinvigorating Science Education" article by Bruce Alberts

www.edutopia.org/appropriate-assessments-reinvigorating-science-education

Videos on comprehensive assessment can be viewed here:

www.edutopia.org/assessment-overview

Stanford professor Linda Darling-Hammond discusses her research on international standards and assessments through two free unique webinar events

www.edutopia.org/assessment-linda-darling-hammond-webinar

A community discussion about these issues is available at

www.edutopia.org/groups/assessment/8306

EDGE THREE: THE TECHNOLOGY EDGE

The Schools That Work series can be found at

www.edutopia.org/schools-that-work

The Maine International Center for Digital Learning's Web site is at

www.micdl.org

America's Digital Schools 2008 Web site is

www.ads2008.org

The One Laptop Per Child, bringing laptops to developing nations, can be accessed at

http://laptop.org/en/

The Escondido school district iRead Web site can be accessed at

https://sites.google.com/a/eusd.org/eusd-iread/

The wiki resource site can be found at

http://wiki.canby.k12.or.us/groups/podusergroup/

Educational wikis site can be found at

educationalwikis.wikispaces.com

Anthony Armstrong's classroom wiki can be viewed at

http://web.me.com/aarmstrong/History/Welcome.html

http://delmarhistory8.wikispaces.com/message/list/Rise+of+Political+Parties+Pt.+II

Information on the Greece, New York school district's Socratic Seminars can be found at

www.greece.k12.ny.us/instruction/ela/socraticseminars/responsibilitiesof participants/htm

http://web001.greece.k12.ny.us/files/filesystem/GRTCN_Socratic_Seminars.pdf

K–12 Online Learning: The report can be accessed at

www.sloanconsortium.org/sites/default/files/k-12_online_learning_2008.pdf

International Association for K–12 Online Learning

www.inacol.org

Edutopia's coverage of online learning can be found at

www.edutopia.org/high-school-dot-com

www.edutopia.org/online-learning-florida-virtual-school

www.edutopia.org/professional-development-through-learning-communities

Scholastic Read180

http://teacher.scholastic.com/products/read180

The Glow network from Scotland can be accessed at

http://Glowscotland.co.uk

EDGE FOUR: THE TIME/PLACE EDGE

The article on Internet-ready school buses can be accessed at

www.nytimes.com/2010/02/12/education/12bus.html

Marco Torres's work with his students can be seen at

www.edutopia.org/san-fernando-education-technology-team

The Generation M2 study and slides can be viewed at

www.kff.org/entmedia/mh012010pkg.cfm

slides.kff.org/chart.aspx?ch=1351

Information about the Two Million Minutes film can be found at

www.2mminutes.com

The West Des Moines school can be viewed at

www.edutopia.org/schools-hubs-community-west-des-moines

The Children's Aid Society partnership with a New York middle school can be seen at

www.edutopia.org/childrens-aid-society-video

More on A New Day for Learning can be found at

www.edutopia.org/new-day-for-learning

More information on TASC's science curriculum and the videos can be found at

www.tascorp.org/section/what_we_do/develop_program_models/science

The Summer Learning Association Web site is

www.summerlearning.org

Descriptions of the award-winners can be found at

www.summerlearning.org/?page=excellence_finalists

The Verde Garden film can be viewed at

 http://vimeo.com/931539

The Center for Ecoliteracy

 www.ecoliteracy.org

The March of the Monarchs project can be viewed at

 www.edutopia.org/journey-north

The Nature Mapping project can be accessed at

 www.edutopia.org/naturemapping

The School of Environmental Studies can be viewed at

 www.edutopia.org/school-environmental-studies

The Henry Ford Academy is profiled at

 www.edutopia.org/it-takes-village-and-museum

The article by Steven Bingler, film about the Zoo School, and an articles by Prakash Nair can be found at

 www.edutopia.org/community-based-school-planning-if-not-now-when

 www.edutopia.org/its-all-happening-zoo-school

 www.edutopia.org/prakash-nair

The Ferryway School film can be viewed at

 www.edutopia.org/ferryway-video

The Edutopia article on students studying the effects of an oil spill can be found at

 www.edutopia.org/project-wise-environmental-science

The National Parks Second Century Commission report can be accessed at

 www.npca.org/commission

EDGE FIVE: THE CO-TEACHING EDGE

National Center for Education and the Economy

 www.ncee.org

Edutopia's coverage of exemplary teacher education programs can be viewed at

 www.edutopia.org/schools-of-education-boston

The film and article about Opening Minds Through the Arts in Tucson can be accessed at

 www.edutopia.org/arts-opening-minds-integration-video

The YES Prep video can be viewed at

 www.edutopia.org/yes-prep-parent-involvement-video

The YES Prep contract can be found at

yesprep.org/downloads/Contract.English.pdf

EDGE SIX: THE YOUTH EDGE

The Web site for Aaron Doering's expeditions is

www.polarhusky.com

Edutopia's Digital Generation coverage is at

www.Edutopia.org/digitalgenaration

The generation YES Web site is

www.genyes.org

Edutopia's film and article about Generation YES can be found at

www.edutopia.org/generation-yes-technology-training

AFTERWORD: TOMMOROW'S EDGE, A 2020 VISION

The Visions 2020.2 report can be accessed at

www2.ed.gov/about/offices/list/os/technology/plan/2004/site/documents/visions_20202.pdf

The 2020 Forecast site can be found at

www.kwfdn.org/future_of_learning

The Beyond Current Horizons Web site can be found at

www.beyondcurrenthorizons.org.uk

ABOUT THE AUTHOR

DR. MILTON CHEN is senior fellow and executive director emeritus at The George Lucas Educational Foundation. During his twelve years as executive director, its Edutopia.org Web site became known as a destination for films, articles, and other resources on innovation in schools. His career has spanned four decades at the intersection of media, technology, and learning as founding director of the KQED Center for Education (PBS) and director of research at Sesame Workshop. Dr. Chen has taught at the Harvard Graduate School of Education and been a Fulbright New Century Scholar at the University of Edinburgh.

He chairs the advisory council for the Fred Rogers Center for Early Learning and Children's Media at St. Vincent College and is a member of the National Park System advisory board. He serves on the board of directors of ConnectEd: The California Center for College and Career and the San Francisco School Alliance. His work has been honored by the Corporation for Public Broadcasting's Fred Rogers Award, Sesame Workshop's Elmo Award, the Association of Educational Service Agencies, the Congressional Black Caucus, and two science centers, The Exploratorium and the Lawrence Hall of Science.

Dr. Chen received an AB in social studies from Harvard College and an MA and PhD in communication research from Stanford University. He and his wife, Ruth Cox, live in San Francisco, and have one daughter, Maggie.

INDEX

Page references followed by *p* indicate a photograph.